"Catch Every Eddy... Surf Every Wave is fun to read, technically advanced, and written so the paddler can learn as he plays and play as he learns."

Bunny Johns, President
Nantahala Outdoor Center

"Catch Every Eddy... Surf Every Wave is awesome. It is a technical "how to" book honed by many years of paddling, teaching paddling and teaching paddlers how to teach paddling. The many diagrams drive the written descriptions home. *Catch Every Eddy... Surf Every Wave* is probably the most credible sourcebook about whitewater playboating that you can find on the market today, and should be required reading for serious paddlers who want to define or refine their technique."

Kim Whitley, Chairperson, National Instruction Committee
of the American Canoe Association

"If you will read this book and practice diligently the skills it describes, you'll be able to paddle like Tom and Kel, and that is a worthy goal indeed! This book progresses from tried-and-true basic technique to cutting-edge playboat tricks, and it does so in a clear, sensible, and wholly admirable style. *Catch Every Eddy... Surf Every Wave* belongs on every paddler's shelf."

Gordon Black, Head of Instruction
Nantahala Outdoor Center

WHAT THE EXPERTS ARE SAYING...

"In *Catch Every Eddy... Surf Every Wave,* Tom Foster and Kel Kelly have combined their years of paddling and teaching to bring us a "how to" book that is up-to-date, clear and easy to read. Beginners as well as experts can use this book as their guide to whitewater playboating. Whitewater instructors, as well as their students, now have a current reference book to use in whitewater playboating."

Bob Foote, ACA Whitewater Instructor Trainer,
Chairperson of the NIC Swift Water Subcommittee

"Catch Every Eddy... Surf Every Wave reveals the technical elements of precision paddling. The authors really help you to understand how the boat, body and river can work in harmony to make paddling easier and more exciting. The 'homework' they assign you on the pond and the river will challenge you and hone your skills."

Randy Carlson, Director, Kayak and Canoe Institute
University of Minnesota at Duluth

"Tom Foster has revolutionized the way ACA-certified instructors are trained, and the way whitewater playboating is taught, much to the benefit of paddlers across the country. In *Catch Every Eddy... Surf Every Wave,* he and co-author Kel Kelly make the latest techniques available to all, in highly readable form. It is the most complete work available on modern paddling technique, a must-have for every paddler who considers paddling a skill-based sport and wants to do it right."

Charlie Wilson, ACA Instructor Trainer,
Co-author of *FreeStyle Paddling*

CATCH EVERY EDDY...
SURF EVERY WAVE

A Contemporary Guide to
Whitewater Playboating

Tom Foster and Kel Kelly

Published by
Outdoor Centre of New England
School of Paddling
10 Pleasant Street
Millers Falls, Massachusetts 01349
Tel: 413-659-3020 Fax: 413-659-3464

Printed in the United States of America

All diagrams and 2-D illustrations by Tom Foster.
3-D illustrations designed by Tom Foster and
drawn by Tabatha McLellan.

Cover photograph by Alan Fortune.

ISBN 0-9645221-4-4 16.95
Library of Congress Catalog Card Number: 95-92033

CONTENTS

ABOUT THE AUTHORS

Tom Foster is the founder and director of the Outdoor Centre of New England, one of the top paddling schools in North America. He teaches canoeing and kayaking both at the Outdoor Centre and at workshops across the country. He is the author of <u>Recreational Whitewater Canoeing</u>, published in 1978 and revised in 1981, and editor of Laurie Gullion's <u>Canoeing and Kayaking Instruction Manual</u>, published by the American Canoe Association (ACA).

Tom is past chairperson of the ACA's National Instruction Committee, a position which he held for ten years. He is an ACA Whitewater Instructor Trainer in kayaking, open canoeing, and decked canoeing.

Kel Kelly is an ACA-certified instructor in whitewater and freestyle canoeing. She has been an avid paddler for decades, and has explored many wilderness waterways on solo canoe-camping trips. She teaches whitewater playboating at the Outdoor Centre of New England.

In her "other life," she is the owner of the Burlington Veterinary Hospital, where she provides medical and surgical care to the four-legged critters of suburban Boston.

A NOTE TO OUR READERS

We are delighted to have some role in your experience of learning whitewater playboating. This sport has given us years of exciting and rewarding experiences on the river, and we look forward to many more. We hope your experience will be as positive as ours. *However, neither the authors nor the publisher of this book can take any responsibility for your safety.* We have made every effort to provide clear, accurate descriptions of playboating technique. But there are inherent dangers in whitewater playboating, and these should be recognized by the participant as risks that he takes upon himself when he chooses to partake of the sport. We cannot over-emphasize the importance of professional on-water instruction, and the value of constant practice of whitewater techniques on calm water. We hope you will take a systematic, disciplined approach to learning this lifetime sport. Your efforts will be richly rewarded!

From Tom:

"The great man is he who does not lose his child's heart, who will run around willows and mess about in boats...."

-- Mencius

From Kel:

"The happiness of your life depends upon the character of your thoughts."

-- Anonymous

From both:

"Love comforteth like sunshine after rain."

-- Shakespeare

WHAT YOU'LL FIND IN
<u>CATCH EVERY EDDY... SURF EVERY WAVE</u>

Contemporary whitewater playboating technique, for both kayakers and canoeists (both open and decked boats)... much of it described without reference to the type of boat or paddle involved, because most of the techniques look the same to the fishes as they look up at our hulls and blades!

Specific strokes and techniques unique to each craft... spelled out in detail in separate chapters on kayaking, solo canoeing and tandem canoeing. Throughout the text, clear diagrams and illustrations help the reader to visualize correct technique.

Universal technique applicable to all skill levels... because intermediate and advanced paddlers should not have to unlearn "beginner technique" in order to progress. Why not learn the correct skills for advanced technique starting the very day you take up the sport?

Contemporary playboating equipment defined in detail... so you can choose your toys wisely -- and you'll need them, as the strokes and techniques we describe will *only* work in heavily-rockered boats with good secondary stability.

Concepts of whitewater paddling... explained in clear, practical terms. The topic is given in-depth attention, as these concepts are the backbone of contemporary technique.

River features and how to read them... current differentials, holes, and other river features described and illustrated in great detail.

Strategies for playing the river "to the max"... from peel-outs to pirouettes, it's all here!

Group organization and individual responsibilities... for both group leaders and participants who want to know more about logistics for river runs, as well as river signals, playboating etiquette, and river rescue. For the new participant, helpful advice on physical fitness and preparedness for playboating.

The most extensive whitewater glossary in print... with concise definitions of the many terms used to describe strokes, maneuvers, river features, and playboat nomenclature.

Everything but the professional on-water instruction... which we consider *essential* for all playboaters, both for their safety and for maximal enjoyment of the sport.

PREFACE

During the ten years I served in the elected position of Chairperson of the American Canoe Association's National Instruction Committee, I had the opportunity to teach and paddle with *great* people all over the United States. For several years, I was able to teach upwards of 150 days per year. As a member of the NIC's National Training Faculty and as the owner of the Outdoor Centre of New England, I have been directly involved in over 100 Instructor Trainer Updates, Instructor Methods Workshops, and Instructor Certification Workshops. The interaction I enjoyed with both faculty and participants in these workshops helped me immensely in the development of my own teaching skills and techniques. Colleagues and students have continually inspired me. My teaching progressions, and the manner in which I present them, have evolved constantly, thanks to their input. In addition to teaching these advanced workshops, I have always found it invaluable to continue to teach entry-level paddlers -- both because it is a joy to watch new paddlers develop enthusiasm for the sport, and because it helps me keep the proper perspective for assisting new instructors and developing instructor trainers.

In this book, I am "giving back" the fruits of my travels and teaching experiences. Although this book is quite technical, it is, thanks to Kel Kelly -- my best friend, paddling partner, and co-author -- presented with a sense of humor. Kel not only is a fluid and graceful playboater, she is a fantastic writer who has enjoyed this endeavor as much as I have, and without her talent and encouragement, this book simply would not be.

I would like to teach and paddle more throughout this beautiful country -- and have been offered plenty of workshops to do so -- but unfortunately, managing a busy school of paddling has diverted much of my time away from the teaching that I love. However, I shall return!

I have never been a follower, and some have even labeled me a renegade. But I would prefer for people to think of me as a leader or teacher who has never been content to accept the status quo. My goal has been to ask always, "Is there a better way?" Therefore, I have attempted, in writing this book, to step above and beyond "the norm"... to help define, redefine, and even re-shape the manner in which whitewater playboating is presented to all good paddler wannabes! Happy reading, my friends, and a sincere Thanks.

Tom Foster

CHARACTERISTICS OF
WHITEWATER PLAYBOATING

Whitewater playboating is...

...An approach to whitewater paddling in which the "goal" is not to go directly from the put-in to the take-out, but rather to make the most of river current differentials and obstacles -- dancing down the river in a creative pattern of peel-outs, jet-ferries, surfing and eddy turns.

...An exciting, challenging lifetime sport that uses a combination of river knowledge and technical paddling skills. One should learn and develop continually -- because techniques and equipment are constantly improving, and the best paddlers have never "finished learning."

...An activity characterized by the ever-present element of danger and therefore requiring good judgment and self-confidence.

...A sport which is increasing in popularity at a tremendous rate. There has been, however, a sharp increase in the number of injuries and deaths, especially among those who attempt it improperly equipped or unaware of its inherent dangers.

...An activity of a very strenuous nature that can use up to 600 calories per hour through a combination of physical exertion and mental concentration.

...An endeavor which requires a high degree of kinesthetic sensitivity and the development of appropriate reflexive responses in order to achieve precise, quick reactions to the many variables such as current differentials, river hazards, wave formations and wind direction.

...A skill-based sport in which one should seek formal instruction, as the self-taught paddler is extremely likely to develop inefficient "coping" habits which make it impossible to paddle well, and dangerous to attempt more difficult rivers.

...An activity which requires considerable "mileage in the saddle" before it is mastered.

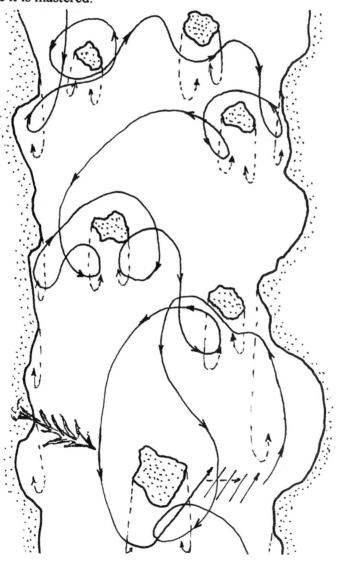

PADDLERS' PERSONAL RESPONSIBILITIES

As a participant you should:

Paddle with a group. Never paddle whitewater alone. Three boats should be considered the minimum size paddling group.

Be honest about your skill level. Select rivers that challenge but do not exceed your abilities. Do not hesitate to portage a rapid that you don't feel comfortable paddling, and support such decisions by others -- no one should ever feel pressured to run a rapid that might be beyond his abilities.

Wear a U.S. Coast Guard approved Personal Flotation Device (PFD). All boaters are legally required to have one PFD (lifevest) per person in the boat. Paddlers should *wear* their PFD at all times, not only for flotation, but also for warmth and for protection against injury if they wind up swimming a rapid. The PFD also provides increased visibility to other paddlers who may be trying to spot you in the water.

Protect your head. Wear a high-quality whitewater helmet at all times to protect against head injuries.

Protect your skin. Cover any exposed skin with sunscreen, since sunlight bounces off the water, increasing your exposure compared to other outdoor activities.

Wear proper clothing. River water can be extremely cold, even in summer, and prolonged exposure can be life-threatening. As a guide, if the sum of the air temperature plus the water temperature is less than 100 degrees Fahrenheit, wear a wetsuit or a drysuit. In all weather conditions, wear synthetic wicking materials next to your skin, since they retain body heat even when wet. This layer will also provide some protection against abrasions when swimming rapids.

Never eat or chew gum while playboating. When a boat capsizes in whitewater, a gasp reflex occurs as the paddler hits the water. The reflex is particularly strong when hitting cold water, and can't be voluntarily prevented. This can result in choking if there is anything in the mouth.

Leave warm, dry clothes in the vehicle at your take-out. There is nothing more satisfying after an exciting day on the river than the comfort of fresh, dry clothes. Dry clothes are also a great help to the paddler chilled from unplanned "fish counts."

Load the boat properly. Whitewater playboating requires greater boat maneuverability in a more chaotic environment than any other type of boating. Therefore, never exceed a boat's design in weight carried or the number of people paddling it. The boat should be trim (sitting as deeply in the water at the bow as at the stern).

Beware of the three W's -- wind, weather, and waves. Windy or gusty days can be hazardous, as they will change the course of your boat (especially an open boat). Wind also changes the appearance of the water surface, making it harder to read the river. In general, if the wind is strong enough to lift a spray of water into the air above the waves, it is too windy to paddle. Cold or rainy weather puts paddlers at risk for hypothermia. And heavy chaotic wave formations, often found in Class III and IV rivers, can knock the boat off course unexpectedly.

Never paddle when the shores are icy. In early spring, the rivers are running but ice ledges often line the shore. In this environment, it can be impossible to get a hand-hold on shoreline rocks or vegetation in order to pull yourself out of the river. Ice ledges usually break off in one's hand, if they can be grasped at all. More importantly, ice ledges are strainers which can trap swimmers underwater. One risks drowning, or at least very rapid-onset hypothermia, when capsized under these conditions.

Be in good physical condition. Work out regularly, with an emphasis on cardiovascular conditioning to increase stamina and endurance, and weight-training to develop upper body strength. Flexibility is also extremely important. Warm up before workouts and before river runs by stretching, with emphasis on the torso muscles and hamstrings. Loosen up so you can easily rotate your shoulder plane 90 degrees by twisting at the waist. Bend sideways to kink one side of your waist while stretching the other side -- try to touch your calf with your fingertips. Reach forward to your toes to stretch out the hamstring muscles. This is just a starting point -- when you take professional instruction, ask for the stretching exercises that will help *you* the most.

Eat and sleep well before paddling. It is absolutely necessary to be well rested and well nourished if you are going to be responsive and alert for several hours on the river. "Carbo-load" at breakfast, and pack high-carbohydrate snacks and plenty of water.

Be aware that drugs and playboating don't mix. Artificial stimulants are contraindicated in a sport that demands acuity, coordination and skill. Whitewater paddling produces its own "high"! Depressant drugs, such as alcohol, make an already dangerous sport absolutely unsafe. Paddlers cannot afford any attenuation of their reflexes, stamina, or mental alertness while on whitewater.

Be a good swimmer. Confidence *in* the water increases your confidence *on* the water. Never attempt to paddle a rapid that you would not feel competent to swim.

Know your self-rescue technique. Develop a fairly reliable roll. Until you have a solid roll, be thoroughly competent at wet-exits and swimming to shore with your boat and paddle in hand. Whenever you complete such a self-rescue, signal to your friends that you are okay by making an "O" with your arms over your head. They'll be relieved, and return the signal with delight!

Carry a personal first aid kit. Assemble a small, simple waterproof kit that you feel comfortable using, given your level of first aid training. (Better yet, first *increase* that level by taking a first aid course.) We suggest you start with Band-Aids, aspirin, antacid (stomach upset or even nausea can occur when a paddler hears a big drop ahead!), a small plastic bottle of disinfectant, moleskin, white tape, a few gauze pads, and a roll of stretch gauze. Additional contents are a matter of personal choice... are you allergic to bees?

River signals. Know the American Whitewater Affiliation (AWA) River Signals System. See the illustrations below. When a signal is given to you, you should repeat the signal back to the sender. Also, when appropriate, transmit the signal to paddlers following you down the river, but wait until you're at the point where the signal has relevance. Remember, *never* point (with your arm or your paddle) *toward* a hazard. Always point toward the course that should be taken by the paddlers you are assisting.

AWA UNIVERSAL RIVER SIGNALS

HELP/EMERGENCY: Assist the signaller as quickly as possible. Give three long blasts on a police whistle while waving a paddle, helmet or lifevest over your head in a circular motion. If you don't have a whistle, use the visual signal alone. A whistle can be attached to one's lifevest for signalling.

STOP: Potential hazard ahead. Form a horizontal bar with your paddle or outstretched arms. Move this bar up and down to attract attention. Those seeing the signal should pass it back to others in the party. Wait for "all clear" signal before proceeding, or scout ahead.

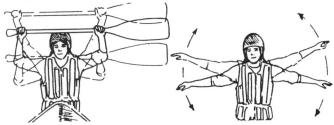

ALL CLEAR: Come ahead. In the absence of other directions, proceed down the center. Hold your paddle or one arm high above your head. Paddle blade should be turned flat for maximum visibility. To signal directon or a preferred course through a rapid, lower the paddle by 45 degrees toward the side of the river with the preferred route. Never point toward an obstacle to be avoided.

ATTENTION: This signal consists of a series of short "chirps" on the police whistle. It is used when no emergency exists, but the need to communicate is urgent. This signal should not be given casually, but only when other forms of communication are having little or no effect.

7

Abide by the River Paddler's Code of Ethics. It is essential that each person in the group understand and abide by these ethics. *(See back cover.)*

Support the etiquette guidelines. Your safety, as well as that of others in your group, depends on the cooperative efforts of each participant. The following informal etiquette guidelines have been established by river playboaters over the years. *You will find greater harmony on the river if you...*

...Yield right-of-way to craft or people with less maneuverability, e.g., rafters, tubers and swimmers.

...Show respect for the various other river users, including swimmers, fishermen, and racers.

...Maintain adequate space between your boat and the boat ahead of you -- 50 to 75 feet in easy rapids; more challenging rapids should be run by one boat at a time.

...Don't pass other craft in narrow sections of the river where navigability is restricted. These sites are best played by one boat at a time.

...Be considerate of other paddlers on the river and try not to hinder them or force them to alter their course. For example, don't "peel out" from shore or an eddy until an approaching craft has passed or stopped; you should not execute a maneuver that might force other boaters to alter their program.

...Avoid obstacles that can damage the boat -- Whitewater playboating should not be a demolition derby!

...Yield right-of-way to paddlers who wish to run straight through a playsite while, at the same time, sharing the site rather than monopolizing it.

...Identify and give wide berth to instructional programs being conducted on the river. Novice playboaters are just learning to read the river and to control their boats!

...Play the river. Practice river maneuvers and learn the joy of spending time on a small section of the river rather than simply paddling or floating downstream -- *Catch every eddy, surf every wave!*

GROUP ORGANIZATION ON THE RIVER

Minimum group size. Whitewater groups should have at least three boats, so that if one paddler gets into trouble, a second paddler can stay and assist while a third goes for help.

Group leader. Select an experienced paddler as the group leader. The leader should be concerned with the overall safety of the group, and be certain that each paddler is capable of the planned river run (with possible short portages around rapids that others in the group may plan to run). He should be experienced in river rescue procedures, as well as group leadership.

Leader preparedness. The group leader should be familiar with the river *at the level it is running* the day the group is paddling it, and should be constantly alert for strainers or other hazards. Rivers are constantly changing, and are especially likely to have new hazards during and immediately after high water. Leaders also need to be aware of the skills and physical abilities of the group, and set the pace of the day accordingly. Good judgment and sensitivity to the needs of the group are prerequisites for this job!

Sweep boat. A second experienced paddler should be designated "sweep," and should carry a first aid kit in his boat. He should be familiar with the planned river run, be experienced in river rescue, and should be comfortable with the use of the first aid kit. The sweep boat is always the last in the group, and is responsible for making sure no one falls behind. The sweep paddler should immediately assist at the scene of any mishap on the river.

Maximum group size. If there are more than six boats in the group, split into smaller groups; each group should have a lead boat and a sweep boat (complete with first aid kit). Since experienced paddlers take longer to play their way down the river than beginners, it may be best to split the group by skill levels, letting the less experienced group start the run first. (Tell them to save some cookies when they reach the take-out!) *Each* group, however, should have experienced paddlers in the lead and sweep boats.

Participants. Each paddler should know which boats are lead and sweep, and should maintain a position between these two boats throughout the run, except when the group is stopped at a playsite. Each paddler should stay well behind the paddler ahead of him, so as not to limit any of the other's playboating options. Similarly, when a following boat approaches an eddy, the paddler in the eddy should either move over or move on!

Shuttle. Set up the shuttle before making the river run, leaving as many vehicles as possible at the take-out (and as few as possible at the put-in). Leave food and dry clothes in the vehicles at the take-out -- both for comfort and for safety, in case anyone is in danger of hypothermia from unpremeditated fish counts or excessive exposure. By leaving most of the cars at the take-out, people can begin loading boats while one car takes drivers to retrieve vehicles left at the put-in. And, you'll find it easier to deal with shuttle logistics at the beginning of the day than at the end of a hard day's play on the river!

Shoreline vehicle. When weather or river conditions are unusually challenging, select a river that runs alongside a road, so a safety vehicle can provide shoreline assistance. If possible, the vehicle should stay within sight of the lead craft, in case a paddler needs help or the leader decides to abort the run. This vehicle should carry dry clothes, food, and a more extensive first aid kit.

PLAYBOATING EQUIPMENT

Before investing in the "toys" of the sport, learn what to look for in a boat, paddle, and accessories. Here are some of the features of contemporary playboating equipment that you'll want to know about before taking the big plunge!

Boat rocker. Look at a whitewater playboat and you will see the characteristics that make it a playboat. Whether it is a kayak or canoe, open or decked boat, some essential features will be the same. First, and most significantly, you will see a "banana shape" from the side view. That is, the bottom of the boat is significantly curved from fore to aft, to the extent that the ends of the boat aren't even in the water! This *rocker*, as it is called, reduces the resistance to lateral movement at the ends of the craft, enabling it to spin easily about its pivot point. This same readiness to spin makes whitewater playboats rather devilish when you try to paddle them in a straight line!

Boat outfitting. Secondly, look inside and you will see the *outfitting* that fits the paddler snugly inside the boat. Outfitting gives the paddler optimum boat control because it allows him to operate his body and his craft as a unit. Good outfitting includes a back support, hip pads, knee or thigh support and foot braces or foot walls. While the canoe playboater has thigh straps to hold his legs down on the bottom of the craft, the kayak paddler adjusts his foot pegs or walls so that his knees and lower thighs are held snugly up against the boat's deck. All playboaters lean their craft by J-leaning their bodies -- a technique explained in detail later. More on outfitting in a bit.

Boat size. Whitewater playboats are narrow compared to open water paddlecraft, ranging from 55 to 80 cm (22 to 32 inches) in

BOAT STABILITY

The Kayak

The Canoe

The round bottom boat...such a design would have neither initial nor secondary stability. The paddler would simply tip over!!

The hard chine boat...such a design would have initial stability, but poor secondary stability.

The soft chine boat...such a design would have more secondary stability but less initial stability.

Good playboats have soft chines where their sides meet the bottoms...such boats handle well when leaned into a turn and they are relatively forgiving.

14

width. Because the boats are narrow, they feel quite tippy to the neophyte playboater. But the paddler overcomes his initial uneasiness when he discovers the secondary stability which is designed into the hull of a good playboat. Secondary stability is the tendency of the boat *not* to capsize when heeled to one side; it allows the paddler to comfortably lean his boat without feeling like he is about to tip over. See diagram of boat stability designs.

Boat length and weight. Another feature of playboats is that they are generally shorter than the boats used in other paddlesport disciplines. Kayaks and decked canoes are only 10 to 13 feet long, and weigh 25 to 45 pounds including outfitting and flotation. Whitewater solo open canoes are 11 to 15 feet in length, and weigh 35 to 70 pounds fully outfitted. Tandem open canoes are 14 to 17 feet in length, and proportionately heavier.

Boat composition. Weight depends on material as well as size of the boat. Lighter craft are constructed of carbon fiber and kevlar, while the heavier ones are made of various types of plastic or fiberglass. Lighter materials come with a higher price tag, but are very often worth it. Plastic boats are more "indestructible," so they have their advantages, too -- depending on the nature of the river and skill level of the paddler!

Kayak outfitting: *The starting point.* At the factory, whitewater kayaks are outfitted with a plastic seat, foot blocks, support walls and grab loops. The designers leave plenty of cockpit room so the boat accommodates a wide range of body types. Foot blocks keep the legs slightly flexed, which sets the lower thighs in contact with the underside of the deck, facilitating lower body control of boat lean. However, every whitewater playboat should be additionally outfitted to fit the owner.

PARTS OF A KAYAK AND PADDLE

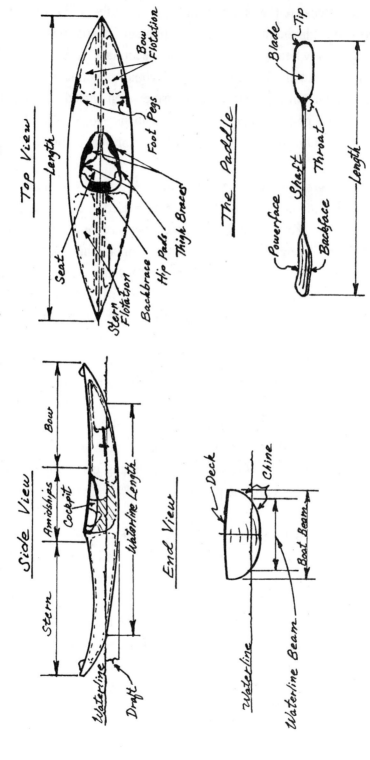

Top View

Bow Flotation

Foot Pegs

Length

Seat

Stern Flotation

Backbrace

Hip Pads

Thigh Braces

Side View

Bow

Amidships

Cockpit

Waterline Length

Stern

Waterline

Draft

End View

Deck

Chine

Boat Beam

Waterline

Waterline Beam

The Paddle

Blade

Tip

Shaft

Throat

Powerface

Backface

Length

Seat and hip pads. Whitewater kayaks should be outfitted with a seat pad, which is a thin layer of foam providing warmth and comfort, and preventing the body from slipping in the seat. Hip pads, which prevent the derriere from slipping from side to side, connect the lower body to the boat to assist in both boat leans and hip snaps.

Back brace. As the most common complaint of kayakers is lower back pain, particular emphasis should be placed on outfitting one's boat with a substantial back brace.

Flotation. Kayaks should be equipped fore and aft with flotation bags to reduce the amount of water taken in when a paddler wet-exits.

Canoe outfitting: ***Pedestal, knee cups and thigh straps.*** When a dealer receives a canoe from the factory, it is usually not outfitted at all. Outfitting is done either by the dealer or the purchaser of the boat. Not a job for the faint of heart, canoe outfitting is both time-consuming and expensive. Whitewater canoes are outfitted with a pedestal seat, on which the paddler sits. The authors do not recommend a kneeling thwart, which extends across the boat, because of the risk of entrapment of the paddler in the boat. Knee cups are needed to support the knees and prevent lateral slippage. Thigh straps run diagonally across the thighs; their function is to hold the legs securely in the knee cups on the bottom of the boat. While many newcomers to the sport prefer a high pedestal, that puts the thighs in a near-vertical position, which causes the thigh straps to slip off too readily. As thigh straps are the means by which one "connects" to the boat for proper boat leans, train your body to accept as low a pedestal as possible; ideally, the legs should bend at least 135 degrees at the knees and the thigh straps should lie about halfway up the

PARTS OF A CANOE AND PADDLE

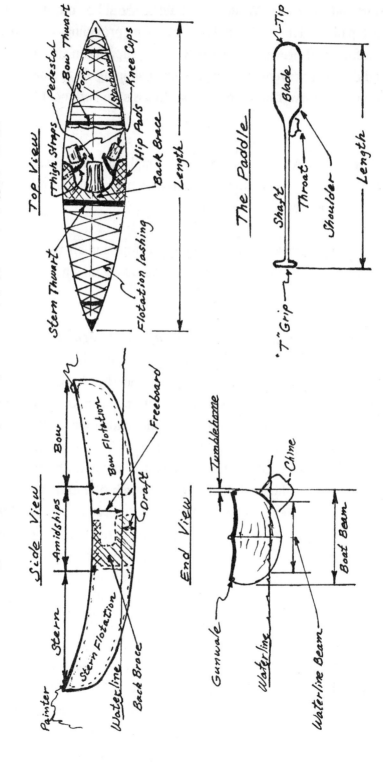

Top View

Pedestal
Bow Thwart
Port
Starboard
Knee Cups
Thigh Straps
Hip Pads
Back Brace
Length
Stern Thwart
Flotation lashing

Side View

Bow
Amidships
Stern
Painter
Bow Flotation
Freeboard
Draft
Waterline
Stern Flotation
Back Brace
Waterline

End View

Tumblehome
Chine
Boat Beam
Gunwale
Waterline
Waterline Beam

The Paddle

"T" Grip
Blade
T-Tip
Shaft
Throat
Shoulder
Length

thighs. Also inspect the location where the thigh straps are attached to the boat. If the lateral attachment points are too high up the wall, the strap will run too vertically across the thigh -- another common cause of straps slipping off the legs. If the anchor point is too low, it may be difficult to make an emergency exit from the boat. Thigh straps should never be attached to the boat farther back than your ankles.

Foot braces and hip pads. Foot braces in open canoes are blocks against which one rests the ball of the foot; they help hold the thighs forward against the thigh straps, connecting the paddler to the boat. Foot braces are especially helpful in performing efficient strokes and are absolutely necessary in rolling an open canoe. Hip pads are an optional feature that stabilize the paddler on the pedestal and enhance his boat leans.

Painters. Open canoes have a "painter" (12 to 15 foot highly visible, floatable rope) at bow and stern, looped and tucked under a bungee cord on each deck plate, so that it can be undone easily when the boat capsizes. Decked canoes have grab loops instead of painters.

Flotation. Both open and decked canoes are equipped fore and aft with flotation bags to reduce the amount of water taken on in heavy water or when capsized.

Paddles. Paddles vary greatly in shape and composition. Because of the torquing force of current transmitted to the paddler's body via the blade, contemporary whitewater paddles have a smaller blade than touring paddles.

Kayak paddles are usually measured in centimeters, and run 190 to 206 cm (76 to 82 inches) in length. A longer paddle puts greater torquing stress on the body, so smaller people should select shorter paddles. The two blades of a kayak paddle are generally not parallel to each other, but are "offset." The offset is expressed in degrees, and is the angle seen between the blades when one peers down the length of the paddle from one blade tip to the other. The greater the offset, the more feathered the non-working blade will be during its recovery phase on power strokes. The price one pays for this advantage is the greater work done by the control wrist to rotate the shaft for each powerphase, especially during the left blade's powerphase (in a right-hand-control paddle). A 90 degree offset would give perfect feathering of the non-working blade, but require the most wrist action. A zero-degree offset paddle would not require any flexion or extension of the control wrist, but the non-working blade would be fully broached (perpendicular to its line of travel) on the recovery phase. Kayak paddles were once typically offset by 90 degrees, but the tendency has been to offset contemporary paddles at 45 to 60 degrees to reduce stress and the possible resulting carpal tunnel syndrome of the control wrist. The "ideal" offset is still being debated, and paddle designs will no doubt continue to change as a result.

Whitewater canoeists use a straight paddle, rather than a bent-shaft, as both faces of the blade are used to power the craft. Canoe paddles are usually measured in inches, and generally are 54 to 60 inches long; they have a T-grip for good control of blade angulation.

Stowage. Canoeists have the luxury of storage space for a spare paddle, and should take advantage of this option. Kayakers paddling on wilderness rivers or leading a group should carry a breakdown paddle, which can be stowed under the stern deck. In all cases, whitewater playboaters should carry water, food and a personal first aid kit. All gear should be secured inside the boat to prevent loss when the boat is capsized.

Purchasing your boat. If you are a beginner, newly-hooked on the sport and thinking about purchasing a boat, you have two options: You can buy a boat designed for beginners, or you can buy a higher-performance boat designed for more experienced paddlers. The primary differences between a high-performance boat and an entry-level boat are their rocker, chines and volume. A high-performance boat is generally both heavily rockered and sharp-chined, and may have relatively low volume compared to an entry-level boat designed for the same size paddler. A boat designed for beginners will have less rocker, softer chines, and higher volume. These features make the beginner's boat more forgiving of incorrect boat leans, and easier to paddle in a straight line. If you only get to paddle a dozen days each year, or you have a conservative outlook in that you find fish counts pretty aversive and you try not to risk them, then you will probably be happiest in an entry-level boat.

Why *would* a beginner buy a high-performance boat? The entry-level boat is more forgiving. But the trouble with a forgiving boat is that you might not really learn from your mistakes, since you won't always be aware of them. The "edgier" boat (one with sharper chines) will *train* your lower body to lean correctly, to sense changes in the side of opposition and respond instantaneously by altering the boat lean. This will cost you -- You will count, and perhaps even *name,* the fish! But you will learn faster, and you'll still be happy with your boat when you become an intermediate or an advanced paddler. The same features that make the beginner's boat forgiving also reduce its responsiveness. The beginner's boat is like a docile pony, while the advanced boat is a hot-blooded racer... more fun, but bound to cost you more spills at the outset. If you are an aggressive paddler and don't mind paying your dues in fish counts, buy the boat you'll want to keep for a few years.

Purchasing other playboating equipment. When you start shopping for gear, you will find that prices vary widely. In general, the least expensive equipment will last one season at best, while the finest gear will last up to four or five seasons (not forever!). *Any* equipment that is handled improperly will be quickly destroyed, though, so treat your gear with respect. We suggest you try to buy medium-priced equipment, which should serve you well for two or three seasons. At the end of that time, you may find that the features you want in an item have changed, so you're ready to replace it anyway.

HOW TO READ THE RIVER

Understanding the various speeds and directions of current at any point on the river will enable you to anticipate the response of your boat. By playing with the river currents instead of against them, you can get almost anywhere on the river with a minimum of effort. In this chapter, we analyze the river currents without getting into boat maneuvers -- you'll find out how to play these currents in the chapter on River Playboating Maneuvers.

The art of river reading. River reading is an art that takes time to develop. It is the ability to discern river currents and underwater obstacles from patterns on the water's surface. Since river reading is an essential skill for all playboaters, it's worth investing some time to become good at it. Start with easy currents, and assess the surface patterns both from your boat and from shore. You'll find that your perspective of the rapid from the boat is quite different than from shore. For challenging rapids, it is very informative to the paddler to get out and scout, but for most paddling, you'll want to be able to read the river adequately without getting out of your boat.

Scouting rapids. When you do leave your boat to scout a rapid, don't climb some high bluff, peer *down* 50 feet to the water, and expect to plan your route. It will look entirely different from what you see once you return to your boat -- you won't even recognize where you intended to go! Scout as close to the water's edge as possible, and squat down so you get something resembling the perspective you will have from the boat. Study the rapid looking *up*river, memorize your route options, and then try to get a look at the same stretch from shore looking *down*river, so you'll know better how the route will appear from the boat.

When to scout. Scout when (1) the river ahead drops out of view, (2) there is an unusual amount of noise ahead, (3) the river has risen since you began the run, and you're not familiar with it at the new level, (4) there has been recent flooding, so there may be new strainers ahead, (5) you wish to evaluate the drop from shore before deciding whether to attempt it, *or* (6) you wish to plan your route more carefully.

The straight river: *Top view.* First, imagine a river that runs perfectly straight, and is of uniform width, with a smooth, convex-shaped riverbed. All of the water flows in the same direction, but not at the same speed! It flows fastest in the middle of the river, and slowest right next to the shore.

Cross-section. If you were a fish looking at that same river in cross-section, you'd find it flows slowly along the bottom, then faster toward the surface; it flows fastest *just below* the surface. Friction with the shoreline and riverbed slows down the water near these boundaries. Friction with air slows down the surface water.

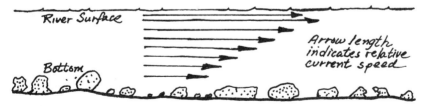

Fastest route. So, the fastest route downstream in a straight river would be mid-river. The easiest way to *ascend* such a river would be to paddle along the shore.

Current differentials. A *current differential* is an interface between two currents of different speeds and/or directions. So, all across this imaginary river, there are current differentials as one goes from the slowest current along the shore to the fastest current at midstream, and into slower current again at the far shore. Paddlers play with current differentials constantly, because they experience differing forces at the two ends of the boat, which can be exploited to play the river.

Eddies. Wherever an obstacle diverts water flowing downriver, a void is created downstream of the obstacle. Current flows upstream to fill the void, and this upstream current is called an *eddy.* An eddy is any area where water flows upstream relative to the main river current. Eddies are found just below obstacles along the shoreline and in the river, whether the obstacles break the surface or are completely underwater.

Anatomy of an Eddy

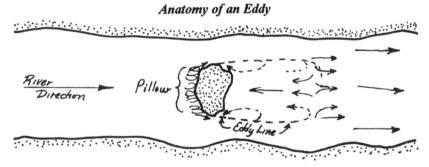

Riverbends: *Top view.* Now picture that same river, but with a bend in it. All the water flowing downstream has momentum that causes it to go straight until deflected by an obstacle. (Newton's First Law of Motion.) So it tends to flow to the outside of the riverbend, where it bounces off the shore and rebounds in the new direction of flow downriver. The result is greater volume and faster current on the outside of riverbends, and slower current on the inside. All this extra flow eventually cuts into the riverbed. That's why the river is generally deep on the outside of a bend, and has a shoal on the inside bend.

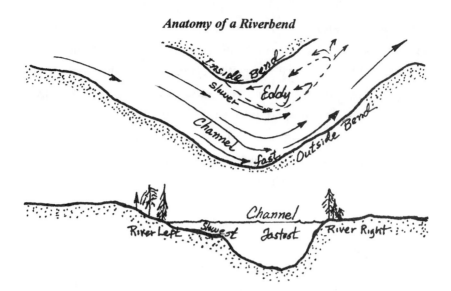

Riverbend eddy. So much water flows to the outside of the riverbend that there's a void created on the inside edge. Some of the water reverses direction to fill this void -- You can actually stand on the inside shore toward the bottom of a riverbend and watch the water rushing upstream! This *riverbend eddy* is one form of a *shoreline eddy*.

Eddy lines. Now we've got a river flowing around a bend, with water flowing *upstream* in the eddy on the inside bend, and the adjacent main river current flowing *downstream*. This is a kind of current differential, as mentioned a little while ago. Wherever there is differential involving current flowing in opposite directions, there's a shear line at the interface between the currents; this interface is called an *eddy line*. When there is substantial current in opposite directions, the eddy line is readily seen as a line of ripples on the surface.

Eddy walls. When there is extremely heavy current, the downstream flow is so fast that it doesn't immediately reverse direction at the top of the eddy but continues downriver, leaving a void that's *not* filled in behind the rock. The water surface in the top of the eddy can be as much as three or four feet below the surface of the downstream current rushing by. At such an eddy, the eddy line is a "wall" of water, and is called an *eddy wall* or *eddy fence*.

Eddy Wall -- Side View

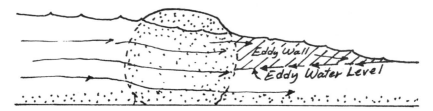

Mid-river eddies. Let's put a rock in the middle of the river. Water flowing downstream is diverted by the rock. As it flows off to the left and right of the rock, a void is left *downstream* of the rock. Just as at the riverbend, some of the water reverses direction and flows upstream to fill the void. This upstream current is another *eddy*, and it has an eddy line to right and left, where it interfaces with the downstream current. This is an absolutely *key* play feature on the river! To paddle past an eddy without "catching" it should be punishable by law.

Chutes. Picture another rock, say, 10 feet to the right of the first one. Water is diverted around both rocks, and the space *between* the rocks gets half the diverted flow from each obstacle. The extra flow is faster than the mainstream current, and is called a *chute*. Since the flow through a chute tends to be smooth and dark, it's also referred to as a *tongue* or a *black tongue*.

Downstream and upstream V's. The eddy lines adjacent to the chute will form a "V" with the apex downstream. *Downstream V's* tend to be safe routes to paddle, whereas *upstream V's* are avoided as they usually are created by an obstacle just below the surface at the apex of the "V".

White eddies. Not all eddies are formed by obstacles that break the surface. An underwater rock deflects the current too, and will create upstream current that can be seen as a *reversal* on the water's surface, where waves may crest and break on their *upstream* side; this is called a *white eddy*. (Eddies behind rocks that are exposed above the surface are sometimes referred to as *black eddies*.)

Surfing waves. If the wave in a white eddy is big enough, with a deep enough depression in the water surface just upstream of the wave, it forms what's known as a *surfing wave* or *surfing hole*. Chances are, when you come across one of these, you'll find a playboater making the most of it! You'll see why, when you get to the chapter on River Playboating Maneuvers.

Standing waves. Another playable river feature is *standing waves*. These are formed wherever fast current is forced to slow down as it encounters a pool of slower-moving water. The waves are fixed in position, though the water rushes through them. They are also referred to as *haystacks,* and are a gathering site for River Gods -- who like to watch as paddlers play the waves like dolphins frolicking in the wake of a ship.

Low Water -- Side View

Black Eddy

Medium High Water -- Side View

White Eddy

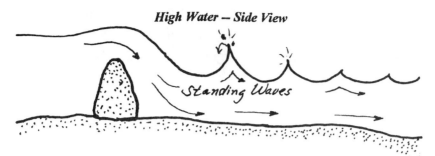

Standing Waves

Holes. All of the current differentials described so far provide great playsites. But there are also a few river features that create danger for the paddler, and should be avoided. One such feature is any very large *hole*. Holes are created by a large volume of water flowing over a dam, ledge, rock, or other underwater obstacle. The water drops over the downstream side of the obstacle, hitting forcefully at the bottom of the drop. This creates a depression on the surface, and upstream flow just downstream of the depression. If you were a fish looking at the area of the upstream flow, you would find that it's like a great big washing machine, with the water rapidly recirculating -- the deeper water flows downstream under the upstream-flowing surface water.

Keepers. When big enough, a hole can trap a boat and the paddler. The upstream current can be extremely powerful, and the depression deep enough to retain sizable objects. For this reason, such a hole is called a *keeper*.

Characteristics of unsafe holes. The primary factor that creates a keeper is the angle of descent of the smooth water after it flows over the obstacle; if it is more vertical than 45 degrees, the hole could be very difficult to get out of. A hole will be particularly hard to escape if the ends of it are upstream of the center, so the depression is shaped like a frown as you look at it from upriver; this frown is a River God warning you away! Another factor to consider is the distance between (1) the point in the depression where the smooth water hits the aerated reversal water and (2) the visible dividing point between the water flowing upstream on the surface of the hole and the water flowing downriver. (See illustration.) This top-view length of the reversal is equal to its potential depth. As a general guide, avoid holes that exceed four feet!

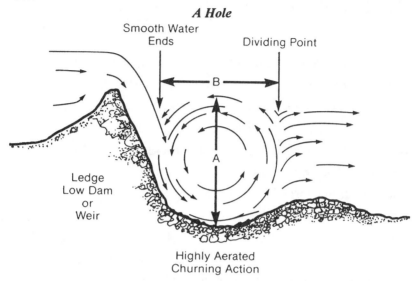

The depth of a hole (A) is often equal to the length of the boiling reversal (B). This length (B) can usually be observed from the boat or shore.

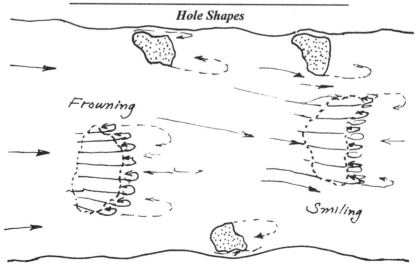

When looking at them from upriver, treat frowning holes with respect!

Stoppers. Smaller holes can be paddled straight through, if approached with enough momentum. If the hole is just large enough to momentarily stop a boat (not a keeper), it is called a *stopper*.

Strainers. The other river feature every paddler should watch out for is a *strainer*, which is any obstacle that will stop objects but permit water to flow through. It is typically a fallen tree extending into the river. Strainers trap boats and paddlers, frequently underwater, making them potentially fatal traps. Always give wide berth to any branches extending into or out of the water, as the underwater component of the strainer may be more extensive than it appears from the surface.

Volume. Finally, get to know your local rivers in terms of their *volume*. Volume of river flow is measured in cubic feet per second, c.f.s. For each section of a river, there is a characteristic flow at any given c.f.s., but this of course does not transfer to another river --- 12,000 c.f.s. on the Rio Grande is a lot easier to paddle than the same volume would be on the creek behind the cabin! Learn what c.f.s. ranges are best for the rivers you frequent.

Gauges. Find the gauges -- or, in the case of dam-controlled rivers, the phone numbers for recorded release announcements -- so you know what to expect in the way of river currents on the day of your run. Local outfitters and experienced local paddlers can tell you the characteristics of the river at various levels on the gauge.

Sometimes a Channel is the Safest Route...

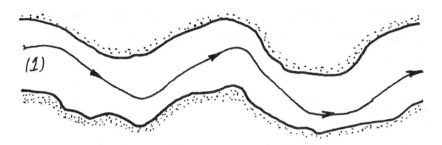

(1)

...And Sometimes It's Not!

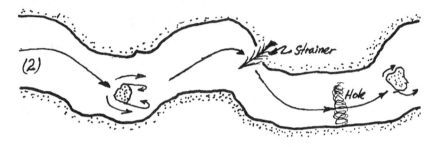

(2)

Strainer

Hole

Two Converging Rivers Form an Unstable Shear Line

Eddy

The Low Head Dam

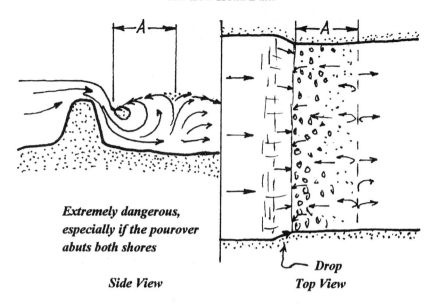

Extremely dangerous, especially if the pourover abuts both shores

Side View

Drop

Top View

The Rock Garden: Playboater's Heaven

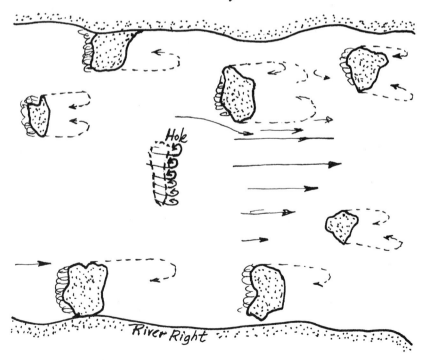

INTERNATIONAL SCALE
OF RIVER DIFFICULTY

RATING	RIVER CHARACTERISTICS	EXPERIENCE REQUIRED
SMOOTH WATER		
CLASS A	**Pools, Lakes, Rivers** Flowing under 2 mph	BEGINNER
CLASS B	**Rivers** Flowing 2-4 mph	BEGINNER WITH RIVER INSTRUCTION
CLASS C	**Rivers** Flowing above 4 mph	INSTRUCTED AND PRACTICED BEGINNER
WHITEWATER		
CLASS I	**Easy** -- River speed 4-6 mph. (River can be ascended by beginners.) A few riffles and small waves. Few or no obstructions.	PRACTICED BEGINNER
CLASS II	**Moderate** -- Frequent but unobstructed rapids. Easy eddies and bends. Course generally easy to recognize. River usually can be ascended by experienced paddlers. Waves up to 3 feet. Some maneuvering necessary.	INSTRUCTED NOVICE
CLASS III	**Difficult** -- Maneuvering necessary. Numerous rapids with high, irregular waves which may swamp open boats. Main current may have dangerous strainers or obstacles. Course not easily recognizable. Scouting advised, from shore or from eddies.	INTERMEDIATE

CLASS IV	**Very difficult** -- Long, extended stretches of rapids. High, irregular waves with boulders directly in current. Difficult broken water, eddies, and abrupt bends. Scouting frequently necessary. Rescue difficult. Should have reliable roll, whether in open or decked craft.	ADVANCED, WITH SEVERAL SEASONS OF EXPERIENCE
CLASS V	**Exceedingly difficult** -- Long, difficult, rocky rapids with completely irregular water that must be run "head on." Very fast eddies, abrupt bends, and vigorous cross currents. Rescue conditions very difficult. Decked boats only. Must have reliable roll.	TEAM OF EXPERTS
CLASS VI	**Limit of navigability** -- Previously listed difficulties increased to the limit. Only negotiable at favorable water levels. Cannot be attempted without risking life.	TEAM OF EXPERTS WITH NO DEPENDENTS OR LOVED ONES

NOTES:

It is rarely accurate to classify an entire river. Classify specific rapids or sections of the river. For example, the Fife Brook section of the Deerfield River in Massachusetts is mostly Class I-II, but the paddler unfamiliar with this river needs to know there is a short but intense Class III rapid about halfway down this section. Also, changes in the water level or the presence of new obstacles or strainers frequently alter the class of a particular rapid, so beware of outdated river classifications.

When planning a river run, it is advisable to add one difficulty class for each of the following environmental conditions: (1) an extremely windy and gusty day, (2) the sum of the air and water temperatures being less than 100 degrees, or (3) a wilderness river run with no immediate vehicle available in case of emergency.

CONCEPTS OF PADDLING

The paddler's goal is to "play" the river with fluidity and grace, through precise, efficient boat control. This requires a combination of intellectual understanding and physical skills. You have begun to develop a knowledge base by studying the fundamentals of river currents. The next step is to examine the concepts of paddling. Those of you who are analytical learners will <u>love</u> this chapter. Those of you who "learn best by doing," we urge you to tackle the intellectual side of the sport -- We will continue to build on these tools toward the playboater's goal of intelligently challenging Mother Nature!

Understand River Currents: Learn to read the river and operate your craft in harmony with it. You should feel connected to the river, working *with* the currents, rather than against them... a wise move, since you can't expect to be stronger than the river. This "connection" isn't learned overnight! See chapter on How to Read the River.

Two Bodies: Paddlers use their upper body to control the paddle position, and their lower body to control the boat position. So, step into your boat and *voila!* you have two bodies. Now, all you have to do is learn how to use them!

One Unit: The boat and your body move as one unit. Your lower body has several contact points with the boat, which should hold you in it tightly but comfortably, much like a foot in a ski boot. With a snug fit, the boat responds immediately to your lower body movements as if it were an extension of your body.

J-leans: Paddlers constantly heel their boat while keeping their upper body approximately over the centerline to keep from capsizing. They do so with a J-lean, which is primarily a lower body function. Let's suppose you're leaning the boat to your right. The right side of your body will be stretched and the left side crimped as you curl your body laterally. Pull up on your left leg to get the full effect -- Your body is now curled in the shape of a "J".

Correct Boat Lean Technique

Incorrect Boat Lean Technique

Side of Opposition: Whitewater playboaters are always J-leaning to elevate the craft's *side of opposition*. That's the side of the boat experiencing greater water pressure at a given moment. This water pressure will tend to capsize the boat or at least slow the boat's movement, if the side of opposition is not raised. For example, when sculling to move the craft sideways, the side of opposition is the side of the boat nearest the working blade. When the boat is turning, the side on the outside of the turn is the side of opposition -- it is the greater resistance (water pressure) on this side that is causing the boat to turn.

Bank Your Craft: *"Proper boat lean prevents fish counts."* Repeat this five times after every swim!! When the bow is turning to the right, J-lean your body to heel the boat to the right. When the bow is turning to the left, lean the boat to the left. Think of it as banking the boat, the way you would bank an airplane, or the way you would lean into a turn on a bicycle. This lower body function is generally independent of what you're doing with your paddle, and is based on the fact that the side of the craft *away* from the direction the boat is turning is *always* the side of opposition.

Use Your Torso: The muscles of your torso have far greater strength and endurance than your arm muscles. So you can paddle with greater power and efficiency by torso rotation than by just using your arms. Torso rotation also protects against shoulder injury. Your arms should remain fairly rigid during the powerphase of a stroke, and simply function as extensions from the torso muscles to the paddle.

The Paddler's Box: Imagine a box in front of your shoulders; the back of the box is your chest. Always keep both hands in the box. To place your paddle blade behind your hips (as in a sweep), rotate your torso so the box projects toward the paddle shaft; i.e., the box rotates too, enabling you to keep your hands in the box. Placing a hand outside the paddler's box risks shoulder dislocation. This is an entirely preventable injury if you concentrate on this concept.

Pivot Point: To control your boat's course more easily, locate its pivot point. It is the point on the hull where a mermaid with a bionic finger could balance you and your boat in midair. If you are in your boat and your boat is trim, the pivot point is generally located near the center of the boat and on the centerline.

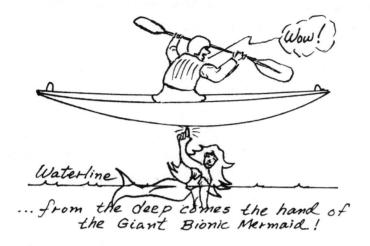

...from the deep comes the hand of the Giant Bionic Mermaid!

Distance from Pivot Point: When you want to turn your boat, the farther you place your paddle blade from the pivot point, the more turn you'll get for a given amount of force on the paddle. So, the most efficient way to turn the boat is with the paddle shaft horizontal, which enables you to stroke farther from the pivot point.

Frontal Resistance: When your craft is under way, the ends respond very unequally due to the different *resistances* at the bow and stern. As the boat travels forward, the bow is plowing through the water and displacing it. (The stern is plowing when going in reverse.) The water presses on the sides of the boat as water is displaced along to the widest part of the boat, which is generally in the same area as the pivot point. This is the *frontal resistance end* of the boat, also referred to as the leading end of the boat. This resistance or pressure is very stabilizing on the half of the boat affected by it, and makes it more difficult to turn the boat with strokes executed at this end of the boat.

Eddy Resistance: From the widest part of your craft aft to the stern, water is swirling in to fill the void left by the boat as it travels forward. This is exactly what water does downstream of a rock -- in other words, the "trailing end" of the boat is in an eddy! That's why we call it the *eddy resistance end* of the boat. There is very little stabilizing lateral pressure on this half of the boat. The trailing end responds as if it were on ball bearings -- A correction stroke executed far from the pivot point, *in the following end of the boat,* will change the boat's course dramatically... in the same boat that seems so stubborn when corrections are attempted at the frontal resistance end!

An Eddy ...or is it?

Current Direction

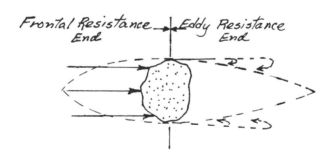

A paddler holding position in the current....
A boat could be thought of as a "moving rock."

The Three Resistances

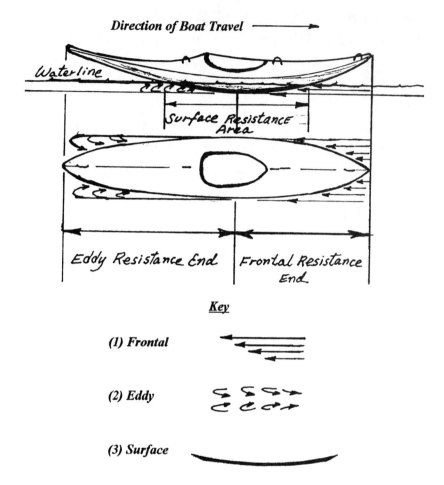

Direction of Boat Travel ⟶

Waterline

Surface Resistance Area

Eddy Resistance End

Frontal Resistance End

Key

(1) Frontal

(2) Eddy

(3) Surface

*Power strokes and power control strokes are
executed in the frontal resistance end of the boat.
Correction strokes are executed in the eddy
resistance or "ball bearing" end of the boat.*

Newton's Third Law of Motion: Newton *must* have had playboating in mind when he wrote, *"For every action there is an equal and opposite reaction."* The *action* is the force applied on the blade by the paddler. The *reaction* is the response of the boat generally in the opposite direction. Efficient strokes and precise boat control are achieved only when the paddler keeps "Uncle Newton" in mind!

Categories of Strokes: There are three categories of strokes: (1) power and control strokes, with a nearly vertical shaft angle and the blade close to the boat, propelling the craft forward or backward; (2) correction strokes, with sloping-to-horizontal shaft angles, executed in the following end of the boat and designed to change or correct a course; and (3) righting-action strokes which prevent the craft from tipping over.

Power and Control Strokes: Strokes that provide significant momentum are done in the frontal resistance end of the boat and are called *power strokes* and *control strokes.* These strokes are generally done parallel to the boat's centerline. Power strokes propel the boat on its established course. Control strokes provide forward momentum while adjusting the boat's course via subtle modifications in blade angulation and/or position.

Correction strokes: Correction strokes are executed in the trailing end of the boat. These strokes *turn* the boat well, but are not considered efficient because they contribute little, if any, to the boat's momentum.

Stroke Components: There are two major stroke components -- the propulsion phase and the recovery phase. During the *propulsion phase*, the paddler is applying force to either the backface or the powerface of the paddle and the boat responds.

During the *recovery phase*, the paddler moves the paddle either through or over the water to another anchor position, to set up for the next powerphase.

Paddle as Anchor: When you are under way, the paddle only moves through the water an inch or so during the powerphase of a stroke -- if you place it next to a bubble on the water's surface at the beginning of a stroke, you'll see it's still next to the bubble at the end of the stroke... while your *boat* will have moved several feet! So, think of your paddle as an anchor and use your lower body to pull the boat to the anchor.

Paddle as Stabilizer: Since the blade functions as an anchor, it also helps stabilize the boat -- the boat is less likely to capsize when you are stroking than when you glide with the blade in the air. The rule to remember is: When in trouble, stroke!

The Paddler's Pie: If your intended direction is straight ahead at twelve o'clock, the paddler's pie is that wedge 30 degrees to each side of twelve o'clock -- that is, eleven o'clock to one o'clock. If you keep your bow within the pie, you'll be able to maintain your desired course by using power and control strokes only. If your boat shifts out of the pie, the most efficient way to get back on course is to resort to a correction stroke, which is executed in the eddy resistance end of the boat. As your paddling improves, you'll make fewer of these correction strokes. *It is the paddler's utopian goal to have such precise boat control that all strokes can be placed in the frontal resistance end of the boat.*

THE CIRCLE CONCEPT

This is one more concept of paddling, but because it is a major new idea in contemporary playboating, it deserves a separate chapter. Paddlers have been "carving circles" for years, but the circle concept itself was not being taught to beginners until fairly recently. Understanding the circle concept will enable you to play the river with a minimum number of correction strokes, using mostly power and control strokes -- you'll get where you want to go more safely and with less effort than you would have thought possible.

Boat design. Whitewater playboats are designed to "carve a circle," not to track in a straight line. Maneuverability is more useful than tracking ability because playboating involves constant turns and spins, and rarely involves paddling in a straight line from Point A to Point B. As a result, your boat, by its design, is just *begging* to be paddled in circles.

The forward stroke. As you try carving circles, you will want to develop a good, *short* forward stroke. If your strokes are too long or too far from the centerline, you will be unable to apply the circle concept on the water; the boat will turn away from the paddle as if you were performing a forward sweep, when your intention is to do a forward stroke. Paddling circles will help you develop a technically correct forward stroke.

Starting a circle. One starts a circle by getting the boat moving forward and turning slightly in the desired direction, and then executing forward and control strokes on the "inside" of the circle (the side to which the boat is turning). Kayakers of course stroke on both sides, but the stroke on the inside of the circle is modified to control the size of the circle (explained in a bit).

Boat lean. *Lean the boat in the direction it is turning.* This is a rule that should be emblazoned in your brain. It will prevent countless fish counts! This rule applies whenever you're traveling *faster than the current* -- which should be most of the time, in good playboating. Whether the paddler or the river causes the boat to turn, the fact that it's turning means there is a side of opposition on the outside of the turn. And you should *always elevate the side of opposition, even if that means you'll be leaning upstream* -- something many paddlers used to be taught not to do!

Where to stroke. Kayakers stroke varying distances from the boat on the inside of the circle, and they use a high shaft angle to stroke close to the boat on the other side. Canoeists stroke *only* on the inside of the circle, using forward strokes when turning to their onside, and cross forward strokes when turning to their offside -- again varying the distance of the strokes from the hull. In either craft, this stroke placement influences the size of the circle.

Boat-designed circle. With regular forward strokes and a slight lean into the turn, a contemporary playboat will carve a circle so small that you won't feel like you're going anywhere! The size of the circle toward which your boat gravitates depends on the design of its hull, and is referred to as the *boat-designed circle*. Modern playboats have boat-designed circles ranging from ten to twenty feet in diameter.

Larger circles. You can shift out of the boat-designed circle by altering your boat lean and/or the distance from the boat that your forward strokes are executed. To increase the circle size, decrease the boat lean (always maintain *some* lean!) and stroke farther from the boat. Of these two factors, boat lean has the greater influence on circle size.

Smaller circles. When you want to paddle a smaller circle, simply increase your boat lean and stroke closer to the boat on the inside of the circle. Don't let your circle get too small, because it's more difficult to open a circle up than it is to make it smaller.

Tandem canoes. In tandem paddling, the size of the circle to be carved is set and controlled by the stern paddler. The bow paddler contributes forward momentum with power strokes. The easier circle to carve is the one turning toward the side on which the sternperson is paddling, since he can apply the same techniques as if he were paddling solo.

Tandem stern's offside circle. If tandem canoe paddlers were to switch paddling sides when carving in the other direction, it would be easy for the stern paddler to control the size of either circle! However, switching sides is a major *faux pas* in contemporary canoe playboating. So the sternperson controls his offside circle by using either a rudder or a pry to increase the size of the circle; this usually forces him to skip one of the bowperson's forward strokes, but the paddlers regain unison paddling on the next stroke.

Figure eights. Practice increasing and decreasing the size of your circles, and then try Figure Eights -- switching from a left circle to a right circle, and back again. More on the use of Figure Eights in later chapters.

Circles on the river. How will these circles apply to the river? Every peel-out, every eddy turn, and even every ferry is an arc, which is *part* of a circle! We're going to show you how to do these river maneuvers "on the circle." You'll control your course by adjusting the size of the circle or changing to the opposite circle. Circle paddling uses power strokes almost exclusively, so you're constantly adding to your boat's momentum -- which enhances your control of the boat's course.

Efficiency. The circle concept is efficient because it eliminates the need for correction strokes done in the eddy resistance end of the boat. You'll get more miles of play out of a single energy bar than ever before.

Safety. The circle concept increases your safety on the river because it teaches you to set the proper lean in the leaving current when circling into or out of eddies. Paddlers take fewer unpremeditated swims when carving circles, as they quickly learn to set the correct boat lean before crossing a differential or eddy line.

KAYAKING

Don't read this chapter!! *...until* you have read the preceding chapters! This entire book (believe it or not!) is designed in a logical progression; when we present you with the material specific to kayaking, we're counting on you to understand all the aspects of playboating covered earlier. So, if you skipped directly from the Table of Contents to this page, WE CAUGHT YOU and we're sending you back to Chapter One.

Introduction. Whitewater playboating is easy!! But it *does* require the development of a number of specific skills. Some people expect to hop into a kayak and be ready for Class IV rivers by the end of their first day. However, after a few hours in the boat, these same people may be convinced those rivers will be forever beyond their reach. *You*, however, are going to be able to paddle those rivers, if you so desire... *after* investing in formal instruction, good equipment, and many exciting and challenging days of practice.

We urge you to start with formal instruction at a reputable school of paddling. It's all too easy to develop incorrect technique if you try to learn completely on your own or from friends. It takes time to master even the most basic skills, so give yourself at least 15 to 20 days of concentrated paddling after your initial lesson before you even *think* about giving up. Otherwise, your initial investment will be wasted, and you may deprive yourself of a most enjoyable and rewarding lifetime sport.

Also remember that everyone learns cognitive and motor skills at his own pace. So believe in yourself, proceed at your own pace, and try not to compare yourself to others. The rate at which you learn has no relation to the ultimate skill level you will achieve!

In this chapter, we're going to cover all the essential skills required for effective boat control -- starting before you even get into the boat, since managing it on land can make you feel like a beached elephant seal with a bad limp! From land, we'll get you into your boat on calm water, where most skills must be mastered before being attempted on moving water. On a lake or calm pool in a river, you can work through the specific strokes and boat movements presented in this chapter. Our logical progression will introduce or review for you the skills needed on the river. In the chapter on River Playboating Maneuvers, we'll show you how to apply these techniques to whitewater.

Fitting Yourself to the Boat. Your kayak should be snug on your lower body. The boat will respond as if highly attuned to your every move if you *wear* it, rather than fitting loosely into it. Start by selecting a kayak that is the right size for your body. There are small boats for kids and large boats for people who weigh as much as 260 pounds, and there are a variety of boats designed for every size in between. Any reputable kayak dealer should be able to help you select a suitable boat for your body type. *But*, we strongly recommend that you take at least a two-day lesson before you consider such an investment. Not only will you then know whether or not you really want to take up the sport, but you will make a more educated choice when you do buy. Your kayak and all the necessary gear may well cost as much as $1200 to $1600, depending on the quality of the items you select. (More on purchasing a boat in the chapter on Playboating Equipment.)

Once you have a boat, you will need it fitted further to your body, because kayaks come generically outfitted, which is generally not sufficient for good boat control on whitewater. Start with it on dry land. Slide into the boat feet-first, setting the balls of your feet on the foot braces or foot walls. Your heels should be next to the walls. Move the braces or walls fore or aft until your knees are held firmly up on the underside of the deck. Your feet should be comfortable, neither crunched up against the braces nor straining to reach them. They should have a slight forward tilt, like the position they would have if you sat on the floor and rested your legs in front of you.

Your knees should be spread as far apart as possible and snugly held up under the deck. Once in position, they should not easily move laterally. If they do, consider installing another set of thigh braces or having knee cups fitted underneath the deck of the boat. Also, make sure the braces are against the thighs no more than six inches above the knee.

Next, check for any space between your hips and the sides of the boat. You do not want any room for slipping from side to side. Have hip pads installed if you're able to move sideways on the seat. Hip pads should make you feel snug in the boat, while not *so* snug that you would have difficulty getting out of the boat when capsized.

The back support deserves close attention, and is one item of outfitting that must be installed in every kayak. A good back brace prevents lower back pain, which is a common complaint of the kayak paddler. A well-designed brace supports your lower back and keeps you sitting erect in your craft. There are two common types: a back band and a mini-foam brace, the latter of which has to be custom installed. Most dealers sell the bands; only a few install the foam. The authors prefer foam back braces, because they remain in place when getting into and out of the boat, they are higher and more comfortable, and they can be designed to be removable so gear can be easily stored in the stern compartments.

Carrying your boat. It is worth learning to carry your boat and gear properly, to prevent injury to yourself or your equipment. Start with your paddle on the ground parallel to the boat. Stand between the boat and the paddle, and bend at the knees so you're crouching between them. With the hand nearest the boat (your *onside* hand), grasp the cockpit rim furthest away from you and place this rim on your shoulder. You'll find this is more comfortable if you wear your PFD! The boat should be at or near its balance point; adjust the boat fore or aft, if necessary, until the balance point rests on your shoulder. Then, still crouching, pick up the paddle with your other hand. Keeping your back straight, stand up. Remember to do all bending at the knees!

Loading and unloading. For the best river karma, always load your boat bow-forward! We don't know why this is true, but it is! The easiest way to get the boat onto the vehicle is to start with it on your head. Here's how to get to that position: Crouch down as you did to put the kayak on your shoulder. But this time, reach across the cockpit with the *offside* hand (the hand farthest from the cockpit) and grasp the far rim, with your thumb on the inner edge of the rim. Then grasp the near edge of the cockpit rim with your onside hand, again placing your thumb on the inside edge. In one smooth but strong motion, swing the boat up over your head and rest the seat of the boat on the top of your head. You'll be more comfortable if you have on your helmet! Straighten your knees to stand up. Remember to keep your back straight. Approach the back of the vehicle and gently set the bow on the "stern" roof rack, and push it forward a couple of feet. Roll the boat over, so the cockpit rim won't catch on the rack as you slide it the rest of the way onto the vehicle's "bow" roof rack. Center the boat on *both* racks, when viewed from the side!

Securing the boat for travel. A minimum of two sturdy lines or straps should be used whenever you tie a boat to a rack. You can buy straps that have a clinch-buckle and are 15 or 20 feet long wherever you buy your paddling gear. These allow for quick, secure tie-down of the craft. One line goes over the boat about six inches forward of the cockpit, and the other goes about six inches aft of the cockpit. They should be tied tightly to the bars of the rack. Additional lines, or the extra length of the first two lines, can be run through each grab loop and tied back to the rack to provide security against the boat sliding forward or backward on a hill or when you change speed suddenly. Remember they will only prevent the boat from shifting if the bow and stern lines go in opposite directions to their tie-down points on the vehicle. When more than two boats are loaded, alternate between bow-forward and stern-forward, because the bows are thicker than the sterns, and this alternating pattern will result in an even-width load on top of the vehicle. (Your river karma will be fine as long as any stern-forward boats are sandwiched between positive-karma, bow-forward boats.) Secure all the grab loops in the front of the vehicle with one line, and all the grab loops in the rear with another, plus the two lines running over the boats amidships. Regardless of whose boats they are and who ties them on, remember, the driver of the vehicle is always responsible for making sure the kayaks will not become airborne on the highway!

Launching and landing. Many beginning paddlers take their first unintended swim as they try to get into their kayak for the first time! Here's how to stay dry and look cool: Place your boat parallel to shore, just barely in the water, but not totally afloat, if possible. If you're on the river, aim the bow upstream to the main current. Set your paddle shaft just behind the cockpit rim, with the backface of one blade resting on land. (Be sure to use the backface, not the powerface, as its contour will conform to the ground, and you will not damage the tip.) The other blade will be off the other side of the boat, out over the water. Crouch down next to the cockpit, place the foot nearer the boat on the bottom in the *center* of the boat, and swing your "behind" onto the back of the boat so you're sitting on the back deck just aft of the cockpit rim. The hand near shore should be on the paddle shaft. Throughout this elegant maneuver, lean slightly toward shore, applying slight pressure to the "land brace" that you've set up with your paddle. (Don't damage your paddle by leaning heavily toward shore.) This will prevent the boat from tipping over and/or slipping away from land. As your balance improves, you'll become comfortable getting into the boat without a "land brace," and your paddle will breathe a sigh of relief.

Now place your other foot in the boat. Straighten both legs and slide your feet down to the foot pegs. *Voila!* You're in!! Reach behind you, pick up the paddle, and place it in front of you on the cockpit. Now you may be afloat if you had to launch into deep water. If so, you'll want to be competent at getting your sprayskirt on quickly after getting into the boat. When possible, launch in shallow water so you can stay a bit aground until your sprayskirt is secured. Landing and getting out of your boat is simply the reverse of the sequence outlined above.

An alternative launching position, off a beach or gradual sloping shoreline, is to set the boat at right angles to shore, with the bow in the water. You can get into the boat without any risk of tipping over, since it's still partially on land! Then, once in the boat, slide into the water by pushing off with your hands. Landings can be done the same way, if you paddle hard as you approach a sandy beach or grassy shoreline.

Securing the sprayskirt. Learning to put on a neoprene

sprayskirt is one of the most frustrating experiences of the beginning paddler. To secure the sprayskirt around the cockpit rim, start by leaning back slightly. Reaching behind you with both hands, tuck the back of the sprayskirt underneath the rim. Work each hand forward along the right and left rims, tucking the sprayskirt in until you have reached about the middle of the cockpit. Then, grasp the very front of the skirt to pull it forward and tuck the front of the skirt under the rim, *making sure the grab loop is out*. If the sprayskirt snaps off behind you, start over. (Ugh!) Wetting the skirt often helps it to go on more easily. With the back tucked in, work your way forward along the sides until the entire sprayskirt is secure. Before leaving terra firma behind, check your efforts by leaning left and right, then tucking forward and leaning back. If the sprayskirt pops loose, go back to square one. (Aarrgh!)

Holding the paddle. Balance your paddle on your head. Honest! This is a good starting point for finding the correct hand positions, so do it! Position your hands on the paddle so that each elbow is bent at a 90 degree angle. Your forearms will be at 90 degrees to the paddle shaft.

Once you have this position, lower the paddle down in front of you, and bring your hands together two to three inches. Make sure your hands are equal distances from their respective blades. There should be about six to eight inches between the pinky finger and the throat of the blade. Maintaining these hand positions, hold the paddle out in front of you with the right blade at right angles to the water surface. Line up the knuckles of your right hand with the top edge of the right blade. This should feel comfortable because paddles are designed with an oval shaft that fits naturally in your palm when your hand position is correct.

Holding the Paddle

Start With Your Hands Here...

...And Then Bring Them Together About to Here

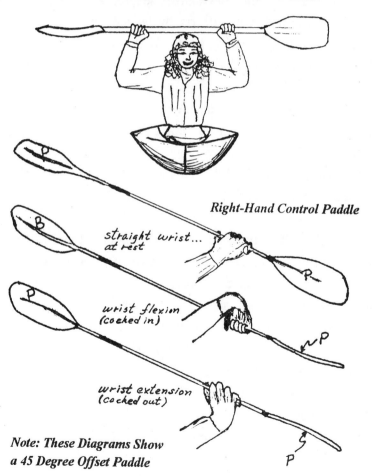

Right-Hand Control Paddle

straight wrist...
at rest

wrist flexion
(cocked in)

wrist extension
(cocked out)

**Note: These Diagrams Show
a 45 Degree Offset Paddle**

Most paddles are designed for right-hand control. That is, blade angulation is controlled by the right hand. The right hand holds the shaft securely at all times (no white-knuckled death grip, please!), and blade angle is controlled by the degree of flexion or extension at the right wrist. The right hand is therefore called the *control hand.* *Cocking out* means raising the hand (*dropping* the wrist, which is *extension* of the wrist); *cocking in* means lowering the hand (*raising* the wrist, which is *flexion* of the wrist). Most of the strokes executed on your left side are done with a cocked-out (extended) wrist. Don't you just hate learning three different ways to say the same thing? But you'll come across all these terms wherever paddlers gather, and we want you to be on top of the lingo!

The left hand grips the shaft securely during powerphases, but loosens when the shaft is being rotated to alter blade angulation. Under no circumstances should either hand shift laterally on the paddle shaft. Entry-level paddlers often benefit from placing colored vinyl tape on the shaft to mark the proper hand positions.

In kayaking, the blade that's in the water at a given moment is referred to as the *working blade*; everything from the centerline of the boat (and the midline of your body) "out" to the working blade is referred to as *onside* -- as in, "the onside edge of the cockpit," "your onside shoulder," or "the onside blade," which is, again, the working blade! The opposite of *onside* is *offside*, which describes everything from the centerline out to the *non*-working blade.

Wet exits. Well, at last you're *in* your boat, and the first thing we want you to practice is getting *out!* These little playboats are tippy critters and they love to take the entry-level paddler to the position of greatest stability -- that's upside-down with the body down too!! So let's go over how to get out when this happens:

Tuck. You must develop the reflex of immediately tucking your body forward whenever you capsize. Tuck all the way forward to the front deck. The tucked position is important for three reasons. First, it is the only position from which you can easily get out of the boat when capsized. Well, that should convince you to do it without even hearing about the second and third reasons, but we'll give them to you anyway. Second, this position minimizes your depth in the water, and is therefore safer. No good being upside-down and head-in-the-mud to boot. And third, if you do hit an underwater object, it will more likely impact the back of your helmet or lifevest, whereas if you leaned back, it could hit your face. When you tuck, try not to let go of your paddle!

Pull. Next, while remaining tucked, take the grab loop of your sprayskirt and pull it forward and up to release it from the cockpit rim. In plastic kayaks, the rim is rounded enough for you to release the skirt just by pulling straight up (actually, straight *down,* since you're upside-down, but everyone gets confused in this position).

Push. Finally, *still* tucked, and preferably still holding onto your paddle with one hand, place both hands on the boat next to your hips, and push the boat vigorously off your body. Push the boat forward toward your head, not up. This will get your legs out so you can start swimming to shore.

Let's review the wet exit: TUCK, PULL, PUSH. Practice it, for there is no such thing as a bomb-proof roll. Every paddler, regardless of his skill level, will sometimes have to call upon the wet exit as his means of self-rescue. Do not proceed until you are completely comfortable doing wet-exits!

The boat boogie-wiggle. To get comfortable J-leaning your boat and get acquainted with its secondary stability, practice vigorously tipping your boat first to one side and then to the other while keeping your upper body centered over the boat. Try to get the edges of your sprayskirt wet! Next set a fixed boat lean to one side, say the right. Try to keep your upper body fairly upright while curling your torso, stretching the right side of your body and kinking the left. At the same time, lift up on your left knee and weight your right hip. This total set of movements comprises the well-known *J-lean.* Next, try holding a left lean with the J-lean. Can you "snap" the boat from one fixed lean to the other? Having fun yet? Did you get a chance to practice your wet exit or roll?

Hip-Snapping From One J-lean to the Other

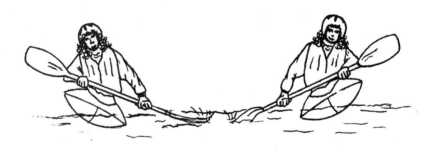

Preventing capsizes: Righting Action Strokes. It's time for a major brain shift. All these years, you've thought of water as a liquid. We want you to think of it as a *solid*, something you can brace on to support yourself and your boat. In fact, it's supporting your boat all the time -- just maybe not always in your preferred upright position! The reason we want you to make this mental adjustment is that you're going to use the water surface to brace your paddle blade when you execute hip snaps to prevent your boat from capsizing. There are two types of braces: high braces and low braces. The difference between these is that on the high brace, the powerface of the paddle hits the water, and your elbows are below the paddle shaft (knuckles up), while on the low brace, the backface hits the water and your elbows are above the shaft (knuckles down).

Righting Action Strokes:

The High Brace

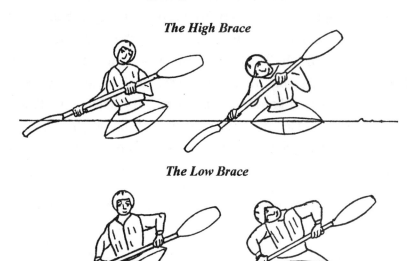

The Low Brace

1.) The high brace. J-lean your boat to the right. Drop (extend) your control wrist and hold the right blade parallel to the water surface with your elbows below the shaft. With your paddle shaft about eight inches in front of your torso and at right angles to the centerline, extend the blade out a bit from the hull. Place your left elbow *on* the sprayskirt next to your left side. Now J-lean a bit further, until you're on the verge of tipping over! At the last moment before capsizing, execute the brace by landing the right powerface on the water. At the same moment, aggressively fling your head toward the working blade. This will cause you to pull down reflexively on your right arm (but don't pull down intentionally), and up on your right leg (i.e., hip-snap), and will right the boat. But remember to keep your head on your shoulder until the boat is fully righted, or you're going to head back down again!

On both the high brace and the low brace, the blade should have a slight climbing angle (the edge of the blade nearest the bow slightly higher than trailing edge), so the blade will stay on the surface during the brace. Since most of the time you will have forward momentum when a brace is needed, the blade will be traveling forward on the water surface as you brace. Bracing with a diving angle could send the blade *down*... to be followed by the paddler!

When a brace is performed, the blade sinks a short distance in the water. In order to pull the blade out of the water without pulling the boat back *down*, feather the blade out by dropping your control hand so the powerface is facing back. This allows the blade to slice cleanly out of the water for the recovery. Practice high braces on the right several times, then on the left several times. Your left high braces will be a bit more difficult, since you have to position the blade so the *left* powerface is at a slight climbing angle. You will have to extend your control wrist as for the right high brace, but you must also bend your right arm at the elbow to raise the control hand level with your collarbone. Don't cheat by rotating your control hand on the shaft!

2.) The low brace. This time, J-lean your boat to the left. Again, hold your paddle about eight inches in front of your torso, with the shaft perpendicular to the centerline. The left blade should be just above the surface of the water with the backface down, and the edge nearest the bow slightly elevated. Your elbows are above the shaft, which is practically resting on the sprayskirt. Lean, lean, lean! At the last possible moment, hit the backface on

61

the water, fling your head toward the blade, and the rest should follow -- a slight downward push with your left hand, and an aggressive upward pull on your left leg. As in the high brace, recover with the powerface facing back as the blade slices to the surface. You'll have to extend the control wrist (raise the control hand) for the recovery. Practice low braces on the left, but you don't really have to practice them on the right, since the low brace is rarely all that useful on the right. Most experienced paddlers develop a conditioned reflex for a high brace on their right and a low brace on their left, because it takes minimal control hand movement to effect these particular braces. To perform a high brace on the right, you simply raise the control hand, and to perform a low brace on the left, you don't have to alter your control hand position from the usual set-up position.

Maneuver: Spin. A spin is a pivot of a boat without forward or astern movement. It is useful for positioning the bow or stern in a particular orientation to ready the craft for another maneuver.

Strokes for this maneuver:

1.) Forward Sweep The forward sweep is a 180 degree arc in which the blade starts at the bow, and ends at the stern. The blade actually hardly moves at all -- it is the *boat* that pivots 180 degrees while the blade stays in place. The paddler lowers the shaft of the paddle, rotates his onside shoulder forward, and anchors the blade as close to the bow as possible with the blade vertical in the water. He then de-rotates his shoulder plane, keeping the shaft parallel to it, until the stern comes to the blade.

Actually, the paddler can think of his boat as a pinwheel with himself at the center. Instead of wind causing the pinwheel to spin, it's the paddler's pressure against his working blade that causes the boat to rotate around its pivot point. As such, the boat should have minimal forward or backward movement nor should the paddle move much through the water -- it simply acts as a lever. To extend the blade farther from the pivot point, the paddler can (1) lean forward slightly at the beginning of the stroke, straighten his body as the shaft comes to right angles with the centerline, and then lean back slightly as he completes the second half of the sweep; and (2) extend his arms comfortably out toward the working blade (without shifting the hand positions on the shaft!) throughout the entire stroke. The sweep ends with the paddle parallel to the boat's centerline and both hands out over the water. Lean the boat slightly toward the working blade during the first half of the stroke, and then slightly away from it during the last half. This elevates the edge of your boat that might otherwise dive underwater as the boat spins -- in other words, your lean will elevate the side of opposition in the end of the boat that is heaviest during each part of the stroke. To make sure you're using full shoulder rotation, keep your eyes on the working blade throughout the stroke. A good exercise for practicing this stroke on *both* sides is to paddle forward using only forward sweeps. The boat will trace a lovely serpentine pattern across the pond! Concentrate on your boat leans, remembering that the lean at the end of one sweep is the same as the lean at the beginning of the next sweep. And rotate your torso -- watch the working blade throughout each sweep.

2.) Reverse Sweep This stroke is simply the reverse of the forward sweep, with the same characteristics: low shaft angle, blade extension from the hull, and boat lean toward the first half of the stroke and away from the second half. The only difference is that the blade is swept at a climbing angle, i.e., the top edge of the blade is tipped forward about 45 degrees throughout the entire powerphase. The blade is initially anchored at the stern,

KAYAK STROKES

EXPLANATION OF ILLUSTRATIONS

Short lines represent a tip-first water entry of the blade with the shaft relatively vertical. Elongated lines represent a more horizontal insertion of the blade. Small arrows adjacent to the paddle blade lines indicate the direction a force is applied during the powerphase of a stroke. Longer bold arrows originating from the side or end of the kayak illustrate the change in the directional movement of the kayak produced by the stroke.

MANEUVER: SPINS

(1) Stroke: Forward Sweep

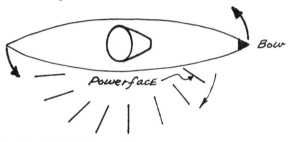

---

(2) Stroke: Reverse Sweep

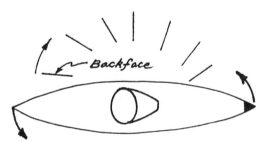

---

(3) Stroke: Stern Sweep

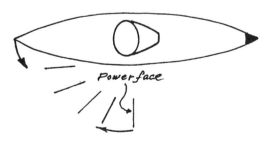

and the powerphase ends as the bow comes to the blade. Practice paddling backwards across the pond, using reverse sweeps alternately on one side and then the other. Again, focus on your boat leans; the lean at the end of one sweep is the same as the lean at the beginning of the next sweep. And remember to watch the working blade throughout each sweep.

3.) Stern Sweep This stroke is just the second half of the forward sweep. It is the ideal correction stroke to use when you're paddling forward and the boat has spun out of the paddler's pie. (Remember that? -- See Concepts of Paddling.) Because it is executed in the eddy resistance end of the boat, it is the most efficient way to make an immediate course correction. It begins with the blade opposite the paddler's hip, and ends when the stern comes to the blade. The paddler leans his boat slightly away from the working blade as the stroke approaches its conclusion. Advanced paddlers, whose craft are almost always operating within the paddler's pie, rarely need to use a stern sweep; rather, they execute only the *first* half of the forward sweep, which is all they need for the minor course adjustment, while at the same time providing increased forward momentum. For a really weird experience, try crossing the pond using just stern sweeps on both sides of the boat. Note how little forward momentum the stroke provides.

Any of the above strokes will spin your craft if you repeat them on a given side. However, the most efficient spins are done with a forward sweep on one side followed immediately by a reverse sweep on the other side. It's fun -- practice spinning your kayak in both directions as you float through the pools between rapids!

Maneuver: Abeam. An abeam is a lateral movement of the craft with no forward or astern movement and no rotation about the pivot point of the craft. It has many uses -- To position your boat for exiting an eddy, to make room for another boat coming into the eddy you're in, or to sidle up to a pal for a chat.

Strokes for this maneuver:

1.) Draw This is a movement of the blade at right angles to the centerline, directly out from the pivot point. The paddle shaft is held nearly vertical, with both hands out over the water on the side to which you intend to draw the boat. You will need to rotate your shoulder plane about 90 degrees so you're facing the working blade. Anchor the blade opposite your onside hip with the powerface facing you, about two feet away from the hull. Both arms are extended, with the offside forearm several inches in front of your forehead. This position will force you to lean the boat slightly toward the blade. This is your starting position. To execute the stroke, hip-snap the boat *to* the blade, which remains anchored. This hip snap elevates the craft's side of opposition as it travels laterally to the anchor. Just before the boat and blade come together, rotate your control hand wrist so the powerface is back, and recover underwater by slicing the blade out to a new anchor position. (Do *not* remove the blade from the water.) The most common mistake in executing this stroke is not keeping both hands out over the water; keeping the offside hand in over the boat causes force on the blade to be more *downward* than directly opposite the desired line of travel, which wastes energy unless you're trying to elevate your boat skyward. Another common mistake is anchoring either too far forward or too far back. This will cause the boat to spin. If your anchor is too far aft, the stern will travel laterally more than the bow, resulting in a spin to the offside. If your anchor is too far forward, the boat spins to the onside. To move straight laterally, you'll need to learn where your pivot point is, and anchor the blade directly out from it. A third error is slicing *aft* during the recovery, so that the subsequent stroke is anchored aft of the pivot point.

MANEUVER: ABEAM

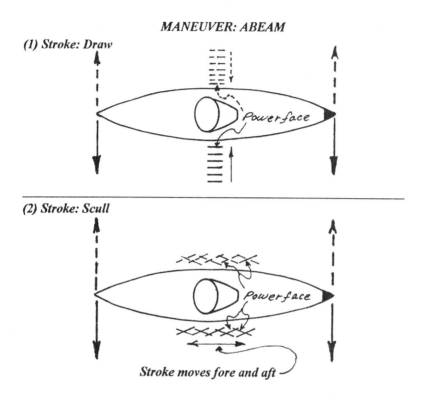

(1) Stroke: Draw

Powerface

(2) Stroke: Scull

Powerface

Stroke moves fore and aft

2.) Scull This is a second way of moving your boat laterally. You already know how to scull. You just don't *know* you know! When you tread water, your palms are sculling to keep you afloat! All you have to do is translate that motion with your palms to the motion of the paddle, with the powerface working as your "palm" -- except that, rather than pushing water down with the powerface to keep the boat afloat, we want to apply a force toward the boat to move the boat laterally. An easy way to get the sculling motion is to imagine that the surface of the water is one huge slice of bread. Your paddle is a knife. And you're going to make an absolutely immense peanut butter sandwich. The only rule is, you can spread peanut butter with the powerface but not with the backface. Smoothly spread the peanut butter with a back-and-forth motion onto the surface. Your blade should be very nearly flat on the surface, and travel about two feet with each spreading motion. The motion should be directly opposite your hip, so the paddle shaft is at right angles to the centerline of your boat. Got it? Great. Now keep on spreading peanut butter, but start raising your offside hand so the blade is operating closer and closer to your boat. When both hands are out over the water, i.e., the blade is almost vertical, operating about eight to ten inches from the hull, you are sculling! Stop, pat yourself on the back, then let's address the fine points -- blade angle, torso rotation and boat lean.

Keep the blade angle slight, as if almost slicing through the water, rather than pushing a lot of water on each stroke. Specifically, the blade should not be more than 15 to 20 degrees from parallel to the centerline. Rotate your shoulder plane rather than moving your arms to generate the back-and-forth motion. This uses your torso muscles, and also keeps your hands within the paddler's box to protect your shoulder from injury. To make the maneuver more efficient, J-lean slightly to raise your side of opposition, which is that side of the boat nearest the working blade. Practice sculling on both sides.

Maneuver: Forward Travel. Whitewater playboaters spend most of their time traveling forward, so of course you'll want to master this maneuver!

Strokes for this maneuver:

1.) Forward stroke This is the most common stroke you will use in river playboating, yet it will take considerable mileage in the saddle before you can paddle in a straight line using the forward stroke. This stroke, like all solo forward power strokes, takes place in the frontal resistance end of the boat. That is, the powerphase is executed in *front* of the paddler. During the execution of each powerphase, the shoulder plane rotates 70 to 90 degrees. The shaft is angled so that one blade is in the water to propel the boat; so of course one arm is higher than the other. The lower arm will be referred to as the *pulling* arm or *onside* arm, since it's on the side of the working blade of a given moment, and is pulling to execute that powerphase -- but because the paddler strokes alternately on each side of the boat, the *opposite* arm is the onside (pulling) arm half the time.

The powerphase begins with the onside arm comfortably straight, and the offside arm bent with the forearm parallel to the water and at eye level. During the powerphase of the stroke, the lower arm does not bend significantly. The upper arm pushes out, beginning at eye level and ending when it is straight and the fist is blocking your view of the bow grab loop. As the offside arm is pushing, the offside shoulder rotates forward, while the onside shoulder rotates back. This shoulder rotation provides most of the power for the stroke. Throughout the powerphase, the working blade *travels parallel* to the centerline, and should be *positioned perpendicular* to the centerline.

The powerphase ends when the working blade is beside your hip, and your onside "pinky" is near the water's surface. At this point, slice the blade out of the water by lifting the onside arm out laterally and then bending it to bring your fist in next to your temple as you prepare for the next powerphase with the other blade. Watch the working blade at the catch position and throughout the powerphase, to make sure that it remains at right angles to the centerline of the boat.

Most new paddlers find they're so busy thinking about all this that they completely forget their body extends below their waist. But the lower body should get into the act, too! In order to propel the boat forward more efficiently, and at the same time reduce its tendency to yaw away from the working blade, use your foot pegs -- push the foot on the onside foot peg during each powerphase -- your feet will be pumping much like peddling a bicycle. At first you may have to keep reminding yourself to use your legs, but it will eventually become a part of your "muscle memory" of the forward stroke.

MANEUVER: FORWARD TRAVEL

(1) Stroke: Forward

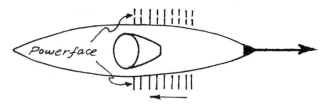

Shaft Angle is About 65 Degrees as Viewed From the Front

What a lot to think about! Let's approach it another way -- we're going to take you from an easy stroke that you know, the forward sweep, and "evolve" that stroke step-by-step into a nice, technically-correct forward stroke.

<u>Step 1.</u> Start by paddling forward using forward sweeps.

<u>Step 2.</u> Shorten the sweeps by eliminating the stern sweep part of the stroke. That is, execute quarter sweeps starting at the bow and ending opposite your hip.

<u>Step 3.</u> Now lock both arms straight at the elbow, and paddle forward but raise the shaft angle to about 45 degrees from horizontal. Remember to stop the strokes opposite your hip. You will be forced to rotate your torso because your arms are locked straight. This is a good exercise to instill the required rotation of your shoulder plane into "muscle memory." Get those feet pumping! When doing this exercise, note that the shaft of your paddle, between your hands, is always parallel to your

shoulder plane.

Step 4. Now relax your elbows slightly, and try executing the powerphase of each stroke parallel to the centerline and close to the boat. *Voila!* You're now doing the forward stroke! The paddle shaft will be at about 60 degrees from horizontal. You will be forced to bend the pulling arm *slightly* during the powerphase. Now go back and review all the components of this stroke, listed above.

2.) Touring stroke You already did it! Step 3 (above) is actually the touring stroke, except that you should relax your elbows slightly, still keeping your arms comfortably straight. Your "pushing hand" remains below eye level at all times. The other components are the same as in the forward stroke. The touring stroke is used by whitewater paddlers in the following situations: (1) for crossing calm water, (2) when ascending a shallow river, and (3) when paddling in Class IV or better, where the unseen underwater currents might tip you over if your blade is inserted deep into the water.

(2) Stroke: Touring forward

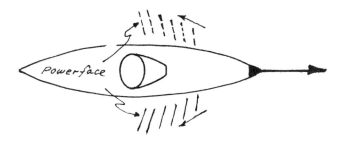

Shaft Angle is About 45 Degrees as Viewed From the Front

The powerphase of the touring stroke has a lower shaft angle than that of the forward stroke, and therefore is not as efficient because the force exerted on the blade is not opposite the intended direction of travel. The blade begins near the bow, and travels at an angle away from the boat, instead of traveling parallel to the centerline. (See illustration.) However, this stroke is popular because it is a relaxing, comfortable stroke.

The Forward Stroke

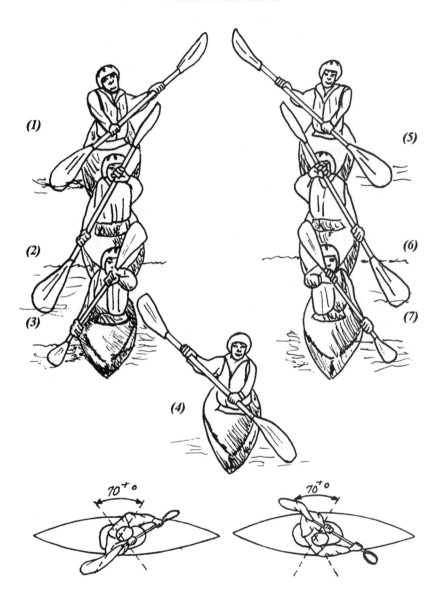

Shoulder Rotation During Powerphase

Maneuver: Reverse Travel. Why be normal? Many river playboating maneuvers are simply more *fun* if you do them in reverse once in a while. In addition, reverse travel can be a valuable skill for situations demanding backferries or turns in which there is not enough room to spin your boat. So, as awkward as it may seem at first, we urge you to become proficient at paddling in reverse.

Stroke for this Maneuver: Back Stroke The efficient back stroke has an even higher shaft angle than the forward stroke (about 70 degrees vs. 60 degrees). The catch position is behind your body, and the powerphase -- which uses the backface -- ends slightly forward of the front of your cockpit. Unlike the forward stroke, the lower arm is *pushing,* and the upper arm is *pulling.*

MANEUVER: REVERSE TRAVEL

Stroke: Back

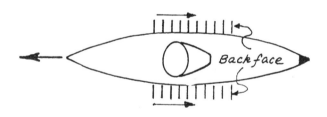

To begin the stroke, rotate your shoulder plane so that it is nearly parallel to the centerline of the boat. Hold both hands out over the water, insert the blade in the water about 18 inches behind your body, push with the lower hand, and pull with the upper hand. Start with a slight backward lean of your torso, and end the powerphase with a slight forward lean. At the beginning of a given powerphase, both arms are *slightly* bent at the elbow. In the course of the powerphase, the lower arm straightens to full extension at the elbow; the upper arm bends as your fist approaches your forehead. Also, in the course of the powerphase, rotate your shoulder plane a full 90 degrees so that it is mostly your torso muscles that power the stroke. Concentrate on keeping the blade close to the boat throughout the powerphase. The stroke ends when the pulling hand is just in front of your forehead, and the pushing arm is straight. Switch quickly to the other side and catch the blade for your next stroke. If you had trouble paddling in a straight line with the forward stroke, you will have the same problem traveling in a straight line in reverse. But with practice, you will develop the boat and paddle sensitivity to maintain a straight reverse course. It just takes time!

Maneuver: Circle Paddling. A form of forward travel, circle paddling is a central feature of whitewater playboating. Because it greatly reduces the need for correction strokes that rob the boat of its momentum, it enables the paddler to play the river with far greater efficiency.

Strokes for this maneuver:

1.) Forward stroke (described under Forward Travel) This stroke is executed on the outside of the circle, while circle size is controlled by control strokes on the inside of the circle.

2.) Forward control strokes These strokes are modified forward strokes. First of all, if you skipped it (or slept through it!), go back and read the chapter on The Circle Concept. Start your boat circling to the right. Set a slight, comfortable boat lean, and see how large a circle you can paddle without starting to turn to the left. To do this, execute standard forward strokes with your left blade (on the outside of the circle), while stroking a good distance from the boat with your right blade. The strokes with your right blade should begin alongside the front of the cockpit

74

and about two feet away from the hull; they end alongside the back of the cockpit. In other words, these strokes begin and end slightly farther aft than your usual forward stroke. Next, practice a large left circle until it feels as natural as your right circle.

MANEUVER: CIRCLE PADDLING
Stroke: Forward Control Strokes

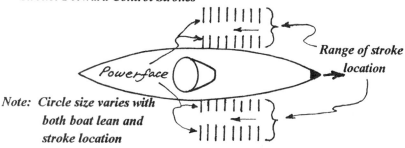

Range of stroke location

Powerface

Note: Circle size varies with both boat lean and stroke location

Most kayak playboats will carve circles as small as eight to ten feet in diameter when standard forward strokes are executed close to the boat on both sides and the boat is leaned comfortably in the direction it is turning. Practice carving little circles; find the smallest circle you can paddle while still maintaining some forward momentum. This will demonstrate for you the range of circle sizes that your boat will carve. Develop boat control by setting a buoy out on the pond. Paddle in circles, hitting the buoy on each pass. Enlarge and shrink your circle, still hitting the buoy on each circle. Practice circling both to the right and to the left.

Maneuver: Figure Eights. This maneuver consists of circle paddling, plus a couple of techniques for changing from one circle to another.

Strokes for this maneuver:

Forward Strokes (described under Forward Travel)
Forward Control Strokes (described under Circle Paddling)
Stern Sweeps (described under Spins)

Place two buoys on the pond, about 30 to 50 feet apart. You're going to paddle figure eights around them, and change from one circle to the other at the moment when you cross the imaginary line connecting the two buoys. To make an immediate change from one circle to another, execute a stern sweep on the inside of the circle you're leaving. Remember to lean your boat away from the working blade as you execute the stern sweep. This sets the proper lean for the circle you are initiating. A *single* stern sweep, properly executed, should change you to the new circle. Continue paddling on the new circle until you have come around the buoy and are about to cross the imaginary line again. Now, execute a stern sweep on the opposite side, to return to your first circle. Develop your precision so that you can change circles exactly at the moment your body crosses the imaginary line.

A more advanced technique for changing from one circle to another is to anticipate the spot where you will switch circles; as you approach it, take several control strokes on the inside of your present circle to enlarge the circle to the point where you actually "lose" it (i.e., your kayak begins turning in the other direction). Continue paddling with control strokes on the inside of your *new* circle, and forward strokes on the outside of the new circle. Again, develop precision in changing circles exactly at the intended point. Practice paddling figure eights with every possible circle size; i.e., continue until you are exhausted!

Maneuver: U-Turns. Playboaters are constantly U-turning (without getting a traffic ticket!) as they dance around the obstacles in the river. For the many different situations you will encounter, the seven turns described below are going to come in very handy. They will enable you to carve a huge arc (without hitting a rock due to lack of momentum), or spin on a dime. We're going to start with the largest-diameter turns, and progress to the tightest turn possible.

1.) Paddling a circle until you've turned 180 degrees is a form of U-turn. It can be a very wide "U" or a fairly tight one. Because it offers such flexibility, this technique comes into use on the river in many of the playboating maneuvers. Its great advantage is that you are adding forward momentum to your boat throughout the maneuver.

2.) Start paddling a circle, then stop paddling, and set a high brace in the air. Make sure you have a climbing angle on the blade, but don't actually drop the blade to the water. We call this an "air brace." The stern will immediately begin to skid out on its "ball bearings," resulting in a fairly sharp U-turn. Amazing -- you stop paddling and your boat skids into a turn!

3.) Start paddling a circle, set a high brace, but this time place the paddle in the water, near the surface. Remember to set that slight climbing angle! Placing the brace on the water creates a slight anchor on the inside of your turn, causing the boat to spin more sharply.

4.) Start paddling a circle, and then set another high brace -- a real one, with the blade on the water -- and, as the pressure on the blade begins to diminish (as the boat slows down), raise your offside hand up and put both hands out over the water. Set the powerface so it faces the bow grab loop, and apply force toward the front of your boat. As soon as the bow comes to the blade, conclude with a forward stroke *under* the boat. This sequence is actually a combination of three strokes: (1) The turning high brace (with a low shaft angle), (2) the bow draw (with a high shaft angle), and (3) the forward stroke. The turning high brace with the low shaft angle (see High Braces, above) helps prevent tipping over, but is not much of an anchor for turning the boat. When you raise your offside arm for the bow draw, the shaft becomes almost vertical, so the blade is more effectively anchored in the water but provides little "anti-capsize" support. At the end of the bow draw, the blade should be far enough forward for you to execute a full-length forward stroke in the frontal resistance end of the boat. By concluding with a forward stroke *under* the boat, you will maintain the boat's original discipline (i.e., turning toward the working blade). If your intention is to continue going forward but turning in the other direction, execute the forward stroke farther from the hull.

MANEUVER: U-TURNS

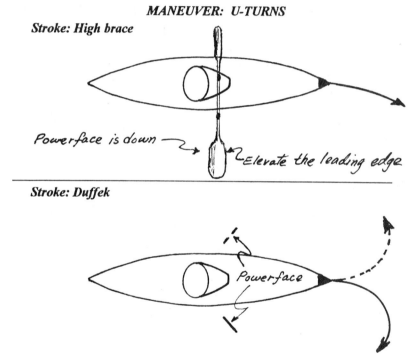

Stroke: High brace

Powerface is down

Elevate the leading edge

Stroke: Duffek

Powerface

5.) Start paddling a circle, and then set a **Duffek stroke**. This is a high-shaft-angle turning high brace (as opposed to the *low*-shaft-angle turning high brace used in Steps 3 and 4). It is a favorite stroke of experienced kayakers, and if executed properly, can be combined with a number of other strokes for playboating maneuvers. Here's how the Duffek stroke is done: Raise your offside hand over your head, keeping your lower arm bent, with the elbow close to the body to minimize the risk of shoulder dislocation. Rotate so that your shoulder plane faces the blade. Place the paddle in the water with the blade next to your knee. The powerface faces the bow grab loop. Your palms will both face away from you. Make sure both hands are out over the water, with the upper hand a bit aft of the lower hand. The back of your upper hand should be about six inches in front of your forehead. The blade that's in the air will be slightly behind your body. You'll need a good boat lean toward the Duffek *before* anchoring the blade -- It's difficult to set an appropriate boat lean once the Duffek is in place. You're going to perform what is known as the *Duffek System*: Start circling forward, then (1) execute the above-described Duffek stroke, (2) apply a force toward the bow, and (3) conclude, when the bow comes to the blade, with a forward stroke. Try to maintain equal force on the powerface throughout all three components of the Duffek System. This type of U-turn, and the two that follow, are intermediate-level skills.

The Duffek Stroke

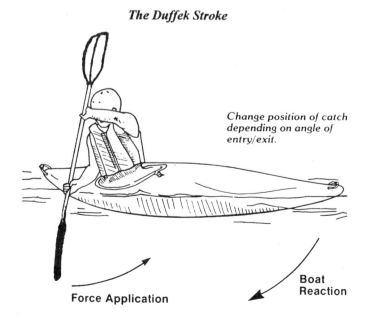

Change position of catch depending on angle of entry/exit.

Force Application

Boat Reaction

6.) Start paddling a circle, then U-turn with a slowly executed *reverse sweeping low brace*. This stroke is very similar to a reverse sweep, except the paddler maintains his boat lean toward the working blade throughout the entire stroke. Again, as in Steps 4 and 5, conclude with a forward stroke. The turn resulting from this stroke is so crisp that you will literally spin the bow directly around to the blade, resulting in a 180 degree turn. This stroke is used in situations which require an abrupt change of direction, common in negotiation of intricate routes.

MANEUVER: U-TURNS (cont.)

Stroke: Reverse sweeping low brace

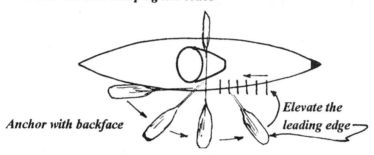

Anchor with backface

Elevate the leading edge

7.) Start paddling a circle. Execute a U-turn with a *compound reverse sweep*. This stroke consists of the first half of a reverse sweeping low brace, which is converted into a Duffek stroke when the blade is opposite your hip. The Duffek is followed by a bow draw and forward stroke, as in Steps 4 and 5. This maneuver will provide the same sharpness of turn as seen in Step 6, but involves more advanced technique.

Maneuver: Sideslip. This elegant little move shifts your boat laterally without altering its directional discipline. Imagine you're paddling down a river when you look up and spot a bald eagle flying over your head. You are transfixed. When your gaze finally returns to the river, you see a rock directly in front of you! Being the cool paddler that you are, you mask your alarm, simply position a stationary draw, and sideslip your boat by the rock, continuing in the same direction you originally were headed in.

This maneuver is an easy intermediate skill, but most kayakers simply have never learned to do it. We suggest that you invest the time on calm water to "wire" the move. You'll find it well worth your effort. Additionally, if you can sideslip your kayak playboat, you will have learned how to sideslip *any* solo boat you paddle, whether it be a touring kayak, or a solo open or decked canoe. The technique and position of the stroke are identical in all solo craft.

Stroke for this maneuver: Stationary draw. The stationary draw is really a modified Duffek stroke in which the blade is placed slightly behind your torso, about six to eight inches away from the boat. Like the Duffek, the stationary draw uses the powerface. Rotate your shoulder plane so it is parallel to the centerline. Place your paddle as if you intend to execute a Duffek stroke, but: (1) anchor the blade farther aft, as described above, and (2) instead of aiming the powerface at the bow, aim it at your body, so the blade is only about 15 to 20 degrees from parallel to the centerline, with the leading edge farther from the hull than the trailing edge.

MANEUVER: SIDESLIP

*(1) Stroke: Stationary draw - **right side***

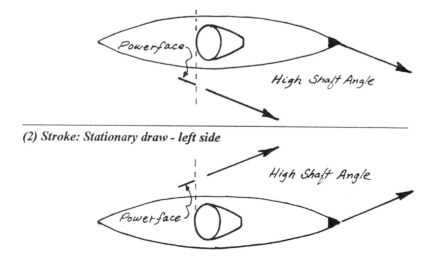

*(2) Stroke: Stationary draw - **left side***

Since the boat sideslips toward the working blade, the side of the craft toward the blade should be elevated for more efficient lateral movement. Lastly, for *any* stationary stroke to be effective, the boat must have forward momentum with respect to the current. You can't just sit on the pond, plant a stationary draw, and expect to go skidding across the water! (You probably knew that. We just want you to remember to get good forward momentum before you execute this stroke.)

Final challenge: Try sideslipping in reverse. Your stationary draws will still use the powerface, but the blade will be positioned near the front of your cockpit. As in forward sideslips, the blade is anchored parallel to the sideslip direction. It's easier than you might think!

A Final Tip! *Remember, boat control is learned on calm water. There is no substitute for "Pond Homework"! All of the strokes and maneuvers presented in this chapter will be valuable tools on the river. Practice them on the pond, in the pools between rapids, or even at an indoor pool when the rivers freeze over. You're going to see them all again in the chapter on River Playboating Maneuvers!*

SOLO CANOEING

Don't read this chapter!! ...*until* you have read the preceding chapters! This entire book (believe it or not!) is designed in a logical progression; when we present you with the material specific to canoeing, we're counting on you to understand all the aspects of playboating covered earlier. (Okay, you can skip the chapter on kayaking.) So, if you skipped directly from the Table of Contents to this page, WE CAUGHT YOU and we're sending you back to Chapter One.

Introduction. We'll tell you the same thing we told the kayakers at the beginning of "their" chapter: Whitewater playboating is easy! But it *does* require the development of a number of specific skills. No one is ready for Class IV rivers at the end of their first day. But almost anyone who is willing to commit the time and effort to learn the necessary skills can paddle those rivers... *after* investing in formal instruction, good equipment, and many fun and challenging days of practice.

Whether you want to paddle an open or a decked canoe, you will find the techniques you need to know spelled out completely in this chapter. Open and decked techniques are essentially identical, except where we indicate specific differences. However, if you are making the *transition* from open *to* decked canoeing, be aware that you are stepping into a new realm of boat responsiveness -- you will need to make all your lower-body movements more subtle or you will count a few fish! The decked boat is lighter and lower-volume; in addition, it is a hard-chined boat. As a result, it will react much more abruptly to any stroke or weight shift. Because decked-boating demands greater paddle sensitivity and lower body sensitivity, we find that the best playboaters -- even those who usually paddle open boats -- *have* spent considerable time developing this sensitivity by paddling extensively in decked boats, whether kayaks or canoes. In short, decked boats will teach you a higher level of sensitivity to both paddle and boat -- and what the boat doesn't teach you, the fish-counts will!

We urge you to seek out formal instruction at a reputable school of paddling. It's all too easy to develop incorrect technique if you try to learn completely on your own or from friends. And don't quit after your first lesson! Give yourself at least 15 to 20 days of concentrated paddling to try to assimilate the skills presented to you, before you even *think* about giving up. Otherwise, your initial investment will be wasted, and you may deprive yourself of a most enjoyable and rewarding lifetime sport. Also, remember that everyone learns cognitive and motor skills at his own pace. Don't compare yourself to others, because the rate at which you learn playboating skills has no correlation to the ultimate skill level you will attain!

In this chapter, we're going to cover all the essential skills required for effective boat control -- starting before you even get into the boat, since managing it on land can make you feel like a complete klutz! From land, we'll get you into your boat on calm water, where most skills must be mastered before being attempted on moving water. On a lake or calm pool in a river, you can work through the specific strokes and boat movements presented in this chapter. Our logical progression will introduce or review for you the skills needed on the river. In the chapter on River Playboating Maneuvers, we'll show you how to apply these techniques to whitewater.

Fitting Yourself to the Boat. You're going to actually *wear* your canoe the way a snail wears his shell, except that you must be able to exit the boat quickly when necessary. (Can snails do that?) The key to a good fit is proper outfitting, but first select a boat that's designed both for your body type and your paddling attitude. Any reputable canoe dealer should be able to help you with this. *But*, we strongly recommend that you take at least a two-day lesson before you consider such an investment. Not only will you then know whether or not you really want to take up the sport, but you will make a more educated choice when you do buy. A new canoe and all the necessary gear may well cost as much as $1500 to $2000, depending on the quality of the items you select. (More on purchasing a boat in the chapter on Playboating Equipment.)

Once you have a boat, you will need it custom-fitted to your body, because canoes come "naked." We urge you to consider a pedestal, thigh straps, knee cups, foot braces and hip support. And don't forget your flotation and spare paddle!

Start by sitting on the pedestal, with your knees in the knee cups and the balls of your feet on the foot pegs behind your body. Your feet should be comfortable, neither crunched up against the foot pegs nor straining to reach them. Your knees should rest comfortably in the knee cups, which should be as far from the centerline as possible for maximal boat control. The knee cups should cradle your knees snugly, preventing any lateral movement of the knees.

The height of the pedestal determines how low your center of gravity is -- and the lower the better! But the lower the pedestal, the more bent the knees will be. Beginning paddlers find a high pedestal to be more comfortable until they become accustomed to sitting for hours with their knees bent 135 degrees or more. If you buy a high pedestal, you can always trim it down as you get your body trained!

Make sure your thigh straps are installed so that, when secured, they are about halfway up your thighs. When the boat is a good fit, your body and boat will move as one unit when you shift your weight quickly. If a thigh strap is more than halfway up your thigh, your knee will come out of the knee cup when you lift your leg (which you do during a hip snap). If the strap is too low, it will tend to slip off your leg.

Finally, check for any space between your hips and the hip pads (if your boat has them). Snug hip pads will make your boat leans and righting actions much more effective.

Carrying your boat. It is worth learning to carry your boat and gear properly, to prevent injury to yourself or your equipment. Decked-boaters, you'll find a good system for picking up and carrying your decked canoe in the section corresponding to this one, in the chapter on Kayaking. Open-boaters, you *can* carry that big boat all by yourself. Or, you can enlist another canoeist to do what we call a "two-canoe-carry," which gets two boaters and all their gear to the water's edge in a single trip.

Let's start with the "solo carry." There are two ways to carry the boat: alongside your body, or on your head. To carry the boat alongside your body, stand next to the boat at its pivot point. With the hand nearest the boat, grasp the gunwale and lift the boat so the hull presses against your leg. Lightweight boats can be carried this way, while you carry gear in your other hand. To carry a heavier boat, you may need to place your other hand on the same gunwale, several inches forward of the first hand. The boat should be lifted at or near its balance point, so neither end hits the ground as you walk. To carry a boat on your head, see the description below, under "Loading and Unloading."

The two-canoe-carry is a nice, sociable way to get from your vehicle to the water, and is easier than a solo carry because the load is evenly balanced on both sides of your body. Simply set two boats side by side on the ground. One person stands between the bows; the other stands between the sterns. Then each person lifts the carrying handles to their right and left. Before picking up the boats, toss in all your gear, and you'll be ready to go when you reach the water. This is certainly the least tiring way to carry a canoe, so we recommend it for long carries or portages, wherever the path is wide enough.

Loading and unloading. For the best river karma, always load your boat bow-forward! We don't know why this is true, but it is. The easiest way to get the boat onto the vehicle is to start with it on your head. Carrying the boat on your head is generally more comfortable if you have on your helmet. Because it's tough on the cervical spine, we don't recommend you carry your boat long distances this way, but it's very handy for short carries. Here are three different ways to get the boat on your head without risk of injuring yourself or the boat:

1.) Crouch down beside the pedestal. Reach across the gunwales (of an open canoe) or cockpit (of a decked canoe) with your *offside* hand (the hand farthest from the canoe) and grasp the far gunwale or rim, with your thumb toward the centerline. Then grasp the near gunwale or cockpit rim with your onside hand, again placing your thumb on the inside edge. In one smooth but strong motion, swing the boat up over your head and rest the pedestal on your head. Straighten your knees to stand up. Remember to keep your back straight! Move your hands forward if necessary, to balance the boat so you can see where you're headed.

2.) Stand next to the pedestal, facing the boat. With both hands on the gunwale nearest you, hoist the boat and bend your legs slightly so you can rest the hull on your thighs. Next, holding onto the near gunwale with the hand farthest aft, reach across to the far gunwale with your other hand. Place both of your thumbs on the inside of the gunwales. Supporting the boat with the hand on the near gunwale, pull the far gunwale up and toward your body to swing the boat up over your head. Gently lower it to rest the pedestal on your head. Slide your hands forward along the gunwales until the boat is slightly elevated in the front so you can see the pathway.

3.) This last method is the best for heavy boats or for paddlers whose muscles have turned to mush after too much playboating! Turn the boat upside-down on the ground, and go to the stern. Lift the end in the air, allowing the bow to dig into the ground a little bit. Lift the stern over your head and grasp the gunwales, thumbs toward the centerline. "Walk" your hands forward along the gunwales until your head is under the pedestal. Lower the boat until the pedestal rests on your head, then continue walking your hands forward until the boat is balanced in the air with the bow slightly higher than the stern.

At last, you've somehow gotten the canoe on your head, and you're ready to put it on top of your vehicle. Approach the rear of your vehicle and gently set the bow on the "stern" roof rack, and push it forward a couple of feet. Back your hands along the gunwales for a new grip on the boat, and slide the boat forward, keeping the bow up so it doesn't catch on the "bow" roof rack. Center the boat on *both* racks, when viewed from the side!

Securing the boat for travel. A minimum of two sturdy lines or straps should be used whenever you tie a boat to a rack. You can buy straps that have a clinch-buckle and are 15 or 20 feet long wherever you buy your paddling gear. These allow for quick, secure tie-down of the craft. One line goes over the boat above the "bow" roof rack, and the other goes above the "stern" rack. They should be tied tightly to the bars of the rack. Additional lines, or the extra length of the first two lines, can be run through each grab loop or tied to each painter, before being tied back to the rack; these lines provide security against the boat sliding forward or backward on a hill or when you change speed suddenly. Remember they will only prevent the boat from shifting if the bow and stern lines go in opposite directions to their tie-down points on the vehicle.

When multiple boats are loaded, all the bows can be secured with one line, and all the sterns with another, plus the two lines running over the boats amidships. Whenever possible, use any safety lines that you may have attached to your boat for tie-downs. Regardless of whose boats they are and who ties them on, remember, the driver of the vehicle is always responsible for making sure they will not become airborne on the highway!

Launching and landing. Many beginning paddlers take their first unintended swim as they try to get into their playboat for the first time! Here's how to stay dry and look cool: Place your boat parallel to shore, just barely in the water, but not totally afloat, if possible. If you're on the river, aim the bow upstream to the main current. Set the shaft of your paddle across the gunwales (or front deck, in a C-1) about 18 inches forward of the pedestal, with the blade toward shore. Facing the bow, bend over and hook both hands over the paddle shaft as you grasp the gunwales or cockpit. Keeping your weight over your hands, set the foot nearer the boat *in* the boat, on the centerline. Ease your derriere onto the pedestal, and bring your other foot into the boat. If you're getting into a C-1, you'll need to place both feet in the boat on each side of the pedestal, place your hands on the front deck, lean forward and then tuck both feet in the boat under the back deck. Settle into the knee cups. Secure your thigh straps. *Voila!* You're in! Now you may be afloat if you had to launch into deep water. If you're in a decked boat, you'll want to be competent at getting your sprayskirt on quickly after getting into the boat. When possible, launch in shallow water so you can stay a bit aground until you're all set to paddle. Landing and getting out of your boat is simply the reverse of the sequence outlined above.

An alternative launching position, off a beach or gradual sloping shoreline, is to set the boat at right angles to shore, with the front two-thirds in the water. You can get into the boat without any risk of tipping over, since it's still partially on land! Then, once in the boat, slide into the water by pushing off with your hands. Landings can be done the same way, if you paddle hard as you approach a sandy beach or grassy shoreline.

Securing the sprayskirt. Once in the boat, decked canoeists have to contend with this irksome contraption before they are ready to paddle. Attaching the sprayskirt is described in numbing detail under this same heading in the chapter on Kayaking.

Holding the paddle. Whitewater canoeists *commit* to paddling as either a "righty" or a "lefty," i.e., they do not indiscriminately switch paddling sides. A "righty" always has his left hand on the grip and his right hand on the shaft, so the paddle is on his right side at rest. The right side is his *onside*, and the left is his *offside*. "Lefties," you're used to hearing the directions for "righties" and then figuring out what to do!

The palm of the control hand should be flat against the grip, with the fingers wrapped over the T-grip, and the thumb hooked under it. Your other hand (the shaft hand) holds the shaft anywhere from four to eight inches above the throat of the paddle. The shaft hand moves a few inches closer to the grip on low-shaft-angle strokes, but you might want to mark your "home" position with a piece of vinyl tape until your shaft hand goes there automatically. Here's a way to find it: Tuck the grip in your onside armpit, and line up your arm along the paddle shaft, with your fingers extended. Mark the spot where your fingertips end. The index finger of your shaft hand will go just below this spot.

Wet exits. Well, at last you're *in* your boat, and the first thing we want to talk about is getting *out!* These little playboats are tippy critters and they love to take the entry-level paddler to the position of greatest stability -- that's upside-down with the body down too!! All "strapped in," some beginning canoeists fear they will be unable to get out when capsized. In fact, in an open boat, even though you're securely connected to the boat when upright, you will tend to fall right out when you're upside-down. In a decked boat, you can exit easily with three simple steps. Decked boaters must be comfortable with wet exits before learning anything else. Open boaters should become comfortable with wet exits in a pond or easy Class I-II rapids before attempting heavier water. Here's how to wet-exit your boat:

1.) Tuck. Whatever type of whitewater playcraft you are in, you must develop the reflex of immediately tucking your body forward whenever you capsize. Tuck all the way forward to the front deck or air bags. The tucked position is important for three reasons. First, it is the only position from which you can easily get out of the boat when capsized. Well, that should convince you to do it without even hearing about the second and third reasons, but we'll give them to you anyway. Second, the tucked position minimizes your depth in the water, and is therefore safer. No good being upside-down and head-in-the-mud to boot. And third, if you do hit an underwater object, it will more likely impact the back of your helmet or lifevest, whereas if you leaned back, it could hit your face. When you tuck, try not to let go of your paddle.

From here on, it's a little different for open vs. decked boaters:

Open Canoe:
2.) *Move your feet.* Shift your feet off the foot pegs so your legs are free.

3.) *Fall out!* In an open boat, the position you're now in will cause your thighs to shift back, the thigh straps to slip off your legs, and your body to tumble out of the boat. Hang on to your boat and paddle, and head for shore.

Decked Canoe
2.) *Pull.* Staying tucked, pull the grab loop of your sprayskirt forward and up to release it from the cockpit.

3.) *Push.* Finally, *still* tucked, and hopefully still holding onto your paddle with one hand, place both hands on the boat next to your hips, and push the boat back vigorously to get your lower legs out. Hang onto your boat and paddle, and head for shore.

That's all there is to it. *Practice* it, especially if you're taking up decked-boating for the first time, because there is no such thing as a bomb-proof roll. Every paddler, regardless of his skill level, will sometimes have to call upon the wet exit as his means of self-rescue. Do not proceed until you are completely comfortable with your wet-exits!

The boat boogie-wiggle. To get comfortable J-leaning your boat and to get acquainted with its secondary stability, practice vigorously tipping your boat first to one side and then the other, while attempting to keep your upper body centered over the boat. Try to make BIG waves! Next set a fixed boat lean to one side, say the right. Try to keep your upper body fairly upright while curling your torso, stretching the right side of your body and kinking the left. At the same time, lift up on your left leg and weight your right hip. This total set of movements comprise the well-known *J-lean*. Next, try holding a *left* lean with a J-lean. Can you "snap" the boat from one fixed lean to the other? Having fun yet? Did you get a chance to practice your wet exit or roll?

The Coasting Position. Also called the running position or ready position, this is a way of gliding downriver in situations where the current will take you just where you intend to go. Bear in mind that when you glide, your boat has little momentum with respect to the current underneath your boat, so you will find it more difficult to suddenly alter your course. (River Devils' watery whisper in your ear: "That's okay, why would you ever want to alter your course? Why not go with the flow?") With that caveat, here's the coasting position: Place the blade parallel to the canoe's centerline, just off the onside hip. Keep both arms relaxed and both hands out over the water with the control thumb back. In this position, the paddle functions much like the centerboard of a sailboat, providing the boat with some lateral resistance to tipping. Practice your righting action strokes (see below) from the coasting position -- execute a righting action stroke, then immediately resume the coasting position, and repeat.

Preventing capsizes: Righting Action Strokes. It's time for a major brain shift. All these years, you've thought of water as a liquid. We want you to think of it as a *solid*, something you can brace on to support yourself and your boat. In fact, it's supporting your boat all the time -- just maybe not always in your preferred upright position! The reason we want you to make this mental adjustment is that you're going to use the water surface to brace your paddle blade when you execute hip snaps to prevent your boat from capsizing -- that's a low brace. And you'll use the water to anchor your blade, when you execute a righting pry. Low braces prevent you from capsizing to your onside. Righting pries save the day when you're tipping over to your offside.

Many beginning paddlers reflexively grab the gunwales for support when they're tipping over. But the gunwales will simply go in the direction of the force applied to them, they won't "support" you; so reach out for the water (with your paddle) instead. Think of it as a solid. Practice both the low brace and the righting pry until they are conditioned reflexes -- with which you respond the moment a River Devil reaches up and pulls down on one of your gunwales! Here's how the righting action strokes are done:

1.) The low brace. There are many degrees of low braces, ranging from minor righting actions done just with the hips to the full brace used as to conclude a 360 degree roll. How fully you need to brace will depend on the amount of tip your boat is experiencing. The low brace presented here is for the sudden tip *beyond the point of no return.* If you can do this brace, you'll be prepared to do a more subtle version of it to match any situation that calls for a low brace. To practice the "ultimate" low brace, start by J-leaning your boat to your onside. Protect your onside shoulder from injury by rotating your shoulder plane so it is parallel to the onside gunwale. Hold your paddle horizontally, perpendicular to the centerline. Shift your arms so that *both* hands are nearly out over the water, with your control thumb pointed away from you so the backface will hit the water when you brace. Now lean further... further... until you're on the verge of capsizing! At the last possible moment, do three things at once: (1) arch your back and *brace* by hitting the water with your *entire* paddle, (2) throw your head down with the paddle and keep looking down, and (3) exert a brisk, forceful upward pull on your onside leg, loading your weight onto your offside leg. The paddle brace will begin to halt your impending capsize. The head throw will create a thrust *toward* the water ("action") which results in a movement of that side of the boat *away* from the water ("reaction") -- courtesy of Newton's Third Law. The head throw will also cause you to push down reflexively on your onside arm, and pull up on your onside leg.

The Low Brace
An onside righting action... immediately after the bracing action

Try *not* to put much weight on the paddle -- you don't want the blade to go down very far in the water. Instead, concentrate on the upward pull of your onside leg. This sudden weight shift will right the boat. Conclude your brace by sweeping the blade forward to the bow, with a slight climbing angle so it'll stay on the surface; "follow" the blade with your body (de-rotate your shoulder plane), leaning way forward and then past the centerline a little to the offside before sitting up. Remember to keep your head down, since picking up the head too early will negate what you're doing with the rest of your body.

Now, when you brace, we want you to get *both hands wet*. In fact, the *perfect* brace gets the control hand wet a few microseconds before the shaft hand, because the paddle is actually angled with the grip slightly closer to the water than the blade. The only way to get your control hand wet is to have the entire paddle (and both hands) out over the water. A common error is the failure to extend far enough out. However, bracing with your control hand over the boat is a real knuckle-cruncher, and will dim your enthusiasm for the sport.

2.) The righting pry. Practice the righting pry by J-leaning your boat to your offside. Start with your paddle in the coasting position. Keeping the shaft vertical, slice your blade into position: set the shaft tight against the onside gunwale beside your torso, with your control thumb pointed aft so the powerface faces the boat.

The Righting Pry

Ready for the canoe offside righting action...
aggressively pull the control hand toward the offside

Open your shaft hand so it's flat and presses the paddle shaft against the gunwale. The open-hand position will prevent a nasty finger pinch as you execute the pry. Lean, lean, lean! As you go beyond the point of no return, plunge the blade down farther into the water by pushing downward on the grip (but leave at least 15 inches of shaft above the gunwale), then yank the grip aggressively toward your offside gunwale. This is done with your control arm horizontal, so the elbow is out from your torso. Go for another pry immediately after the first, if you're not quite up. But you'll rarely need two in a row -- the pry really works!

Maneuver: Spin. A spin is a pivot of a boat without forward or astern movement. It is useful for positioning the bow or stern in a particular orientation to ready the craft for another maneuver.

Strokes for this maneuver:

1.) Forward Sweep The forward sweep is a 180 degree arc in which the blade starts at the bow and ends at the stern. Force is applied to the powerface, but the blade actually hardly moves at all, since in fact the stern pivots around to the blade. With the paddle shaft nearly horizontal, lean forward slightly, rotate your onside shoulder forward, and anchor the blade as close to the bow as possible, with the blade vertical in the water. Point your control thumb toward the sky. Now de-rotate your shoulder plane, keeping the shaft parallel to it, until the stern comes to the blade. During the last part of the sweep, lean back slightly and rotate toward the onside gunwale. The sweep ends with both your shoulder plane and the paddle shaft parallel to the centerline, and both hands out over the water.

Actually, the paddler can think of his boat as a pinwheel with himself at the center. Instead of wind causing the pinwheel to spin, it's the paddler's pressure against the blade that causes the boat to rotate around its pivot point. As such, the boat should

SOLO CANOE STROKES

EXPLANATION OF ILLUSTRATIONS

Short lines represent a tip-first water entry of the blade with the shaft relatively vertical. Elongated lines represent a more horizontal insertion of the blade. Small arrows adjacent to the paddle blade lines indicate the direction a force is applied during the powerphase of a stroke. Longer bold arrows originating from the side or end of the canoe illustrate the change in the directional movement of the canoe produced by the stroke.

MANEUVER: SPINS

(1) Stroke: Forward Sweep

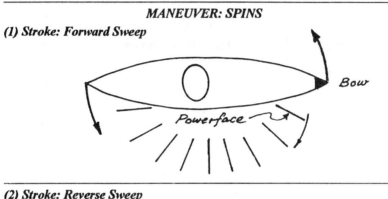

(2) Stroke: Reverse Sweep

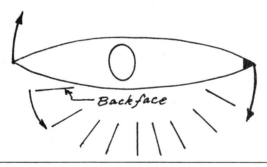

---

(3) Stroke: Stern Sweep

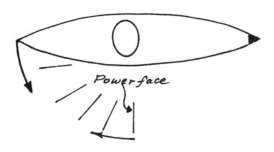

have minimal forward or backward movement nor should the paddle move much through the water -- it simply acts as a lever. To extend the blade farther out from the pivot point, slide the shaft hand up several inches toward the grip. Lean the boat slightly toward the blade during the first half of the stroke, and then slightly away from it during the last half. Concentrate on your boat leans, remembering to change the lean as the blade passes its halfway point in the sweep. Also remember to rotate your torso; one way to achieve this is to watch the blade throughout each sweep.

2.) Reverse Sweep This stroke is simply the reverse of the forward sweep, with the same characteristics: low shaft angle, blade extension from the hull, and boat lean toward the first half of the stroke and away from the second half. The primary difference is that the blade is swept at a 45 degree angle to the water, i.e., the top edge of the blade is tipped forward and kept at this climbing angle throughout the entire powerphase. The blade is initially anchored at the stern, and as the force is applied to the *backface*, the bow swings around to the blade. Again, focus on your boat leans; change the lean as the blade passes its halfway point in the sweep. And watch the blade throughout each sweep to make sure you're rotating your torso.

3.) Stern Sweep This stroke is simply the second half of the forward sweep; it's actually a quarter or 90 degree sweep. It is the ideal correction stroke to use when you're paddling forward and the boat has spun out of the paddler's pie. (Remember that? -- See Concepts of Paddling.) Because it is executed in the eddy resistance end of the boat, it is the most efficient way to make an immediate course correction. It begins with the blade opposite your hip, and ends when the stern comes to the blade. Start with your boat level, then gradually lean the boat slightly away from the blade as you execute the stroke. Advanced paddlers, whose craft are almost always operating within the paddler's pie, rarely use a stern sweep; they execute only the *first* half of the forward sweep (90 degrees) which is all they need for minor course adjustments, and provides increased forward momentum. The stern sweep itself provides little forward momentum.

Any of the above strokes will spin your craft if you repeat them. But the most efficient spins are done with either the forward or the reverse sweeps, depending on which direction you wish to spin. A good place to practice your spins is in the pools between rapids. Concentrate on your boat leans while you practice spinning your canoe in both directions. See how many complete spins you can get from five forward sweeps; and then try five reverse sweeps to see which stroke wins!

Maneuver: Abeam. An abeam is a lateral movement of the craft with no forward or astern movement and no rotation about the pivot point of the craft. It has many uses -- to position your boat for exiting an eddy, to make room for another boat coming into the eddy you're in, or to sidle up to a pal for a chat. All abeams are performed with a slight elevation of the boat's side of opposition, which is that side nearest the boat's destination. This will increase the efficiency of the boat's lateral movement, often as much as 20 percent, by improving the boat's hydrodynamics.

Strokes for this maneuver:

1.) Draw The draw is a movement of the blade at right angles to the centerline, directly out from the pivot point. Rotate your shoulder plane so it faces your onside gunwale. Hold the paddle shaft nearly vertical, with both hands out over the water on the side to which you intend to draw the boat. Anchor the blade with the powerface facing you, about two feet away from the hull. The control arm is over your head, and both arms are extended. This position will force you to lean the boat slightly toward the blade. That's your starting position. To execute the stroke, hip-snap the boat *to* the blade, which remains anchored. The hip snap elevates the craft's side of opposition as it travels laterally to the anchor (blade). Just before the boat and blade come together, rotate your control thumb out so the powerface faces aft, and recover underwater by slicing the blade out to a new anchor position. (Don't remove the blade from the water!)

The most common mistake in executing the draw is not keeping both hands out over the water. Keeping the control hand in over the boat causes force on the blade to be more *downward* than directly opposite the desired line of travel, which wastes energy unless you're trying to elevate your boat skyward. Another common mistake is anchoring either too far forward or too far back; this will cause the boat to spin. If your anchor is too far aft, the stern will travel laterally more than the bow, resulting in a spin to the offside. If your anchor is too far forward, the boat spins to the onside. To move straight laterally, you'll need to learn where your pivot point is, and anchor the blade directly opposite it. A third error is slicing *aft* during the recovery, due to incorrect "aim" of the control thumb. The subsequent stroke is then anchored aft of the pivot point.

MANEUVER: ABEAM

(1) Stroke: Draw

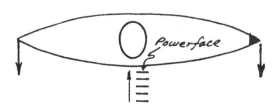

2.) Cross draw A cross draw moves the boat to the paddler's offside. Its components are the same as those of the onside draw -- but applied on the offside. As with all cross strokes, the cross draw is done *without* changing hand positions on the paddle! It is, though, one of the few exceptions to a more flexible guideline -- that your control thumb points in the direction of recovery. The underwater recovery for the cross draw is easier to do with your control thumb pointing *toward* your body as you slice the blade away from your body for the next stroke.

MANEUVER: ABEAM

(2) Stroke: Cross Draw

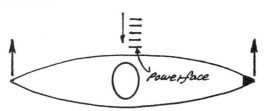

3.) Pry This is a means of moving your canoe to your offside, while keeping the paddle on your onside. A pry is any stroke that places the shaft of the paddle against the boat and uses it as a lever to apply the force to the blade. All pries move the boat away from the paddle, and a pry anchored directly out from the pivot point will move the boat laterally... an abeam. The force on all pries is against the backface. To begin, rotate your shoulder plane to face your onside gunwale. Place the powerface of your blade flat against the chine of the boat just a tad forward of your hips, with both hands over the water. Your control arm is extended a bit farther out than your shaft hand, which is holding the shaft vertically against the boat. The control thumb points toward the stern. To effect the *powerphase*, simply pull your control hand across the front of your body but *stop* when it reaches the centerline. You just gave your boat an abrupt shove! Now, without taking the blade out of the water, *recover* by aiming your control thumb out from whence it came and slicing the blade back under the chine area for another anchor. Repeat over and over! Keep the offside of your boat slightly elevated -- this won't take much effort, since the pry itself exerts a downward force on the onside gunwale, raising the offside for you.

Note that this is a short, quick stroke. It has to be, to minimize boat bobble. It's easier if you lean back slightly. The shaft remains nearly vertical throughout, starting with the control hand about six inches farther out than the shaft hand and ending with the control hand over the centerline of the boat. The shaft hand holds the gunwale throughout the stroke. The most common mistake is pulling the grip beyond the centerline. Doing so results in a *righting* pry (described above) which causes a lot of boat bobble, slowing the boat's abeam movement.

4.) *Scull* This is a second way of moving your boat laterally to your onside. This technique is more fluid since it moves the boat without any bobble. And you already know how to scull. You just don't *know* you know! When you tread water, your palms are sculling to keep you afloat! All you have to do is translate that motion with your palms to the motion of the paddle, with the powerface working as your "palm" -- except that, rather than pushing water down with the powerface to keep the boat afloat, we want to apply a force toward the boat to move the boat laterally. An easy way to get this motion is to imagine that the surface of the water is one huge slice of bread. Your paddle is a knife. And you're going to make an absolutely immense peanut butter sandwich. The only rule is, you can spread peanut butter with the powerface but not with the backface... so keep your knuckles toward the sky. Smoothly spread the peanut butter with a back-and-forth motion onto the surface. Initially, your blade should be fairly flat on the surface, and travel about two feet with each spreading motion. The motion should be directly opposite the front of your body, so the paddle shaft is at right angles to the centerline of your boat. Got it? Great. Now keep on spreading peanut butter, but start raising your control hand so the blade is operating closer and closer to your boat. When both hands are out over the water, i.e., the blade is almost vertical, operating about eight to ten inches from the hull, you are sculling! Stop, pat yourself on the back, then let's address the fine points -- blade angle, torso rotation and boat lean.

Keep the blade angle slight, as if almost slicing through the water, rather than pushing a lot of water on each stroke. Specifically, the blade should not be more than 20 degrees from parallel to the centerline. Rotate your shoulder plane rather than moving your arms to create the back-and-forth motion. This enlists your torso muscles, and also keeps your hands within the paddler's box, protecting your onside shoulder from injury. To make the maneuver more efficient, J-lean slightly to raise your side of opposition, which is that side of the boat nearest the blade.

MANEUVER: ABEAM (cont.)

(3) Stroke: Scull

Directional Key

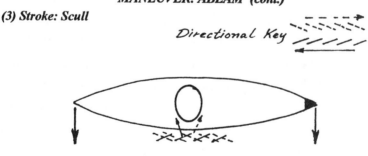

(4) Stroke: Cross Scull

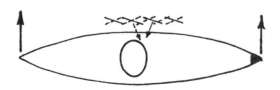

Practice sculling on both sides. *Cross sculling* moves the boat to your offside. The technique is the same as the onside scull, except the paddle is placed on your offside, again with the powerface toward the hull. The stroke may seem a bit awkward at first, but if you "choke up" (i.e., move your shaft hand up a few inches toward the grip), it will be easier to get your blade back behind the pivot point for the aft half of the stroke. Keep your control hand not only out over the water but also in front of your body, and you won't have to rotate quite so far. Did you remember to raise your side of opposition?

Maneuver: Forward Travel. Whitewater playboaters spend most of their time traveling forward, so of course you'll want to master this maneuver!

Strokes for this maneuver:

1.) Forward stroke This is the most common stroke used in river playboating, yet it will take considerable mileage in the saddle before you can do it without constant vigilance against incorrect technique. Eventually you will develop the "muscle memory" to do the stroke correctly without thinking.... and whatever form of forward stroke you may have done in the past, we promise you it will be worth your while to re-learn it, as the biomechanics behind this version of the forward stroke make it both efficient and powerful. That's why it is the stroke used by most of today's best racers.

This stroke, like all forward power strokes, takes place in the frontal resistance end of the boat. That is, the stroke is executed in *front* of the paddler. During the execution of each powerphase, the shoulder plane rotates 60 to 80 degrees.

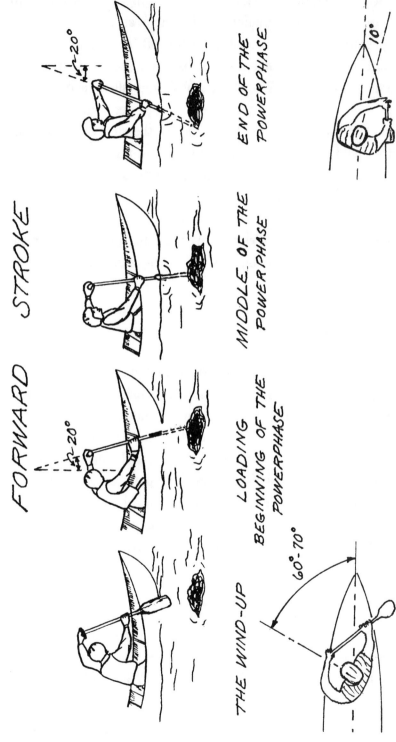

FORWARD STROKE

THE WIND-UP

LOADING
BEGINNING OF THE
POWERPHASE

MIDDLE OF THE
POWERPHASE

END OF THE
POWERPHASE

~20°

~20°

10°

60°-70°

To facilitate your understanding of this essential stroke, let's take it one step at a time:

Step 1. The Wind-up - Start with your control hand above your head and over to your onside (i.e., the "control forearm" is across the centerline). Point your control thumb toward the bow. "Wind up" by rotating your onside shoulder forward, letting your offside shoulder rotate back. Make sure your shoulder plane rotates at least 60 degrees (top view) to your offside. A helpful hint: let your head and neck rotate with your shoulder plane, so you end up looking somewhat to your offside. Lean forward as you rotate, keeping your back straight and unweighting your offside hip. A forward lean of up to 35 degrees is fine. Keep both arms comfortably extended (not locked at the elbows), and keep the blade feathered (control thumb forward) until the blade is over the "load" or "catch" position. Do not reach forward with the blade too much by bending the control arm back, because that will set you up to exert too much *downward* pressure during the powerphase, which is inefficient. At the end of the wind-up, your control hand should be above and to the offside of your head.

Step 2. Loading - Placing the blade in the water is called *loading*, because when done properly, it actually loads force on the powerface. The correctly loaded blade provides two things: (1) it adds significantly to propulsion, and (2) it inhibits the potential boat bobbing effect of the forward lean. If you wind up properly, you will have the ideal loading angle, about 70 degrees from horizontal (20 degrees from vertical on side view), with the shaft hand forward of the control hand. To load the blade, quickly swing the control hand out over the water and rotate the control wrist so the blade is perpendicular to the boat's centerline and you're looking at the powerface. Drive both hands down, still keeping both arms comfortably straight. Concentrate on slicing the blade into the water cleanly, without creating a splash. After loading, you should still be leaning forward and rotated at least 60 degrees to your offside as you were at the end of the wind-up.

Step 3. Powerphase - This step provides most of the propulsion, and is powered by the torso muscles, not the arms. You must perform _three_ simultaneous movements during the powerphase: (1) unwind your shoulder plane all the way to your onside about 10 degrees, (2) pull aggressively on your shaft arm and push with your control arm but _do not significantly bend either arm_, and (3) pull your boat up to the paddle blade by bringing your torso to an upright position (sort of a pelvic thrust with your lower body). When the powerphase is completed, the shaft angle will again be about 70 degrees, but in the opposite direction from the load angle, with the control hand now tilted forward. The blade should be beside your _knee!_ Most new paddlers feel they're just getting "into" the stroke at that point, but we want you to do a very short stroke, only about 12 to 15 inches. (The faster you want to go, the shorter the stroke must be. Racers commonly stroke only six or eight inches before winding up for the next one!) During the powerphase, the shaft hand actually serves as the fulcrum while the shaft angle changes from the backward tilt of 20 degrees to the forward tilt of 20 degrees for a total arc of about 40 degrees.

MANEUVER: FORWARD TRAVEL

(1) Stroke: Forward

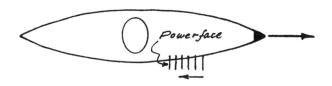

Step 4. Recovery from the water - Slice the blade laterally away from the boat without lowering your control arm and without bending either arm. This might seem awkward at first, but it is more efficient to keep your control arm high than to "pump" up and down with every stroke! At the same time, slowly turn the control thumb forward so that as the blade exits the water, it carves an arc. You are now headed into the wind-up. Return to Step 1 and repeat, and repeat, and repeat!! Remember, these steps have been artificially established.... In reality, the entire stroke is a combination of all of the above movements blended together in a seamless, continuous cycle.

What a lot to think about! Let's approach it another way -- by listing some of the more common mistakes paddlers make when learning this stroke. Don't make _any_ of these mistakes, and you'll do just fine!

Thou shalt not...

...Bend either arm significantly at any time during the stroke. Rather, keep the arms relatively straight so they "connect" your torso muscles to the paddle. There's a lot more strength in your back than in your arms!

...Bend the control arm on the wind-up. This creates a shaft loading angle closer to 45 degrees (side view) which results in too much downward force during the load. By the time the shaft comes up to the proper angle, the torso has just about finished rotating so all that great torso power is wasted!

...Forget to _push_ with the control hand and _pull_ with the shaft hand during the loading and powerphase. That's the only way to get the benefit of the fulcrum effect at the shaft hand, and failure

to do so results in downward pressure (waste of energy!) during the stroke. You can tell you're making this mistake if the shaft doesn't rotate its full 40 degrees during the powerphase.

...*Continue the stroke past your knee.* The powerphase ends when the blade is beside your knee. To continue past the body results in too much yaw, and also puts upward force on the blade, which wastes energy.

...*Execute the powerphase far from the boat.* The powerphase should be executed with the blade very close to -- and in some cases even *under* -- the boat, to minimize yaw. Stroking far from the centerline usually causes the boat to turn away from the paddle.

...*Lean forward during the entire stroke.* You must learn the total dynamic use of your body -- er, bod*ies* -- upper *and* lower. If you are still leaning forward at the end of the powerphase, you forgot the "pelvic thrust." "Upper body action back, boat reaction forward," says Uncle Newton, and that's your goal with the pelvic thrust.

...*Move the upper body forward during the powerphase.* This is common with people who have never had contemporary lessons. And, once the habit is ingrained, it's a difficult one to break! "Upper body action forward, boat reaction backwards," says Uncle Newton, who will happily send your boat in the opposite direction of your torso movement. As long as you're stroking, your boat won't really go backward, but its forward movement will certainly be diminished by this error.

...*Sit like a statue during the entire stroke.* The upper body rotates and tilts forward during each wind-up, and unwinds and

110

sits up during the powerphase.

...Drench thyself or thy neighbors by splashing water when loading the blade. This usually is the result of loading at too great an angle. Have a friend check your loading angle, viewing your boat and paddle from the side.

...Forget to feather the blade during the recovery and wind-up. Many paddlers simply don't feather, and the importance of feathering remains a subject of active debate among leading paddlers. The strongest argument *against* feathering is the amount of wrist action required to do it. The choice is yours. But a broached blade hitting a wave on your recovery will quickly turn the boat off course. We feel it's more efficient to slice the blade to a new anchor, through air and/or water, than to keep it broached. Feathering on all strokes is *required* for certification as an American Canoe Association instructor. And it looks classy!

...Forget to hold the feather until over the load position. Many people think they are feathering, but simple do a token move. They set the feather, but then immediately remove it as they wind-up, so they are actually broaching the blade during most of their wind-up.

...Pull the control hand down below the head on the recovery and wind-up. This excess motion wastes energy! Keep your control hand at least forehead-height throughout the entire stroke.

...Bend the lower arm on the recovery from the water. It takes less energy to simply slice the blade out laterally as the feather is set. And keeping the lower arm straight facilitates a good torso wind-up with the onside shoulder.

...Choke your best paddling friend, the paddle, by gripping its throat with your shaft hand. It is difficult to push and pull with your arms spread so far apart. Also, it's hard to move quickly into other strokes or righting actions from this hand position.

...Push the control hand up during the powerphase. The control hand should push straight out at eye level. Pushing up results in the blade being only partially in the water; it is easier to stroke in this manner, but not too efficient. This is a fairly common problem with people who use a paddle with too much blade surface area. We suggest you change to a smaller blade; you'll be a lot more comfortable and you'll use your paddling muscles more efficiently.

...Forget to keep the blade at right angles to the centerline of the boat during the powerphase. Keep Uncle Newton happy; apply your force on the anchored blade exactly opposite your desired direction of travel. It's more efficient.

...Frown!!! Look like a fish and you'll wind up among them! We're convinced a frown on your face puts a negative mindset in your head, and that leads to more fish counts. So, when we "score" a student who frowns during a maneuver, we only give nine points (on a ten point scale) -- even if the execution is otherwise perfect!

2.) Cross forward stroke The second most common solo canoe stroke is the cross forward. If you've never had formal instruction, or you took your lessons years ago, this may be news to you! Over the past decade, advanced whitewater playboaters and slalom C-1 racers have learned to perform offside maneuvers with the same degree of comfort and effectiveness as onside moves. This has been possible because of technique development

112

leading to the realization that it is simply more efficient to paddle on your offside *without* switching hand positions on the paddle.

To become comfortable with offside maneuvers, you'll have to overcome your initial feelings that the positions are awkward and that the boat is going to tip over. The awkwardness will disappear as you develop upper body flexibility and familiarity with the positions. And as you get to know your boat better, you'll realize it has the secondary stability (stability in a heeled position) to support offside maneuvers very nicely!

In addition, much of the control of high-performance contemporary playboats is achieved by the paddler's development of forward momentum. Older paddling techniques emphasized course corrections at the *expense* of forward momentum. Slowing the boat gives the current more control over the boat's course -- meaning it's harder for the paddler to go where he wants! Cross strokes are a means of correcting course by turning the bow back toward the onside while *adding* forward momentum to the craft. This makes the cross strokes valuable for onside turns as well as offside ones, especially if you are paddling within the "paddler's pie."

When crossing the paddle to your offside, try to slice the blade cleanly and low across the bow. Start by flipping your control hand so the control thumb points to your offside. With the control hand low (in front of your torso), swing your paddle to your offside, keeping the blade parallel to the deck. This helps prevent hitting the gunwales as the blade is crossed. As the blade crosses, start leaning your torso forward, in anticipation of your loading position for a cross forward stroke.

CROSS FORWARD
a "lefty"

Beginning of powerphase

20°

35°

20°

End of powerphase

When returning the paddle to your onside after *any* type of cross stroke, again aim your control thumb in the direction of the blade's travel, and feather the blade over the bow parallel to the deck. The control thumb position again reduces the risk of hitting the boat with the leading edge of the blade.

Here are the components of the cross forward stroke:

Step 1. Loading - This is the set-up for the powerphase, and is also referred to as the "catch." Insert the blade in the water near the bow on your offside, right next to the hull. You should be leaning forward about 35 degrees. Aim the powerface aft, with the shaft angled about 20 degrees from vertical (side view), the grip farther aft than the blade -- the control hand should be about six inches aft of the shaft hand. Both arms are held nearly straight (but not locked at the elbows), extending forward from the shoulder plane. Both hands should be out over the water. The powerface should be angled so that it faces the *offside* of your body; i.e., the blade is not quite at right angles to the centerline, but is turned a little bit toward the hull.

Step 2. Powerphase - Having anchored the blade, now pull the boat to the blade by forcefully pulling your hips forward to sit straight up. This "pelvic thrust" is what propels the boat forward. Your arms merely transfer the strength of the large muscles of your back, abdomen, and shoulders. Keep your arms comfortably straight. The powerphase ends when the blade is next to your thigh. At this point, your paddle angle is again 20 degrees from vertical, but with the grip *forward* of the blade. That is, the control hand is now about six inches forward of the shaft hand.

Let's look at an analogy. Pretend you're kneeling on a skateboard and propelling yourself along the sidewalk using only the parking meters. Assume you are a "righty" and the parking meters are on your left. Lean forward and grasp the first meter, left hand (control hand) above your right hand (shaft hand). Keep your arms straight (but not locked at the elbows) and use your hips to thrust the skateboard forward. As you glide forward, lean forward and reach for the next meter. Then repeat. Watch out for meter maids! Do you feel the power of using torso instead of arm muscles on your offside? That's what powers the cross forward!

MANEUVER: FORWARD TRAVEL (cont.)

(2) Stroke: Cross Forward

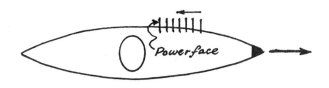

Step 3. Recovery - An underwater blade recovery is the key to efficiency in this stroke. The powerphase ended with the blade just in front of your hips. Turn your control thumb forward, and lean your torso forward while at the same time slicing the blade forward *in* the water to the catch position. Do not alter your arm positions; keep both arms extended, as they were in the powerphase.

Two common errors during the recovery: (1) Hitting the hull with the blade. This results in a "jam" position, which sends the unprepared paddler down for a sudden fish count. Prevent the jam by aiming your control thumb straight forward or even slightly away from the boat, so the blade slices away from the hull as it goes forward. (2) Lifting the blade out of the water during the recovery. This not only wastes motion, but results in downward force (waste of *energy!*) during the catch and powerphase of the subsequent stroke.

116

3.) Traveling J-stroke This onside stroke is designed to keep a canoe traveling in a straight line, and is used for crossing open stretches such as the pools between rapids. It consists of the complete forward stroke described above, followed by a quick correction of the yaw caused by the forward stroke. The fact that there is more than one powerphase component makes this a *combination* stroke.

MANEUVER: FORWARD TRAVEL (cont.)

(3) Stroke: Traveling J

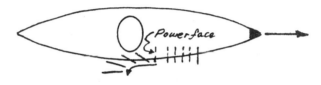

There are probably as many ways of doing a traveling J as there are Kellys in Killarney. But they all have two common features: (1) they use the powerface throughout the powerphase and, (2) the J takes place with the blade a bit behind the paddler while the forward stroke is done in front of the paddler. The J-stroke that we are going to present will enable you to keep your original stroke cadence, with only slight speed reduction. Let's begin by doing a complete forward stroke as described above, but don't take the blade out of the water at the conclusion of the powerphase (by your knee). Instead, rotate your control thumb toward the bow and let your blade continue slicing back close to the boat, powerface still loaded, until slightly aft of your body. From this position, with your control hand high, in front of your body and still over the onside gunwale, begin the lateral exit of the blade by gracefully pulling the grip toward the offside gunwale; this results in a pry (shaft against the gunwale) and continues the load on the powerface in a lateral direction. When the grip is near the centerline, stop pulling laterally and begin the

117

wind-up for the next stroke; the blade is still in the water but it is already feathered and ready for a forward exit from the water. Practice this stroke until you can perform it in one continuous motion with no "hitch" either as you convert to the J or as you wind up for the next stroke. This is a beautiful stroke when it is done correctly, but you'll need many "miles in the saddle" to perfect its subtleties.

4.) *Traveling Pry* This is another onside combination stroke that starts with the forward stroke as described above. The correction for the yaw caused by the forward stroke again occurs behind the paddler and is the pry component of the traveling pry. The main difference from the traveling J is that the paddler switches the force on the blade surfaces from the powerface to the backface immediately after the forward stroke; this is done by turning the control thumb *aft,* instead of toward the bow. Then the blade is quickly positioned slightly behind the torso and a pry is executed as described above in the Traveling J. The traveling pry is more powerful but not as fluid as the J. It is more common in big water paddling than in technical playboating.

MANEUVER: FORWARD TRAVEL (cont.)

(4) Stroke: Traveling Pry

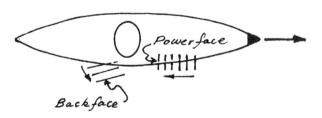

Maneuver: Reverse Travel. The contemporary playboater needs a repertoire of back strokes to help him perform various maneuvers -- for example, to arrest forward travel downriver, or to instantaneously slow his travel to less than that of the current while maintaining a downstream discipline. In addition, experienced playboaters enjoy doing reverse circles and other reverse figures on the river! Reverse paddling also enables you to catch an eddy where you don't have room to spin your boat for an eddy turn.

Strokes for this Maneuver:

1.) Back Stroke Start by rotating your shoulder plane about 70 degrees toward the onside gunwale. With your control thumb pointing out (so force will applied to the back face), and each elbow bent about 45 degrees, place the blade in the water about 18 inches behind your torso, and begin the powerphase, during which you must do three things simultaneously: (1) Unwind your torso and continue beyond your resting position until you're in the catch position of the forward stroke -- fully 130 degrees of torso rotation during this powerphase! (2) Push hard on your shaft hand and pull with your control hand, to quickly bring the paddle to a vertical position (side view), and maintain this vertical position as you complete the powerphase. (3) Start with a slight backward lean, and end with a distinct forward lean.

MANEUVER: REVERSE TRAVEL

(1) Stroke: Back

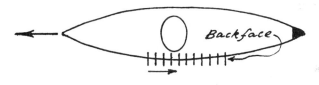

The powerphase ends at the catch position of the forward stroke, with your onside shoulder in a similar position to that which you had during the loading of the forward stroke. The shaft arm is comfortably straight at the end of the powerphase. Make sure your blade is at right angles to the centerline of the boat during the powerphase; failure to do this is the most common mistake of the back stroke. Note that there is more rotation of the shoulder plane with this stroke than in the forward stroke -- about 60 degrees more!

For the recovery, slice the blade out of the water away from the boat; trace an arc by gradually turning your control thumb back. At the last minute before loading for the next stroke, quickly turn your control thumb away to slice the blade into the water perpendicular to the centerline of the boat.

2.) Cross Back A technically correct and efficient cross back is pretty difficult to do with thigh straps on, unless you are part rubber band. But it's worth the effort, as this stroke, coupled with the back stroke, enables you to back ferry in powerful currents.

MANEUVER: REVERSE TRAVEL (cont.)
(2) Stroke: Cross Back

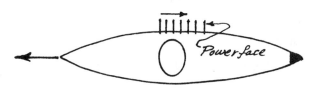

Feather the blade across the boat (control thumb pointing in the direction of travel over the bow), and place it in the water close to the boat on your offside, slightly behind your body. The control thumb points out so force will be applied to the powerface. This position, comfortable or not, will rotate your shoulder plane almost 90 degrees to your offside! You should have a slight backward lean as you begin the powerphase, and end with a slight forward lean, but most of the powerphase is done with a combination of unwinding your torso, pushing with your control hand and pulling with your shaft hand. It's a short stroke, ending at your knee. The recovery is underwater, with the control thumb pointing forward -- one of the few strokes in which your control thumb does not point in the direction of the blade's recovery.

3.) *Compound Back* The compound back stroke, coupled with the reverse J (described below), is a great combination to start your craft moving in reverse from a dead stop, or to quickly arrest your forward movement when in swift water. It is a *compound stroke* because the force is applied to first one blade surface, then the other, during the powerphase. The stroke is executed on your onside.

MANEUVER: REVERSE TRAVEL (cont.)

(3) Stroke: Compound Back

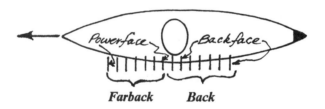

Farback   Back

Rotate your shoulder plane as far as possible to your onside, hopefully beyond 90 degrees. Place the blade in the water as "far back" behind your body as possible, with the control thumb pointed toward the boat. You should be looking at the powerface and leaning back slightly. Now pull the boat to the blade, keeping the shaft as vertical as possible, until the blade is almost beside your back. At this point, quickly flip your control thumb so it points away from the boat, and continue the powerphase by executing the back stroke described above. Recovery is the same as for the back stroke, except it continues all the way to the "far" catch position. Occasionally, some paddlers do just the far-back stroke, which is the first component of the powerphase described above; the recovery for the far-back is *underwater* with the control thumb pointing in the direction of blade travel. Practice start-ups from a dead stop using the compound back stroke coupled with the reverse J, described next.

4.) Reverse J This stroke is a fluid means of traveling in reverse. It is often used in conjunction with the compound back to arrest downriver movement. But once under way, the paddler eliminates the farback component of the compound back, and continues with just the back stroke and the reverse J. This stroke is a modification of the back stroke in which the paddler corrects the reverse yaw by continuing to apply pressure to the backface while turning the control thumb down toward the gunwale, and executing a pry at the end of the powerphase. The pry is efficient only if executed at the end of a powerphase placed well under the boat. Recovery is the same as for the back stroke. Practice traveling in reverse in a straight line, using the reverse J to cross the pools between rapids.

MANEUVER: REVERSE TRAVEL (cont.)

(4) Stroke: Reverse J

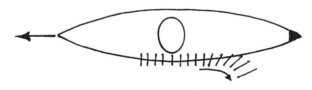

Use backface throughout powerphase

Maneuver: Circle Paddling. A form of forward travel, circle paddling is a central feature of whitewater playboating. Because it greatly reduces the need for correction strokes that rob the boat of its momentum, it enables the paddler to play the river with far greater efficiency.

Strokes for this maneuver:

1.) Forward stroke (Described under Forward Travel)

2.) Forward control stroke This is a modified forward stroke, the difference being the distance of the blade from the hull during the powerphase. In the forward control stroke, the blade is placed farther from the hull to decrease the tendency of the boat to turn too tightly toward the blade as you paddle. If you're thinking the boat always turns *away* from the side on which you paddle, WE CAUGHT YOU AGAIN! You must have skipped (or slept through!) the chapter on The Circle Concept. You'll have to go back and read it before proceeding!

Start your boat circling to your onside. Set a steady, comfortable boat lean, and see how large a circle you can paddle without losing your circle altogether. To open up your circle to the max, you will need to stroke a considerable distance out -- about two feet away from the hull. To maintain this large circle, you might continue paddling with a normal forward stroke. The forward control strokes end slightly farther aft than your usual forward stroke. Next, practice carving little circles; with the blade almost *under* your boat during each powerphase, find the smallest circle you can paddle while still maintaining some forward momentum. This will demonstrate for you the range of circle sizes that your boat will carve.

3.) Cross forward stroke (Described under Forward Travel)

4.) Cross forward control stroke This is a similar modification,

MANEUVER: CIRCLE PADDLING

NOTE: Circle size is a function of (1) boat lean and (2) forward stroke position (control strokes).

(1) Stroke: Forward -- Small Circle

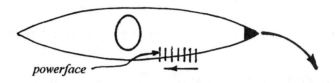

Maximum boat lean, stroking <u>under</u> the boat

---

(2) Stroke: Forward -- Large Circle

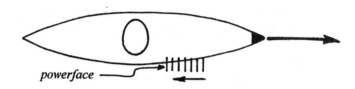

Minimum boat lean, <u>normal</u> forward stroke

---

(3) Stroke: Forward -- Small Circle to Large Circle

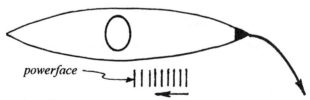

Decrease boat lean to minimum and stroke <u>away</u> from the boat

---

(4) Stroke: Forward -- Large Circle to Small Circle

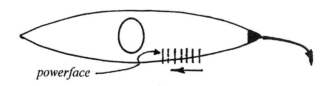

Increase boat lean to maximum and stroke <u>under</u> the boat

applied to the cross forward stroke. Greater distance of the blade from the boat produces a larger offside circle. Practice stroking varying distances from the hull on your offside until you can paddle any size circle you choose.

Homework: Develop boat control by setting a buoy out on the pond. Paddle in circles, hitting the buoy on each pass. Enlarge and shrink your circle, still hitting the buoy on each circle. Practice circling both to the onside and the offside.

Maneuver: Figure Eights. This maneuver consists of circle paddling, plus several techniques for changing from one circle to another.

Strokes for this maneuver:

1.) Forward Stroke (described under Forward Travel)

2.) Forward Control Stroke (described under Circle Paddling)

3.) Stern Sweep (described under Spins)

4.) Cross Forward Stroke (described under Forward Travel)

5.) Cross Forward Control Stroke (described under Circle Paddling)

6.) Shallow Water Pry This is a correction stroke executed well aft of your body, with a low shaft angle. It is similar to the correction component of the traveling pry, except the grip is held low (near the onside gunwale) so the blade is *well* aft and just below the water's surface. It need not be preceded by an onside stroke -- the blade can be crossed from the offside and inserted in the water behind the paddler's body for a quick pry to initiate a boat turn toward the onside.

7.) Cross Forward Sweep   This is the ultimate forward control stroke. Awkward, ungainly, and ineffectual until you learn to do it *perfectly*, it is the quintessential cross stroke. You may never learn to love it, but it is an extremely useful stroke for getting the boat turning to your onside. It is often used in situations where the boat is continuing to turn to the offside despite several cross forward control strokes intended to "lose" the offside circle. Here's how it's done: On your offside, place the blade in the water as close to the bow as you can (lean forward!), with the control thumb pointing down. As with *all* cross strokes, you will be using the powerface of your blade. To get good extension toward the bow, you'll need a low shaft angle -- lower the grip to the front of your chest -- and "choke up." Then sweep the blade *away* from the bow as you sit up straight. You will inevitably bring the blade aft somewhat during this powerphase (as in a cross forward), but the more it travels out from the hull, the more effective your sweep will be. The goal is to turn the bow away from the blade, so just keep Uncle Newton in mind.

The recovery is above water with the control thumb forward. Used appropriately, you'll generally need only one cross forward to get the bow turning to your onside, so the subsequent stroke is going to be on your onside. Therefore, we tend to think of the recovery as a feathering across the bow to the catch position for the forward stroke.

With these *seven magnificent strokes* in your bag of skills, you're ready to do all kinds of figure eights. Place two buoys on the pond, about 30 to 50 feet apart. You're going to paddle figure eights around the two floats, and change from one circle to the other at the moment when you cross the imaginary line connecting the two floats. Start by paddling your onside circle. Anticipate that you want to change to your offside circle -- open it out to a huge-diameter circle -- then do a single stern sweep. This will kick the bow over to your offside, at which point you should immediately switch boat leans. Or, a more advanced way to change circles is to execute two to four control strokes well away from the hull, so that you "lose" your onside circle. The moment your boat starts turning to your offside, switch paddling sides. This enables you to change circles without making a single correction stroke. After either technique of changing circles, immediately switch to an offside lean and start stroking with cross forwards.

Now that you're on your offside circle, anticipate the switch back to your onside circle by opening up the size of the circle. Execute a quick onside stern pry to turn the bow to your onside. A more advanced technique is to do a cross forward sweep instead of a pry, since it increases your forward momentum. Either way, switch to an onside boat lean, and carve your onside circle until it's time to switch again.

Homework: Develop precision by practicing with larger and smaller circles on each half of the figure eight and changing from one circle to the other exactly as your body crosses the imaginary line connecting the two buoys. This precision will be invaluable when paddling technical rapids!

Maneuver: Onside U-Turns. Playboaters are constantly U-turning (without getting a traffic ticket!) as they dance around the obstacles in the river. For the many different situations you will encounter, the various turns described below are going to come in very handy. These will enable you to carve a huge arc (without hitting a rock due to lack of momentum), or spin on a dime instantaneously. We're going to start with the largest-diameter turns, and progress to the tightest turn possible.

1.) Paddling an onside circle until you've turned 180 degrees is a form of U-turn. It can be a very wide "U" or a fairly tight one. Because it offers such flexibility, this technique comes into use on the river in many of the playboating maneuvers. Its great advantage is that you are adding forward momentum to your boat throughout the maneuver.

MANEUVER: U-TURNS
Stroke: Forward — Varying Size Circles

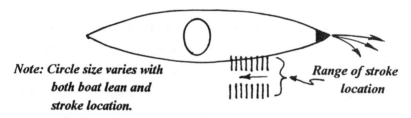

Note: Circle size varies with both boat lean and stroke location.

Range of stroke location

2.) Start paddling an onside circle, and then set a *Duffek stroke*. This is a high-shaft-angle turning high brace (as opposed to the *low* shaft angle of a reverse sweeping low brace described below). It is a favorite stroke of experienced canoeists, and if executed properly, can be combined with a number of other strokes for playboating maneuvers.

Here's how the Duffek stroke is done: Rotate your shoulder plane about 45 degrees to your onside. Raise your control hand so the shaft is nearly vertical, and place the paddle in the water with the blade opposite your knee. Now your shoulder plane should be facing the blade. Aim the powerface toward the bow. Make sure both hands are out over the water, with the back of your control hand about ten inches in front of your forehead.

Keep your shaft arm bent, with the elbow fairly close to your body to prevent the risk of shoulder dislocation. You'll need a good boat lean toward the Duffek *before* anchoring the blade -- It's difficult to set an appropriate boat lean once the Duffek is in place.

MANEUVER: U-TURNS (cont.)

Stroke: Forward to <u>Duffek System</u>

First: Duffek
Second: Bow draw
Third: Forward

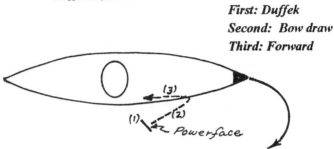

The *Duffek System* is as follows: (1) execute the above-described Duffek stroke, (2) rotate your onside shoulder forward to apply a force toward the bow, and (3) conclude, when the bow comes to the blade, with a forward stroke. The paddler should try to maintain equal force on the powerface throughout all three components of the Duffek System.

3.) Start paddling an onside circle, then U-turn with a slowly executed *reverse sweeping low brace*. This stroke is very similar to a reverse sweep, except the paddler maintains a consistent boat lean toward the blade throughout the entire stroke. Again, as in Step 2, conclude with a forward stroke. The resulting turn is so crisp that you will literally spin the bow directly around to the blade, resulting in a 180 degree turn. This stroke is used in situations which require an abrupt change of direction, common in negotiation of intricate routes.

The reverse sweeping low brace is extremely valuable in playboating because it allows the paddler to use an extreme boat lean (as long as he trusts the bracing aspect of the stroke!), which will both turn the boat *and* arrest its forward momentum much more quickly than a Duffek. The mechanism behind this effect is as follows: Dropping the gunwale to water level on a turn orients a greater portion of the bottom of the boat to oncoming opposition; the surface area of the underwater hull thus exposed to the water is several times greater than the surface area of the blade on a Duffek. This is similar to stopping on a pair of skis by turning both skis at right angles to the direction of movement and forcing the uphill edge of the skis against the direction of travel to bring yourself to an abrupt stop.

MANEUVER: U-TURNS (cont.)

Stroke: Forward to <u>*Reverse Sweeping Low Brace*</u> (*RSLB*)

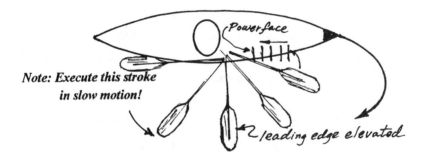

4.) Start paddling an onside circle. Execute a U-turn with a *compound reverse sweep*. This stroke consists of the first half of a reverse sweeping low brace, which is converted into a Duffek stroke when the blade is opposite your hip. The Duffek is followed by a bow draw and forward stroke, as in Steps 2 and 3. This maneuver will provide the same sharpness of turn as seen in Step 3, but involves more advanced technique.

Stroke: Reverse Compound Sweep

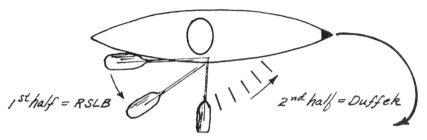

$1^{st} half = RSLB$ $2^{nd} half = Duffek$

Maneuver: Offside U-Turns. Well *of course* you should be equally proficient at U-turns to your offside. They're almost half your playboating repertoire! They're fun, classy, and invaluable in technical rapids.

1.) Paddling your offside circle with cross forward strokes until you've turned 180 degrees is again the first form of U-turn. It is generally more difficult to paddle a large circle to the offside, so you will tend to make tighter U-turns to your offside than your onside when circle paddling. But this is a valuable method for U-turning while adding forward momentum to your boat throughout the maneuver.

MANEUVER: OFFSIDE U-TURNS

Stroke: Cross Forward -- <u>Varying Size Circles</u>

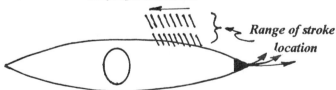

Range of stroke location

Note: Circle size varies with both boat lean and stroke location

2.) Start paddling an offside circle, and then set a *cross Duffek stroke*. This is an offside version of the Duffek stroke introduced above, and looks exactly the same to the fish viewing it from below! As in the onside Duffek, the blade is anchored beside your knee (but on your offside), again with the powerface aimed at the bow. Make sure both hands are out over the water, with the control hand a bit aft of the shaft hand. Rotate so that your shoulder plane faces the blade. Force the bow to come to the blade by de-rotating your shoulder plane. Make sure the boat and blade come together far enough forward to execute a powerful cross forward stroke. As with the onside Duffek, set your boat lean *before* anchoring the blade. Conclude the cross Duffek stroke with a cross forward stroke with the blade *under* the boat.

Occasionally, a second Duffek or cross Duffek is needed to complete the desired turn. Practice setting a Duffek, then, instead of going into a forward stroke, slicing the blade out diagonally *underwater* to the catch position for another Duffek stroke. Try spinning your craft with multiple Duffeks, first on one side and then on the other. Concentrate on your shoulder rotation to power the strokes. For your onside Duffek, the recovery is done with the control thumb "back," i.e., pointing in the direction of blade travel. For the cross Duffek, the thumb points forward (one more of those rare exceptions to the guideline). Both recoveries are underwater.

Maneuver: Sideslip. This elegant little move shifts your boat laterally without altering its directional discipline. Imagine you're paddling down a river when you look up and spot a bald eagle flying over your head. You are transfixed. When your gaze finally returns to the river, you see a rock directly in front of you! Being the cool paddler that you are, you mask your alarm, simply position a stationary draw, and sideslip your boat by the rock, continuing in the same direction you originally were headed in. This maneuver is an easy intermediate skill, but most canoeists simply have never learned to do it. We suggest that you invest the time on calm water to get it "wired." You'll find it well worth your effort. As a bonus, if you can sideslip your canoe, you will have learned how to sideslip *any* solo boat you paddle, whether it be a kayak or a canoe. The technique and position of the stroke are identical in all solo craft.

Strokes for this maneuver:

1.) Onside: Stationary draw The stationary draw is really a modified Duffek stroke in which the blade is placed slightly behind your torso, about six to eight inches away from the boat. Like the Duffek, the stationary draw uses the powerface. Rotate your shoulder plane so it is parallel to the centerline. Place your paddle as if you intend to execute a Duffek stroke, but: (1) anchor the blade farther aft, as described above, and (2) instead of aiming the powerface at the bow, aim it at your body, so the blade is only about 15 to 20 degrees from parallel to the centerline, with the leading edge farther from the hull than the trailing edge.

MANEUVER: SIDESLIP
(1) Stroke: Stationary Draw

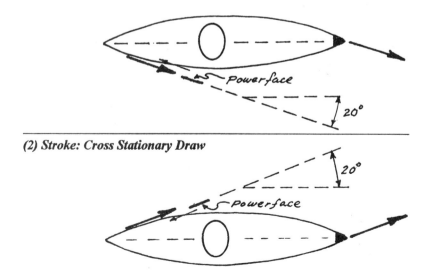

(2) Stroke: Cross Stationary Draw

Since the boat sideslips toward the blade, the side of the craft nearest the blade should be elevated for more efficient lateral movement. Lastly, for *any* stationary stroke to be effective, the boat must have forward momentum with respect to the current. You can't just sit on the pond, plant a stationary draw, and expect to go skidding across the water! (You probably knew that. We just want you to remember to get good forward momentum before you execute this stroke.)

2.) Offside: Cross Stationary Draw This stroke is similar to the cross Duffek, except again the blade is anchored slightly aft of your torso. You will have to "choke up" with your shaft hand and keep the control hand in front of your torso, in order to place the blade correctly. It's basically the cross version of the stationary draw described above, and as such should look identical to the fishes looking up at the boat and blade!

Challenge of the day: Now that you know how to sideslip your craft to your onside and offside *traveling forward,* how do you sideslip in reverse? The blade placement is the key. Use the powerface, and place the blade in the *following end* of the boat (usually about even with your knee). The blade angle? Parallel to the direction of the desired sideslip. This is one of those moves known by so few paddlers that you can impress *anyone* once you have the move "wired." You'll be looking for excuses to use it!

A Final Tip! *Remember, boat control is learned on calm water. There is no substitute for "Pond Homework"! All of the strokes and maneuvers presented in this chapter will be valuable tools on the river. Practice them on the pond, in the pools between rapids, or even at an indoor pool when the rivers freeze over. You're going to see them all again in the chapter on River Playboating Maneuvers!*

134

TANDEM CANOEING

Don't read this chapter!! ...*until* you have read the preceding chapters! This entire book (believe it or not!) is designed in a logical progression; when we present you with the material specific to tandem canoeing, we're counting on you to understand all the aspects of playboating covered earlier. (OK, you can skip the chapter on kayaking. BUT, you must read the chapter on solo canoeing. More on that in a minute.) So, if you skipped directly from the Table of Contents to this page, WE CAUGHT YOU and we're sending you back to Chapter One.

Introduction. Whatever your reasons for wanting to learn tandem canoeing, the key to success is to first become a good *solo* paddler. Because, until you fully understand the craft's response to *your* actions, you will blame everything on your partner!! All alone in the boat, you will develop sensitivity to its dynamics, and you will master 90 % of the skills that you need as a tandem paddler.

Here's how the two are related: Paddling solo, you carry out all the functions of bowperson whenever your blade is in the leading end of the boat, and all the functions of the sternperson whenever it's in the following end of the boat. For example, when a solo canoeist executes a forward sweep, he is doing the bowperson's quarter sweep and then the sternperson's quarter sweep. So, after learning to paddle solo well, you will be equally competent in *either* tandem position! No more of that "I'm just a bow paddler" nonsense!

One of the primary reasons we recommend taking up solo before tandem canoeing is the importance of developing "lower body sensitivity," i.e., a kinesthetic sense of the boat's movements and a set of learned reflexes for adjusting your J-lean in response to the actions of the current on the boat. Beginning tandem paddlers who *lack* solo experience tend to cancel out each other's boat leans, thus preventing each other from developing this kinesthetic sensitivity!

Also, it's a lot easier for tandem paddlers to communicate and work as a team when they both understand how to make the boat "behave." This enables one to call out to the other, "Let's catch the eddy behind that big rock," whereas the paddler with a less-skilled partner is forced to shout, "Sweep! Sweep!!!" -- And is liable to hear back from such a partner the useless warning, "Rock! Rock!!!"

So, start by mastering solo open or decked canoeing or kayaking. *Then* take up tandem open or decked canoeing. In both solo and tandem paddling, formal instruction is essential to develop safe and efficient technique, and to prevent those negative "coping" habits that can hold a paddler back from the more advanced maneuvers or bigger water. When you paddle tandem, learn to paddle both positions, so that you fully understand what your partner can and cannot do in a given situation.

We are going to *count* on you to learn the basics, such as sweeps, the forward stroke, etc., in the Solo Canoeing chapter, since they're not repeated here! In this chapter, we describe how to employ those strokes to carry out tandem canoe maneuvers. We also describe the functions of the bowperson and sternperson during onside and offside turns -- but without defining the strokes, except to indicate any differences from the way they are executed in solo craft.

Orientation to tandem paddling. In tandem canoeing, *onside* and *offside* are defined in reference to the bowperson's paddling side. For example, if the bowperson is a "lefty," the left side of the craft is the onside, and the right is the offside. All tandem boats illustrated in this chapter are paddled with a "lefty" in the bow, so the *left* is *onside.*

Picture the potential area in which an individual can place his paddle blade as being a circle, with the paddler's body at the center. This circle is divided into four quadrants, the boat's centerline dividing the circle in half, and a perpendicular line through the paddler's body further dividing the circle into four quadrants. In general, the bowperson paddles in the two quadrants forward of his body on his onside and offside, while the sternperson paddles only in the two quadrants on his paddling side -- power and control strokes in his front onside quadrant, and correction strokes in his aft onside quadrant. This generalization serves as a good starting point for making the transition from solo to tandem canoeing.

Communication between paddlers. Imagine standing on a bridge as two tandem boats run the river below you. In the first boat, the paddlers are in "call and response" mode, advising each other of obstacles, and calling out eddy turns and spins as they go. They succeed at most of the moves they attempt; when they do miss a move, one of the paddlers quickly calls out an alternative destination. You're impressed by their teamwork.

Then the second boat passes under the bridge and comes into view. These paddlers are also playing the river extensively, spinning their boat to hop onto surfing waves, making dozens of peel-outs and eddy turns... but they're not talking at all! Mad at each other? Not with those grins on their faces! How do they do it? These paddlers are more advanced, and more accustomed to paddling together than the first pair that went past. They are attuned to each other's movements, the boat, and the current, so that they carry on a constant nonverbal "dialogue" as they play the river. For example, as they peel out from an eddy, the angle set by the sternperson telegraphs to the bowperson whether to maintain a ferry angle to that big mid-river boulder, or to anchor a cross Duffek for a sharp turn downstream. Similarly, the sternperson readily identifies the bowperson's desire to surf a hole by the aggressive stroke cadence and the shallow angle maintained as they exit an eddy just below the hole.

As you and your paddling partner develop your tandem skills, you will find less need to talk on the river... which makes it easier to keep that big grin on *your* face!

Bowperson's responsibilities. The bowperson's primary responsibility is to provide power, so most of his strokes are power strokes. Stroke *cadence* is the timing of the strokes, and is set by the bowperson, since the sternperson can easily watch and match the bowperson's tempo. (This remains true when paddling in reverse!) Both paddlers are responsible for maintaining boat lean. The bowperson establishes *how far* to lean when the boat is turning toward his paddling side. He should not counteract *offside* leans set by his partner!

The bowperson's vantage point also makes him the best one for spotting rocks and other hazards to be avoided; it is his job to keep his end of the boat away from all hazards. The sternperson responds appropriately to avoid the same obstacle; both paddlers should be reading the river. In rare instances, the obstacle to be avoided may require an immediate maneuver, in which case the bowperson should call out to the sternperson specifically what to do to alter the boat's course.

Sternperson's responsibilities. The sternperson's primary responsibility is to keep the canoe headed in the proper direction. This depends, of course, on the maneuver being executed, but generally he is responsible for craft angulation and positioning. Because the sternperson is paddling in the eddy resistance end of the boat (except when doing a back ferry or traveling in reverse), he has far greater control over the boat's course than the bowperson, so it's logical for him to be responsible for keeping the boat on course. The sternperson also provides power, matching the stroke cadence set by the bowperson but skipping a stroke when necessary to make a correction such as a pry at the end of a forward stroke.

When the bowperson alters the boat's course, the sternperson makes the appropriate correction to either keep the boat aligned with the current (when traveling directly downriver), or to complete the maneuver (such as an eddy turn) initiated by the bowperson. Both paddlers are responsible for maintaining boat lean. The sternperson establishes *how far* to lean when the boat is turning toward his paddling side. He should not counteract *onside* leans set by his partner! The sternperson shares responsibility for spotting obstacles on the river, since he will sometimes see things missed by the bowperson.

Getting started. As in any paddlesport discipline, start your tandem canoeing on calm water, where most skills must be mastered before being attempted on moving water. Develop your paddling "teamwork" by practicing the specific strokes and boat movements that will keep you upright and enable you to play the river. Then move on to the chapter on River Playboating Maneuvers to learn how to apply these techniques to whitewater.

Fitting yourself to the boat. Each paddler should fit in his chosen position in the same manner as a solo canoeist. If you and your paddling partner differ in weight by more than 40 or 50 pounds, then we recommend that the heavier person be in the stern. (We really don't mean to contradict our earlier advice that you learn to paddle both positions, but some teams are "stuck" by their relative physiques!) Again, we strongly recommend that you take at least a two-day lesson before you buy, so that you can make a more educated decision on the right gear for the two of you. Read the chapter on Playboating Equipment for additional information on purchasing a boat.

Launching and landing. Whether paddling an open or decked canoe, you will suffer fewer launching-point fish counts if one person steadies the boat while the other gets in; then, the second paddler gets in. It makes no difference which paddler gets in first if the boat is parallel to shore. When launching with the boat perpendicular to shore, the paddler taking the position farther from shore should enter first. Before getting in, make sure the entire canoe is in the water -- it's extremely tippy if just the end is resting on the bank. Both paddlers can adjust thigh straps (and sprayskirts) at the same time -- a good chance to get used to the feel of someone else's movements rocking the boat! Upon landing, the first person out of the boat steadies the boat while the second gets out.

Wet exits. Exiting the capsized canoe involves the same movements as outlined in the previous chapter -- starting with the all-important *TUCK!* Open boaters should practice their wet exits before paddling in significant currents. Decked boaters must be comfortable with their wet exits in calm water before paddling on moving water. Upon wet-exiting the boat, each paddler should call to the other to make sure both are okay. Then each swimmer holds onto his paddle and swims aggressively to shore, one paddler also pulling in the boat. On whitewater, the swimmer closer to shore often has greater control of the boat during the self-rescue, because he is generally in slower current. This person should grab the nearest end of the boat and, with the paddle and painter (or grab loop) in one hand, swim aggressively to shore. Swim with the right arm if swimming to river right and vice versa for the left; this keeps you facing downstream to see where you're going. If one paddler is a significantly stronger swimmer than the other, the team should agree beforehand that the stronger swimmer has primary responsibility for getting the boat to shore in the event of a wet-exit. More on self-rescue in the chapter on River Rescue.

The boat boogie-wiggle. To get comfortable J-leaning your boat with your partner, practice vigorously tipping your boat first to one side and then the other, while keeping your upper body centered over the boat -- in other words, J-leaning to each side. Try to make BIG waves! Next, hold a fixed J-lean to the right, and then to the left. Try to "snap" the boat from one fixed lean to the other. Because you are practicing on a pond, the only way for each paddler to know when to change leans will be by verbal communication. On the river, the team learns to respond in unison to changing resistances on the boat, J-leaning to raise the side of opposition. When the side of opposition changes, both paddlers will quickly -- and hopefully simultaneously -- switch gracefully from one lean to the other without having to say a word.

The Coasting Position. In tandem canoeing, the coasting position is maintained by each paddler holding the paddle exactly as he would if paddling solo. The boat has the additional stability of an anchored blade on each side of the hull -- training wheels!

Preventing Capsizes: Righting Action Strokes. If you've already developed your solo righting-action reflexes, this is going to be a piece of cake. To prevent the boat from capsizing to the onside (remember, that's the bowperson's paddling side), the bowperson executes a low brace while the sternperson executes a righting pry. When capsizing to the offside, the bowperson pries as the sternperson low-braces. In other words, each paddler does exactly what he would do if he were alone in the boat! Practice these on a pond. Try to fake your partner out by executing your righting action stroke only at the _last_ possible moment before capsizing -- he'll put more power into _his_ righting action as a result... especially if the water's real cold!

Maneuver: Onside Spin. The boat is kept level during tandem onside and offside spins -- As each paddler rotates and reaches out to execute his sweep, one body lean cancels out the other. Practice executing the sweeps in cadence with your partner. Please study the illustrations as you read the descriptions of tandem maneuvers.

Strokes for this maneuver:

Technique 1: Sweeps
1a.) Bowperson: Reverse quarter sweep Begin the sweep with your blade straight out from your body, and sweep the blade to the bow. In other words, this is just the second half of a solo reverse sweep.
1b.) Sternperson: Forward quarter sweep The sternperson's forward quarter sweep is the same thing as a solo stern sweep. The stern sweep is more efficient for an onside spin than an entire forward sweep, because the sternperson's stroke has far greater power to alter the course of the boat if it is executed behind his body. Any correction stroke the sternperson executes in front of

his body places the blade too near the pivot point of the boat.

Technique 2: Draws

2.) Both paddlers: Draw   When both paddlers execute simultaneous onside draws, the result is an onside spin. Stay in cadence with your partner to spin the boat without excessive "bobble."

MANEUVER: ONSIDE SPINS

(1) Strokes: Both paddlers - Sweeps (actually quarter or 90 degree sweeps)

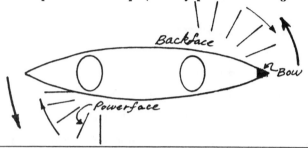

(2) Strokes: Both paddlers - Draws

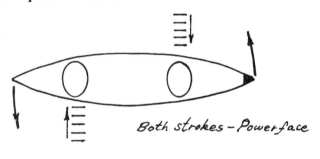

(3) Strokes: Both paddlers - Sculls

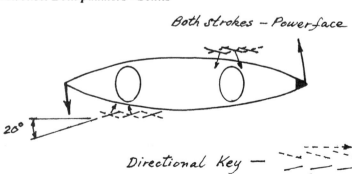

Technique 3: Sculls

3.) Both paddlers: Scull Smoother than the draw, onside sculls executed by both paddlers will gracefully spin the boat to the onside. This stroke is not considered to have a cadence that needs to be matched by the two paddlers. (If the sternperson sculls faster than the bowperson, won't the stern catch up with the bow?)

Maneuver: Offside Spin.

Strokes for this maneuver:

Technique 1: Sweeps

1a.) Bowperson: Forward quarter sweep Begin the powerphase at the bow, and end it when the blade is opposite your body. The rationale for not continuing beyond your body is the same as outlined above for the sternperson's forward quarter sweep -- it is inefficient to continue the stroke near to the boat's pivot point.

1b.) Sternperson: Reverse quarter sweep This reverse sweep begins at the stern, and ends opposite your body.

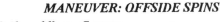

MANEUVER: OFFSIDE SPINS

(1) Strokes: Both paddlers - Sweeps

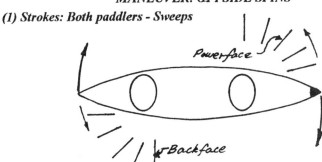

Technique 2: Pries

2.) Both paddlers: Pries When both paddlers pry simultaneously, the boat's response is the opposite of when they execute draws.

144

Again, try to minimize boat bobble by staying in cadence and keeping the powerphase of the pries short.

(2) Strokes: Both paddlers - Pries

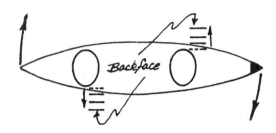

Maneuver: Onside Abeam. All tandem abeams are performed with a slight elevation of the boat's side of opposition, which is that side nearest the boat's destination. Paddlers must learn to apply equal forces at bow and stern in order to move the craft straight laterally.

Strokes for this maneuver:

Technique 1:
1a.) Bowperson: Draw
1b.) Sternperson: Pry

MANEUVER: ONSIDE ABEAMS
(1) Strokes: Bowperson - Draw; Sternperson - Pry

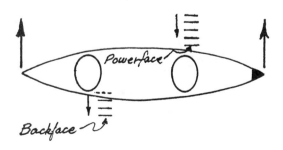

Technique 2:

2a.) Bowperson: Scull

2b.) Sternperson: Slices (dynamic pries)   Oh my goodness, a new stroke! The movement of the blade during this stroke is somewhat similar to sculling, except that the forward slice uses the powerface (as in sculling) while the reverse slice uses the backface.

Any slice, whether using forward or reverse movement of the blade, has a blade angulation of about 30 degrees from the centerline of the boat, with the leading edge of the blade closer to the hull than the trailing edge. This drives the shaft against the boat during the powerphase, forcing water diagonally away from the hull. The boat responds by moving away from the blade. A forward and reverse slice combination is a very powerful dynamic action.

Slices are used almost exclusively by open boaters; a decked boat tends to tip too much in response to a slice.

MANEUVER: ONSIDE ABEAMS (cont.)

(2) Strokes: Bowperson - Scull; Sternperson - Slices (dynamic pries)

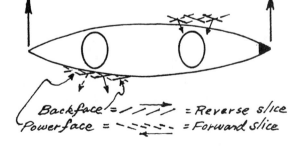

Maneuver: Forward Travel.

Strokes for this maneuver:

Technique 1:
1a.) Bowperson: Forward stroke
1b.) Sternperson: Traveling J-stroke If both paddlers were to simply do the forward stroke, the boat would turn to the onside, because the sternperson is stroking on the offside in the eddy resistance end of the boat and causing the boat to yaw. By executing a traveling J-stroke, the sternperson can maintain a course that is either straight-ahead or turning slightly toward the offside. This is used primarily by open boaters.

MANEUVER: FORWARD TRAVEL

(1) Strokes: Bowperson - Forward; Sternperson - Traveling J

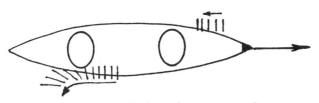

Both strokes use powerface

Technique 2:
2a.) Bowperson: Forward stroke
2b.) Sternperson: Forward slice This stroke has less forward power than a traveling J-stroke, but has a shorter powerphase, making it easier for the sternperson to stay in cadence with the bowperson while maintaining a straight course or turning slightly to the offside. This is again a stroke used primarily by open boaters.

(2) Strokes - Bowperson - Forward; Sternperson - Forward Slice

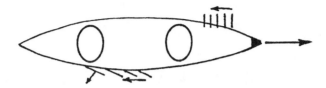

Both strokes use powerface

Technique 3:

3a.) Bowperson: Forward stroke

3b.) Sternperson: Traveling pry   Commonly used by the sternperson in a decked canoe (C-2), the traveling pry prevents the boat from turning to the bowperson's onside, with a minimum amount of time spent on the corrective action itself.

Maneuver: Reverse Travel.   During reverse travel, the sternperson is stroking in the frontal resistance end of the boat, and the bowperson is stroking in the eddy resistance end of the boat.   Therefore, it is the responsibility of the bowperson to keep the boat on course.   Open boaters should practice reverse travel extensively on calm water, since they apply this skill frequently to backferry on the river.

Strokes for this Maneuver:

1a.) Bowperson: Reverse J   Depending on which way the boat is turning, the bowperson will employ either a reverse J or a reverse quarter sweep to maintain a straight course.   The reverse J will be used more extensively since tandem boats always tend to veer away from the power stroke being executed in the following end of the boat.   The reverse J uses the backface only, and has the same effect as the sternperson's traveling J-stroke during forward travel. Some paddlers actually get more power from the J action by prying off the gunwale at the end of the powerphase.

1b.) Sternperson: Back stroke

MANEUVER: REVERSE TRAVEL

(1) Strokes: Bowperson - Reverse J; Sternperson - Back

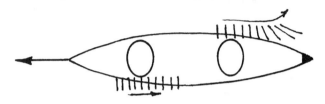

Both strokes use backface

Maneuver: Onside Circle. Circle paddling is as valuable in tandem canoeing as it is in solo. Because he is stroking in the eddy resistance end, the sternperson has primary control over the size of the circle. His technique for controlling the offside circle will be identical to paddling his *onside* circle in a solo boat; the bowperson simply adds forward momentum. Controlling the boat's onside circle will be more difficult. The sternperson must skip occasional strokes to execute a correcting pry or rudder. As in solo craft, the degree of boat lean and the distance of both paddlers' power strokes from the hull will influence circle size.

Strokes for this maneuver:

1a.) Bowperson: Forward stroke As in solo canoeing, the boat will carve a smaller onside circle if the onside strokes are placed closer to the hull. Open up the circle by stroking farther from the hull. Because the bowperson's strokes are entirely in the frontal resistance end of the boat, he cannot open up the circle much unless the sternperson assists him with an occasional correction stroke.

1b.) Sternperson: Forward control stroke with corrections The sternperson adds forward momentum with forward strokes, and keeps the circle from tightening down by executing a pry or rudder whenever needed.   To decrease the circle size, the sternperson strokes farther from the boat... but with caution, because once the stern starts skidding out on its "ball bearings," the circle will quickly tighten down almost into a spin!

MANEUVER: CIRCLE PADDLING

(1) Strokes for onside circles: Bowperson - Forward;
Sternperson - control strokes with an occasional pry or rudder
to keep the desired circle size.

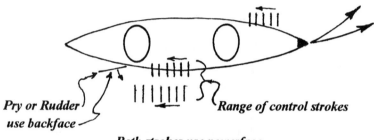

Pry or Rudder
use backface

Range of control strokes

Both strokes use powerface

Maneuver: Offside Circle. As mentioned above, this is the easier circle to control. The boat is turning to the sternperson's paddling side, so he can control it just as if he were paddling solo. Develop control of both your onside and offside circles with plenty of pond practice, using a buoy to test your precision.

1a.) Bowperson: Forward
1b.) Sternperson: Forward control strokes

150

(1) Strokes for offside circles: Bowperson - Forward;
Sternperson - Forward control strokes

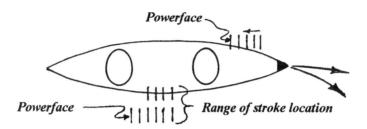

Maneuver: Figure Eights. The sternperson changes the boat from an onside circle to an offside circle by executing a pry, and changes back to an onside circle with a shallow water draw (which is the last half of a stern sweep) or a forward sweep. As you did in solo canoeing, set out two buoys about 30 to 50 feet apart, and develop precision by practicing with larger and smaller circles on each half of the figure eight. Remember to change from one circle to the other *exactly* as your boat crosses the imaginary line connecting the two buoys. And above all, don't forget to switch the lean when your boat changes from one circle to the other!

Maneuver: Onside U-Turns. As a general rule, the person paddling on the side to which the boat is turning is responsible for setting the correct amount of lean for the turn. Both paddlers then maintain that lean. So the bowperson sets the boat lean for onside U-turns.

Strokes for this maneuver:

Technique 1:
1a.) Bowperson: Duffek
1b.) Sternperson: Forward sweep This stroke is more or less just

to give the sternperson something to do. That Duffek in the bow will pivot the boat beautifully all by itself, as long as the U-turn is approached with the boat already carving an onside circle, and heeled to the onside! Increase the boat lean and the boat will turn even faster.

MANEUVER: ONSIDE U-TURNS
(1) Strokes: Bowperson - Duffek; Sternperson - Forward Sweep

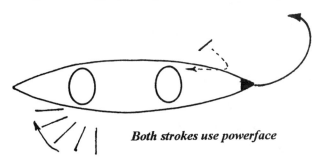

Both strokes use powerface

Technique 2:

2a.) Bowperson: Reverse sweeping low brace This stroke is preferable to a Duffek when the paddlers wish to heel the boat maximally. This will be the case when entering an eddy at high speed or when entering a very small eddy. (Hang in there -- it'll all make sense when you get to the chapter on River Playboating Maneuvers!) A reverse sweeping low brace allows the bowperson to set an extreme boat lean (as long as he trusts the bracing aspect of the stroke!), which will spin the boat and arrest its forward momentum much more quickly than a Duffek. The mechanism behind this effect is as follows: Dropping the gunwale (or seam in a decked boat) to water level during a turn orients more of the bottom of the boat to oncoming opposition. The surface area of the underwater hull thus exposed to the water is several times greater than the surface area of the blade on a Duffek. So the Duffek effect is amplified several-fold. This is similar to stopping on a pair of skis by turning both skis at right angles to the direction of movement and forcing the uphill edge of the skis against the direction of travel to bring yourself to an abrupt stop.

2b.) *Sternperson: Forward sweep*

MANEUVER: ONSIDE U-TURNS (cont.)

(2) Strokes: Bowperson - Reverse Sweeping Low Brace (RSLB);
Sternperson - Forward Sweep

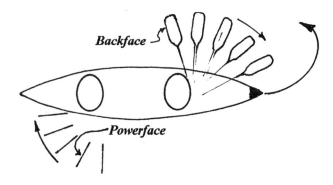

Maneuver: Offside U-Turns. The sternperson sets the proper boat lean for these maneuvers, which are turns to his own paddling side. He played only a supporting role for the *onside* U-turns, while the bowperson really ran the show. Here, the roles are reversed, and the bowperson can take a nap!

Strokes for this maneuver:

Technique 1:

1a.) Bowperson: Forward sweep Something to make the bow paddler feel useful, nothing more. Try the same offside turn with and without a forward sweep in the bow, and see how much it actually influences the turn. A forward stroke instead of a sweep is commonly used to maintain more forward momentum throughout the turn.

1b.) Sternperson: Reverse sweeping low brace   This stroke allows the sternperson to heel his side of the boat down to water level -- The boat will spin on a dime and immediately lose most of its forward momentum.   Substitute this boat lean for a cross Duffek in the bow!

MANEUVER: OFFSIDE U-TURNS

(1) Strokes: Bowperson - Forward Sweep; Sternperson - RSLB

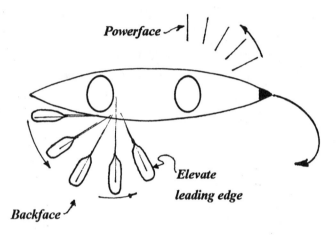

Technique 2:

2a.) Bowperson: Cross Duffek   The boat *didn't* spin right where the sternperson intended? Then try the same maneuver again, this time executing a cross Duffek at the front. But be careful -- you both might end up counting fish! We really do not recommend a cross Duffek in a heavily-rockered playboat if the sternperson intends to heel the gunwale to water level. We have found it best for the bowperson to just continue forward stroking, since the turn is really 98 percent in the control of the sternperson. Remember to use maximal boat lean on these turns!

2b.) Sternperson: Reverse sweeping low brace

(2) Strokes: Bowperson - Cross Duffek; Sternperson - RSLB

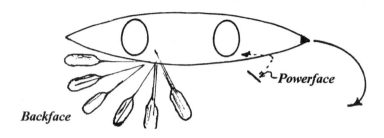

Backface

Powerface

Maneuver: Onside sideslip. As in solo paddling, sideslips are a complete mystery to many experienced tandem canoeists. Yet they are both elegant and fun! Because tandem canoes are longer than solo boats, the ability to sideslip past an obstacle can be particularly useful in narrow routes. Remember to raise your side of opposition slightly, which is the side toward your destination on the sideslip.

Strokes for this maneuver:

1a.) Bowperson: Stationary draw Place the blade just in front of your torso, about 12 inches from the boat. The blade position is similar to that of a Duffek, except the angle from the centerline is only 15 to 20 degrees.

1b.) Sternperson: Stationary pry This is similar to the stationary draw, except the blade is angled so the leading edge is closer to the hull than the trailing edge; as in the stationary draw, the blade is parallel to the direction of the sideslip, which means it is *also* parallel to the bowperson's blade. Place it in front of your torso, by your onside knee; start with a small angle of 15 degrees, until the boat begins its sideslip. Then increase the angle by as much as 30 degrees. An alternative to the stationary pry is for the sternperson to use a rudder. Again your blade will be parallel to the bow blade, but it will be behind your body.

MANEUVER: ONSIDE SIDESLIP

(1) Strokes: Bowperson - Stationary Draw;
Sternperson - Stationary Pry or Rudder

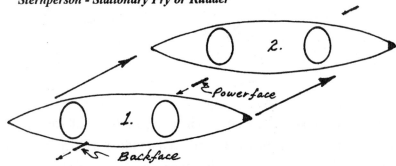

Maneuver: Offside sideslip.

1a.) Bowperson: Stationary pry Place the blade next to your knee, initially parallel to the gunwale. (Check to make sure your T-grip is parallel to the gunwale.) Once the boat starts sideslipping, you can open up the angle 30 degrees or so.

1b.) Sternperson: Stationary draw Place this stroke behind your torso by rotating your shoulder plane exactly as if you were doing a solo sideslip.

MANEUVER: OFFSIDE SIDESLIP

(1) Strokes: Bowperson - Stationary Pry; Stationary Draw

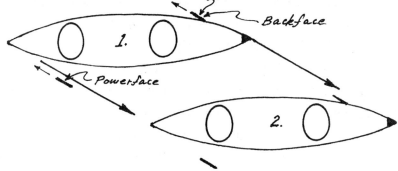

Challenge of the day: All right, you've done it all, solo and tandem -- spins, circles, U-turns, you name it! BUT, can you and your paddling partner sideslip your craft to your onside and offside *traveling in reverse?* Only then can you impress the most jaded boater you will ever run into on the river. Save it for when you're about to go under a bridge with a dozen pedestrians on it!

A Final Tip! *Remember, the key to contemporary tandem playboating is boat control learned on calm water. And, at the risk of sounding like a broken record, we'll say once again that you can only become a great tandem paddler by first learning solo playboating. The most-sought-after paddling partners are canoeists who playboat with equal confidence when paddling solo!*

THE THREE HUNDRED SIXTY DEGREE ROLL

Rolling your kayak or canoe isn't a "necessary skill," although it is a great skill to have. An ability to roll your boat will free you to playboat more confidently in challenging rapids.

Can everyone learn to roll? Everyone can certainly learn the first half... that is, the first 180 degrees. That's the half which once completed allows you to count the fish! It's the next 180 degrees that requires some skill.

To master the three hundred sixty degree roll takes time and a genuine commitment. The average paddler puts in one full season of extensive paddling before he begins to develop a good reflexive "combat roll" (a successful roll on the river after an unexpected capsize). No one part of it is difficult to do; it's just a complex *set* of movements that feel rather bizarre until learned. At the outset, you'll need feedback from an educated observer, because you won't be able to observe yourself and assess your position... unless you've mastered the out-of-body experience.

Part of the challenge lies in the fact that people *think* they're oriented to a three-dimensional world, but in fact our brains are evolved to operate in only two dimensions most of the time -- moving along the surface of the earth or water. We humans tend to get mixed up in no time when the third dimension is thrown in, as when we find ourselves upside-down in the river. This makes it difficult to convert verbal instructions into the correct body movements. So, your best bet is to find a certified instructor who is trained to guide you through the progressions at your own pace and give you the feedback you need until you have the "muscle memory" to roll your boat almost without thinking.

THE KAYAK ROLL

The following descriptions and illustrations refer to a right roll or onside roll with the control hand forward on the set-up (right-hand control paddle).

1. THE HIP SNAP ROLL.   This is the most common roll used by today's kayakers. It's also known as the "C to C" roll. This roll works best for people who are heavier from the waist down or are relatively equally weighted between upper and lower body. The roll works best for individuals with good lateral flexibility. Therefore, the "C to C" roll seems to be easiest for women and lean men! Those of you who are "top-heavy" or not very flexible will want to concentrate on the Sweep roll, which we describe after the "C to C" roll.

The components.   There are three steps to this roll: (1) The Set-up, (2) The Sweep to Right Angles, and (3) The Hip Snap. Before putting them together, let's examine each component and work through a logical progression that begins with the Boat Boogie Wiggle and ends with a complete roll.

3. The hip snap.   Let's start with the hip snap, even though it's Step 3, because this is the key to the roll and must be understood and mastered before proceeding to the other steps. You've done hip snaps before. When you did the Boat Boogie Wiggle you used hip snaps to switch from one J-lean to the other. The hip snap is an upward pull on one knee and a simultaneous push down on the opposite buttock. It is used to set boat leans, to help right the boat that has begun to tip over, and to actually right the capsized boat. The hip snap is what rights the boat whenever you do any kind of brace. Therefore, it is a fundamental skill to master at the very beginning of your kayaking career.

Practicing the hip snap. Here is a sequence of exercises that will help you develop a fluid and dynamic hip snap. When you're comfortable with one exercise, you're ready to move on to the next. You'll want to practice in calm, preferably warm, water. Start with your boat perpendicular to a low support such as the edge of a low dock or the bow of a friend's boat. Position yourself with the support on your right. Place your hands on the support with the fingers of both hands forward, left hand on top. Place your right ear on top of your hands and keep it there! Keep your shoulder plane forward; that is, don't rotate your upper body toward the support. At this point your boat should be partially tipped toward the support. Now practice your hip snap by pulling on the offside (left) knee to tip the boat over the rest of the way and then practice a more aggressive pull on the onside (right) knee to bring the boat to its original semi-upright position. Remember to keep your head on your hands! Concentrate on weighting the buttock opposite the knee doing the pull; it will help if you push on the offside foot peg. Practice, practice, practice!

Rolling with a PFD. Once you feel your body has begun to memorize this righting action, practice the hip snap using a rolled-up PFD as the support. Grasp the PFD with both hands, keep your arms straight, and tip over to the right. Keep the lifevest at right angles to the front of your body. Your head should be tipped so your left ear is on your left shoulder and your head is near the water surface. This is the "first C" of the "C to C" roll, so-called because your body is curled in the shape of a "C". See illustration. Now you're ready to hip-snap to right the boat. For your righting action to work, you must hip snap *and* fling your head to your right shoulder and *leave it there*. It will take several attempts before you can do this fluidly. Practice it until you can do at least five consecutive rolls before you go to the next step.

Rolling with an aided paddle. Make an aided paddle by cutting a piece of mini-foam about two inches thick, six inches wide, and about as long as your blade. Form-fit this to the backface of your right blade and secure it with duct tape. Now ask a friend to stand in the water to the right of your boat. Place your hands in standard paddling position on your paddle, then hold the paddle vertically, with the left blade in the water by your left thigh and the right blade in the air with the powerface facing to your right. Your right forearm will be to your offside and just in front of your forehead, and your left thumb should be against the left side of the boat. Tip over to the right and land the powerface of the aided blade on the surface at right angles to your boat, just a bit forward of your torso.

As you tip over, shift your left arm onto the bottom of the boat above your hip, keeping your left thumb against the hull at all times. Set your body in the "first C" with your left ear against your left shoulder. Take a moment to relax in this position and contemplate your next move.

Now have your friend support the tip of the aided blade while you aggressively hip-snap into the "second C" -- in which your body is curled in the shape of a "C" that's a mirror image of the "first C." As you hip-snap, remember to fling your head to your right shoulder *and keep it there!* Without the head fling, you have no "second C" and your boat will just tip back over.

When you've done five successful rolls, try it with your buddy standing nearby but not holding the blade. You'll make it! When you can do several unassisted rolls with your aided paddle, you're ready to move "forward" from Step 3 to Step 1. (Oh well, we told you things get weird when you're upside-down!)

1. The Set-up. The purpose of both the set-up and the sweep to right angles (Steps 1 and 2) is to get your paddle positioned properly before you effect your hip snap. These steps must be executed correctly for your roll to work. To roll up on the right side, you'll need to set up on the left side of the boat. Initially, practice setting up *before* tipping over, although you won't have that luxury on the river. Tuck your body forward, and place the paddle along the left side of the boat, with the powerface of the forward blade up so you can see it. The whole paddle should be in the water (so it'll be in the air after you tip over). The edge of the blade farther from the boat should be *slightly* deeper in the water than the edge nearer the boat. The blade will then be at a *slight* climbing angle after you tip over. That's the set-up position. Hold the paddle tightly so the position doesn't shift, and tip over. Once you are upside-down, your entire paddle should be in the air, with the forward blade at a slight climbing angle for the next step.

You'll want to later practice tipping over and *then* setting up, since that's what you'll have to do when you capsize unintentionally. Wearing a diver's mask initially will make you more comfortable with underwater orientation. Take your time setting up; failure to do so is a major cause of foiled rolls.

2. The Sweep to Right Angles. From the set-up position, sweep the paddle, preferably in the air, to the position you were in when you practiced hip-snapping with an aided blade. That is, your left arm is wrapped around the bottom of the hull, you're in your "first C," and the right blade is at the water surface just in front of your torso. Try to keep the entire paddle in the air during the sweep. Many people don't have the flexibility to do this, but attempting to

THE HIP SNAP ROLL
OR "C" TO "C" ROLL

The set-up

Climbing angle

Sweeping to right angle
Body swings to right angle too

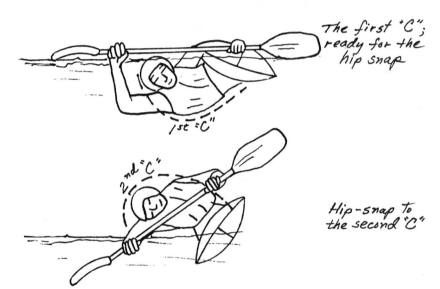

The first "C"; ready for the hip snap

1st "C"

2nd "C"

Hip-snap to the second "C"

Roll complete; still in second "C"

do so will at least keep your body and blade as close to the surface as possible. If your blade tends to sweep out *in* the water, be sure you have set a slight climbing angle on the blade so it will seek the surface.

Attempt to keep your ear on your left shoulder and your head near the surface, as you sweep out *both* the paddle and your body to the right angle position. After sweeping out, you're in the famous "first C." You're now ready to right the boat with your magnificent hip snap, which will put your body in the "second C." As you hip-snap, remember to _fling_ your head to the right shoulder and keep it there until the boat is fully upright and your buttocks are evenly weighted in the boat.

Your head should be the last thing to come out of the water; don't pick it up merely because you want air. Instant gratification is for non-believers.... Be patient and the River Gods will help you!

Common Natural Mistakes. Well, we warned you that the "C to C" roll entailed some complex movements. As a result, there are several common mistakes made by paddlers learning to do this roll. The number one problem is picking the head up during the hip snap. This is often caused by pulling down on the paddle with the right arm; a sudden downward pull causes a natural upward movement of the head. Keep in mind that it is not pressure on the blade that rights your boat -- it's your hip-snap. Relying only on the blade is sometimes called a muscle roll and is seldom successful because when the head is jerked up (the action), the boat simply goes back down (the reaction). Work *with* Uncle Newton, not against him! One way to keep your head down throughout the hip snap is to grasp the right shoulder of your lifevest with your teeth and hold onto it until you're evenly weighted in the upright boat. Another way is simply to make yourself watch the working blade throughout the entire roll.

The second most common problem is rushing the set-up, and as a result not getting the paddle above the water prior to the sweep-out. This can result in the blade diving too low in the water, especially if you sweep out with a diving angle on your blade. A rushed set-up can also make an upstream roll (i.e., one in which the bracing blade is upstream of the boat) more difficult because you have not given yourself enough time to gain current speed, so you are rolling against upstream opposition.

A third mistake is sweeping the paddle beyond 90 degrees, past the torso. It is difficult to properly position the body for an aggressive hip snap when leaning back; stop your body at right angles to your boat, in the "first C," and keep your paddle in front of your torso.

Now you can see why we recommend professional instruction when you're learning to roll -- You'll find it difficult to identify what you're doing right or wrong without the feedback of a skilled observer.

2. THE SWEEP ROLL. This type of roll is better suited to individuals who are "top-heavy" and/or have little lateral flexibility. It consists of just two steps: (1) the set-up, and (2) the forward sweeping high brace with a hip snap. Before proceeding, develop your hip snap using the exercises presented above in the hip snap roll.

1. The Set-up. The set-up is exactly the same as that of the hip snap roll described above. Tip over and remember to (1) tuck your body forward, (2) position the paddle in the air on the left side of your boat, and (3) watch the powerface of the forward blade to make sure it is almost flat on the surface of the water, with the edge farthest from the boat slightly elevated toward the sky (this sets a climbing angle).

2. The Forward Sweeping High Brace.   This is two simultaneous movements: (1) a huge sweep starting with your torso tucked forward and ending with a backward lean and (2) a fluid and smooth hip snap. The blade travels on or near the surface of the water, beginning close to the boat and ending a bit behind the paddler's body when the boat is righted. The working blade must have a slight climbing angle *throughout* the sweep, which is achieved by slowly cocking the onside wrist in during the sweep.

Unlike the standard forward sweep, this sweep pivots on the offside (left) wrist, which is held *near* the boat (but not over the boat) and just in front of your hip throughout, while the onside arm does the sweeping arc. The paddler hip-snaps just a moment after the blade begins to sweep, but unlike the aggressive hip snap of the "C" to "C" roll, this hip snap is slow-motion and graceful, continuing throughout the entire sweep. The boat will be nearly upright when the sweep reaches about 90 degrees (right-angles to the boat's centerline). Continue the sweep, keep leaning back and watching the blade until the boat is under you. Both the hip snap and the sweep end together.

To minimize the risk of a facial injury from underwater obstacles, keep your eyes on the working blade throughout the entire sweep. But don't pull your head up abruptly at the end of the sweep; bring it up gradually so the boat doesn't tip back down to your onside.

Common Natural Mistakes. Like the Hip Snap roll, the number one problem is picking the head up too soon. Keeping your eyes on the working blade until you're almost upright will help, and try to get in the habit of bringing your head up *slowly*. A second common problem is for the blade to dive during the sweep. To prevent this, remember to (1) set-up in the air, (2) set a climbing angle and maintain it by gradually cocking your wrist in during the powerphase, and (3) resist pulling down with the onside arm when sweeping -- if anything, push *up*. Finally, don't forget the gradual, fluid hip snap during the sweep; this is really what rights the boat. Without it, you will be upside-down again -- this time to name the fish!

THE FOOTE CANOE ROLL

*The following descriptions and illustrations
refer to a right roll, executed by a "righty."*

The Foote Canoe Roll is somewhat similar to the Hip Snap kayak roll described above, but with two important differences. First, the canoeist rolls up on a low brace, while the kayaker executes a high brace. Second, the kayaker rights his boat with a hip snap, using the muscles along the sides of his body, while in the Foote canoe roll, the paddler rotates his shoulder plane to face the paddle and rights the boat by contracting his abdominal muscles as in a sit-up. (Both paddlers also pull with their leg muscles as they roll.) The reason the canoeist rotates his shoulder plane is that by facing the paddle he reduces the stress on the onside shoulder, minimizing the risk of injury.

The Foote Canoe Roll can be done in an open or decked canoe. We also describe another method for rolling your decked canoe later in this chapter.

The open boat rolls more slowly than a decked canoe -- it has greater resistance to turning upright because it is bulkier. In fact, it will be *harder* to roll if you try to rush it. It might help to think of the open canoe as a heavy log -- roll the log to an upright position with your lower body and then swing your upper body up over it.

The components.   There are four steps to this roll: (1) The learning set-up, (2) the sweep to right angles, (3) the conversion to a low brace, and (4) the roll.

1. The Learning Set-up. Practice this set-up initially while sitting

THE FOOTE CANOE ROLL

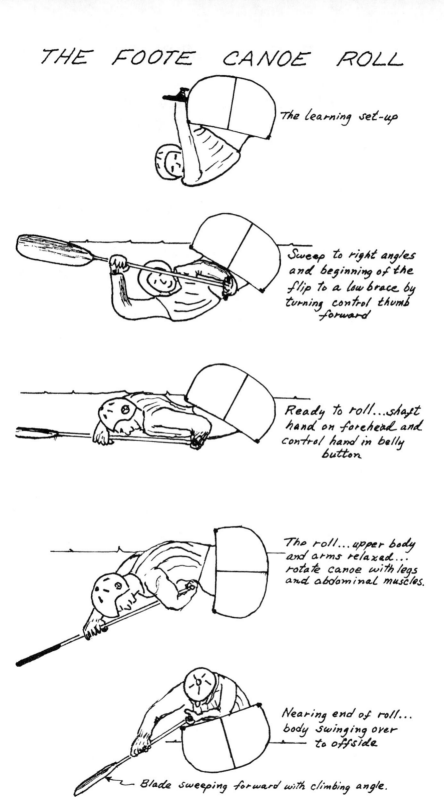

The learning set-up

Sweep to right angles and beginning of the flip to a low brace by turning control thumb forward

Ready to roll...shaft hand on forehead and control hand in belly button

The roll...upper body and arms relaxed... rotate canoe with legs and abdominal muscles.

Nearing end of roll... body swinging over to offside

Blade sweeping forward with climbing angle.

1. The Learning Set-up. Practice this set-up initially while sitting in your boat on dry land. Tuck your torso forward to the front deck or flotation. Cross your paddle to your offside and lay it (and both hands) on the ground near the left side of the boat, powerface up, with the shaft parallel to the centerline of the boat. Your control hand will be close to your left hip with your knuckles on the ground; the shaft hand is forward of the control hand. You are now in the "learning set-up," and if you were upside-down in the water both hands *and* the paddle would be in the air.

Next, practice this while sitting in your boat on the water. Try to put the paddle underwater so when you are upside-down the paddle will be in the air. Finally, tip over, tuck forward, and resume the set-up, again with both hands out of the water. (You might find it more comfortable and less disorienting to practice this wearing a diving mask.) Practice this until you begin to develop "muscle memory" for the set-up position.

2. The Sweep to Right Angles. You are now ready to follow the set-up with a sweep of the blade to right angles to the centerline. This is sort of an upside-down version of the forward quarter sweep. It is very important to sweep the paddle near the surface of the water, so set a slight climbing angle by turning your control thumb up a bit. As you sweep the blade, sweep your torso out so it, too, is at right angles to the boat, with your head pressed against your left shoulder.

3. The Conversion to a Low Brace. At this point, you need to convert the paddle to a low brace position. You're looking up from below at the paddle on the water surface. To convert to the low brace, roll your shoulders over on top of the paddle shaft (that is, rotate your shoulder plane 90 degrees to your onside).

Bring your control hand down to your belly button, switching your control thumb from facing *back* to facing *forward*. The backface is now down (observers watching from shore would be looking at the powerface). But *you're* no longer looking at the paddle -- look straight down at the bottom of the river, with your forehead actually touching the back of your shaft hand. Don't turn your head right or left. Concentrate on letting your upper body relax in this position, with your back arched so your upper body is shaped like a "C".

Take a moment to assess your position: (1) Your control hand is at your belly button, thumb pointing toward the bow. (2) Your shaft arm is bent so the shaft hand is tight against your forehead. (3) You're looking *down*. (4) Your shoulder plane is parallel to the boat's centerline. (5) Your back is arched and your upper body is relaxed. You are now ready to roll!

4. The Roll. Imagine your canoe is a roll of paper towels, and your upper body is a paper towel hanging from the free end of roll. To roll your canoe up, you're going to take the same approach as you'd use to get the last paper towel back onto the roll -- don't push on the towel, just *roll* the *roll*. To roll the canoe, leave your arms, shoulders and neck as limp as the paper towel would be, floating out to the side of the boat, and exert force on the canoe with your legs. Push down with your offside knee and pull up with your onside knee. Tighten your abdominal muscles, but *don't* push down on the paddle. This will roll the boat and pull you in. Don't even *think* about lifting yourself up or pushing down on the paddle until your head is drawn all the way to the side of the canoe and you can read the logo under the gunwale!

At this point, sweep both your paddle and your upper body

forward, with the blade at a climbing angle. Swing all the way past the centerline, keeping your head so low that your nose almost grazes the deck or air bag! Don't sit up until your body has passed the centerline and your boat is level.

Don't rush the boat. Begin the push and pull with your legs, and as the boat starts to roll, increase the force to get it moving faster. A good analogy is to think of the way you start a car rolling in order to jump-start the engine. You don't run up to it full-speed and throw yourself at the rear bumper; you lean and start pushing, then lean harder and move faster as the car begins to roll. The canoe will pick up speed in the same way.

You can practice with a rolled-up PFD in place of your paddle, for extra support. Tip over toward the lifevest and rest your chest on it. Rotate your shoulder plane 90 degrees to your onside, arch your back, and relax your arms and shoulders. Using just your legs and abdominal muscles, roll the canoe as far as you can. You should be able to bring the onside gunwale up to the surface of the water or even out of the water, while your upper body is still resting on the PFD. Keep your arms and shoulders relaxed -- let them just *float*. Practice rolling the boat slowly and smoothly. You'll find that if you try to roll it quickly or abruptly, there will be much less positive response to your efforts. Repeat this exercise until the movement is natural and you develop "muscle memory" for the position in the water.

The Slice Set-up. This is the preferred set-up of the experienced canoeist, but it is more difficult to master at the outset. It has the advantage of permitting a faster roll. Here's how it's done. Tip over to your offside (most of the time you'll go to that side until you've developed a fast reflex for the righting pry), but instead of setting up as described above, simply slice the blade under the boat and on up to the surface at right angles to the boat, in front of your body. Rotate your upper body into the low brace position as the blade nears the surface. Make sure your position is correct, and execute the roll. As in any roll, remember not to pull down on the blade; it's your legs and abdominal muscles that'll get you up every time! If you master the learning set-up and tip over enough, you'll probably find yourself naturally developing the slice set-up.

Common Natural Mistakes. The number one mistake is that of all rolls -- picking the head up too soon. "Head up, boat down," per Uncle Newton. Remember to keep looking down until your head has been pulled all the way back to the side of the boat.

A second common mistake is letting the paddle dive too deep -- once it gets beyond 45 degrees, back down you go. It is usually the result of pushing down on the paddle; this is called a muscle roll, and is based on the notion that downward pressure on the blade will right the boat. Wrong! The key is the push and pull of your legs and the tightening of your abdominal muscles. When you're ready to roll, say to yourself, "I will not push down on the paddle, I will not push down on the paddle, I will not push down on the paddle."

Another common mistake is to sweep the upper body forward before the boat is righted enough. Down you go again! The boat needs to be *at least* 80 percent upright before swinging your body forward. An experienced instructor can tell if this is your problem, since most paddlers who make this mistake are unaware they are leaning forward too soon.

There is an excellent video on this subject, *The Open Canoe Roll*, by Bob Foote. It presents the low brace roll in detail, using

174

above-water and underwater shots, slow motion and regular speed to help you analyze the moves. The technique can also be applied in a decked canoe. It is available from most canoe outfitters.

THE DECKED CANOE ROLL

The following descriptions and illustrations
refer to a right roll, executed by a "righty."

The Decked Canoe Roll is quite similar to the Hip Snap kayak roll described earlier. It also is referred to as a *low brace "C to C" roll*.

Decked canoe rolls are generally somewhat faster than kayak rolls, primarily because setting the brace with the canoe paddle is such a piece of cake -- no non-working blade to get out of your way! In addition, the shaft of the canoe paddle is at a more favorable angle, with the shaft angled *up* from underwater to the blade on the surface. The kayak paddle, on the other hand, is set up with the non-working blade on top of the boat and the shaft angled *down* to the water surface. The difference between the canoe and kayak shaft angles just prior to rolling up is a good 30 degrees, which makes the canoe roll somewhat easier to master.

The components. There are four steps to this roll: (1) The learning set-up, (2) the sweep to right angles, (3) the conversion to a low brace, and (4) the hip snap.

THE DECKED CANOE ROLL

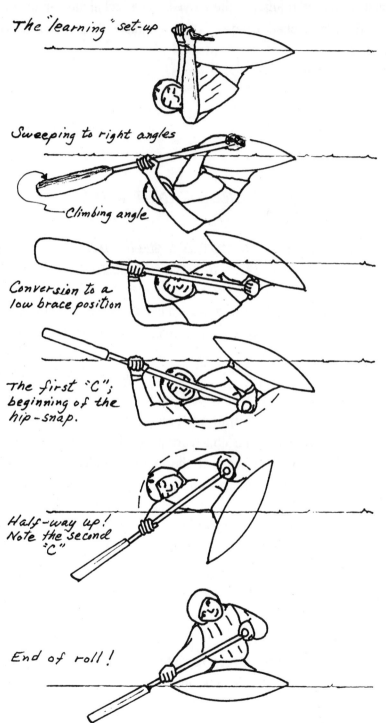

The "learning" set-up

Sweeping to right angles

Climbing angle

Conversion to a low brace position

The first "C"; beginning of the hip-snap.

Half-way up! Note the second "C"

End of roll!

1. The Learning Set-up. See "The Learning Set-up" in the description of the Foote Canoe Roll. It's identical in the decked canoe roll.

2. The Sweep to Right Angles. Again the same -- see the Foote Canoe Roll.

3. The Conversion to a Low Brace. Continue to face forward with your body curled laterally in the shape of a "C". Convert the paddle to a low brace position by switching your control thumb from facing *back* to facing *forward*; the backface is now down. Lower your control hand to your belly button. Keep your eyes on the blade to assure that it remains on the surface. And stay focused on it until your body is evenly weighted in the upright boat. You are now ready to effect the famous hip snap to right your craft! See illustration of Decked Canoe Roll.

4. The Hip Snap. Practice the hip snap supporting your hands on the bow of a friend's boat or on the edge of a low dock or swimming pool. All the exercises described under the Hip Snap Kayak Roll will strengthen your technique, and should be practiced diligently even before you start working on the above learning set-up. The canoe roll requires a fairly brisk hip snap, but it is easier to do if the boat is outfitted with both hip pads and thigh straps. To effect a hip snap, simultaneously *fling* your head to your onside shoulder, *pull* on your onside knee and *push* on your offside knee.

Remember to keep your head on your onside shoulder until the boat is upright and you're evenly weighted. When your boat is almost upright, sweep your torso forward across the front deck all the way *past the centerline* before sitting upright. Keep your body so low that your nose almost scrapes the deck!

The Slice Set-up. This is the preferred set-up of the experienced canoeist, but it is more difficult to master at the outset. It has the advantage of permitting a faster roll. Here's how it's done. Tip over to your offside (most of the time you'll go to that side on unpremeditated spills), but instead of setting up as described above, simply slice the blade under the boat and on up to the surface at right angles to the boat, in front of your body. Your low brace (control thumb forward) is set as the blade nears the surface; make sure your T-grip is near the belly button, and you're ready for the hip snap. Watch the blade, and make sure it's near the surface as you initiate the hip snap. As in any roll, remember not to pull down on the blade; it's your hip snap that'll get you up every time! If you master the learning set-up and tip over enough, you'll probably find yourself naturally developing the slice set-up.

Common Natural Mistakes. The number one mistake is that of all rolls -- picking the head up too soon during the execution of the hip snap. When this is done, you end up returning your body to the "first C," which results in the boat capsizing. After you fling your head to the onside shoulder, you must leave it there so your body remains in the "second C." Try wrapping a velcro band around your head and another on your onside shoulder; this will help keep your head down after the fling!

A second common mistake is letting the paddle dive too deep -- once it gets beyond 45 degrees, back down you go. It is usually the result of the paddler pushing down on the paddle; this is called a muscle roll, and is based on the notion that downward pressure on the blade will right the boat. Wrong! The key is to effect a positive and steady hip snap. When you're ready to hip snap, say to yourself, "I will not push down on the paddle, I will not push down on the paddle, I will not push down on the paddle."

Another common mistake is to sweep the upper body forward before the boat is righted enough. Down you go again! The boat needs to be *at least* 80 percent upright before leaving the "second C" by swinging your body forward. An experienced instructor can tell if this is your problem, since most paddlers who make this mistake are unaware they are leaning forward too soon.

LEARNING TO ROLL YOUR PLAYBOAT ON THE RIVER

Practice your kayak or canoe roll on a pond until you can do it almost without thinking, that is, until you have developed "muscle memory" of the moves involved. As a rule of thumb, we suggest you do 25 consecutive rolls three times a week for six weeks. Then you've got it. You're ready to develop your combat roll.

By now you should be *thoroughly* comfortable sitting in your boat upside-down in the water. You should be able to relax in this position, run through a short shopping list in your head, or consider what you want to do after getting into dry clothes. (If you're freezing in the water, just savor the thought, "Ah, dry clothes!") You should be unrushed in your set-up, accurate with your paddle placement, and fluid with your hip-snap.

Above all, you should be confident that you *will* come up when you hip-snap. Rolling is, more than any other maneuver, an "upper upper body" function -- It only works when you believe it is going to! So, clear your head of any doubts. On the rare occasion when your first attempt doesn't work, believe in your second attempt.

Start at a practice site at the base of a rapid, where the water is flowing swiftly into a pool, causing a wave train formation. The water is usually deep at such a site, so you can tip over safely. Peel out of an eddy, and tip over. Take your time setting up, so your boat is moving with the current by the time you roll up. This prevents upstream opposition to your boat. Advance to more difficult rapids only when you're performing consistent consecutive rolls in easier water.

Once you have a solid combat roll, you will find yourself playing more adventurously on the river, because you will be more willing to risk capsizing. This can greatly accelerate the learning process, as you challenge yourself intelligently and confidently.... And that's what playboating is all about!

RIVER PLAYBOATING MANEUVERS

This is it! At last, you're going to apply everything you've learned -- about current formations, about concepts of paddling, about strokes and maneuvers -- <u>on the river</u>. Many whitewater paddlers know only a tiny fraction of what you have <u>already</u> learned. You now have the skills to negotiate the river from put-in to take-out with greater finesse than the majority of boaters out there. You're ready for more. You're ready for PLAYBOATING!

Spins These are perhaps the best maneuvers for starting to get acclimated to the feel of your boat on moving water. Spins are useful for changing your boat orientation -- For example, to change from a downstream to an upstream discipline in preparation for a forward ferry; you might execute a mid-river spin, and ferry to your destination from there.

Practice spins on a stretch of fast-moving current where there are few, if any, obstacles. Let the current carry you downstream as you sweep with your paddle. Kayakers, the most efficient spins involve a forward sweep with one blade, followed immediately by a reverse sweep with the other blade. Canoeists execute repeated onside sweeps which are either forward or reverse depending on the desired direction of spin. Practice until you are equally comfortable spinning in both directions -- and equally dizzy! If you're paddling a solo craft, remember your boat leans!

Intermediate paddlers should practice spinning their craft while riding haystacks -- Sweep so that your boat spins while on the crest of a wave, where lateral resistance to spinning is minimal, vs. the trough of the wave, which tends to hold your boat in its initial discipline.

Circles Most playboating maneuvers incorporate the circle paddling that you invested so much time to master on the pond... so it was time well-spent! Although only about half a circle might be paddled during a given playboating maneuver, the arc will feel much more natural once you are comfortable paddling entire circles on easy whitewater.

To get used to paddling circles on the river, again pick a stretch of unobstructed fast-moving current. Start paddling in a circle, and continue circling as you move downriver. Unlike the spins, circles give your boat forward momentum with respect to the current, so you will now begin to realize the effects of unequal forces at the bow and stern as you paddle. The current will tend to enlarge your circle when your boat has a downstream discipline, and tighten it during your upstream discipline. Remember what you know about current differentials; as you paddle these circles, figure out why the boat and current interact as they do!

CIRCLES

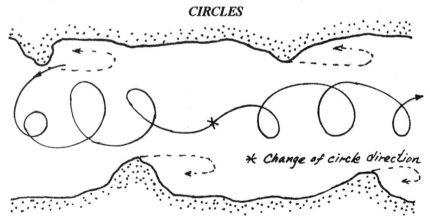

* *Change of circle direction*

Practice circling in both directions, varying your circle sizes and switching from one circle to the other at a specific point. Apply the skills you developed when practicing figure eights on the pond. In Class II rapids, a big wave can exert enough lateral force on the bow of your boat to knock you off your circle, but you'll regain it by executing one or two control strokes.

C-turns A C-turn is simply about half of a circle. It is a maneuver in which the boat is turning in one direction *or* the other from start to finish. C-turns are a great way to hop from one eddy to another eddy a short distance downriver, or return to the eddy you just left. Or, with enough momentum, you can C-turn out of one eddy and into another eddy right beside it, by carving an arc *above* the obstacle that's creating your destination eddy. Your C-turn will generally begin in an eddy, so it begins as a peel-out (which is detailed below). As you continue to C-turn, though, guess where you'll wind up? If the eddy you just left is large enough, you'll end up right back in it! So the C-turn is both a peel-out and an eddy turn (also explained in detail below).

C-TURNS

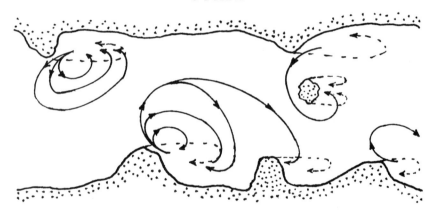

Practice carving C-turns of every possible diameter, to your right and to your left. Start in a large shoreline eddy. C-turn out and back into the same eddy. The tighter your turn, the higher in the eddy you will be at the end of the maneuver. Then use the C-turn to go from one shoreline eddy to the next eddy along the same shore. Then use your C-turn to charge upriver a short distance, pass upstream of an obstacle, and eddy out below that same obstacle. Your boat should be carving a circle in the same direction from beginning to end of the maneuver. Find a large eddy on the other side of the river, and repeat the same program... until you're completely comfortable carving C-turns in either direction.

S-turns When you change from one circle to the other (as you practiced on the pond by doing Figure Eights), you're doing an S-turn. S-turns enable you to catch any eddies that you might have missed on your C-turns! For example, you can start carving one circle as you leave a shoreline eddy, change to the other circle as you head downstream, and eddy out on the opposite shoreline. Or, go from shore to the same mid-river eddy that you C-turned into, but do it by starting a smaller circle than on the C-turn, switching circles as you approach the mid-river obstacle, then paddling into the eddy on the new circle.

S-TURNS

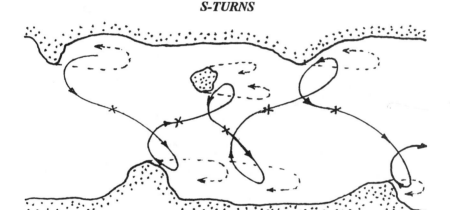

x = point where paddler changes circles

Forward ferries Ferries are the most common maneuver done on the river. To ferry means to cross from one river bank to the other (or from one eddy to another, including mid-river eddies), keeping the same end of the boat upstream from beginning to end. On forward ferries, the bow is always upstream of the stern. The traditional description of ferrying has you set your boat at a fixed angle to the current, which you maintain from start to finish.

184

That's a lot of work! You fight the current when you force your boat to hold the same angle all the way across, because the current force on your bow is *not* equal to the current force on your stern; at first, there's greater downstream force on the bow, then there's greater downstream force on the stern.

But there is a much easier way to ferry. Have you noticed how some paddlers seem to glide across the river almost effortlessly, while others muscle their way across, working against the current as if it were their mortal enemy? The graceful paddlers are using the technique of circle paddling and working *with* the current rather than against it.

When the boat is set at an angle to the current, the current is deflected off the boat, creating a lateral force that contributes to its movement across the river. This will work equally well whether the boat angle remains constant or changes a bit in the course of the maneuver. Carving two graceful, partial circles, you can easily maintain an upstream discipline with a varying angle, using the current's lateral force to full advantage -- but you're relaxing the traditional, fixed angle into a graceful, sweeping "S" as you cross the river. See the Forward Ferry illustrations.

As in other playboating moves such as the C-turn or the S-turn, you should set your circle before leaving the eddy. When ferrying, it is especially important to leave the eddy at a shallow angle (aimed nearly straight upstream). For the first portion of the ferry, your boat will be gradually turning more broadside to the current. Let it turn a little, but maintain the bow-upstream discipline, or your ferry is going to turn out to be a peel-out. (Remember, if that happens, try to look like that was what you *meant* to do!)

That's a lot of work! You fight the current when you force your boat to hold the same angle all the way across, because the current force on your bow is *not* equal to the current force on your stern; at first, there's greater downstream force on the bow, then there's greater downstream force on the stern.

But there is a much easier way to ferry. Have you noticed how some paddlers seem to glide across the river almost effortlessly, while others muscle their way across, working against the current as if it were their mortal enemy? The graceful paddlers are using the technique of circle paddling and working *with* the current rather than against it.

FORWARD FERRIES

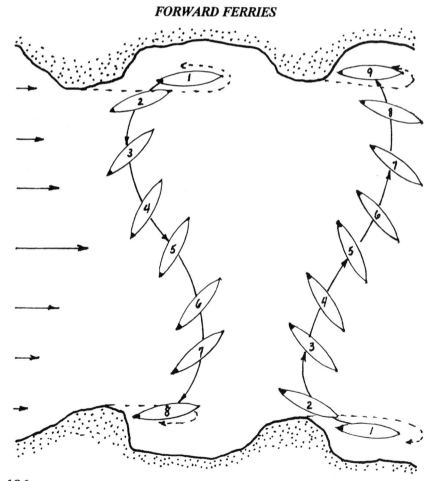

The initial circle will get you farther across the river than the second circle, which will carve your boat into its destination. The same S-shaped ferry will help you cross at a riverbend, but consider the current dynamics, and adjust the shape of your "S" accordingly. When crossing from the inside of the riverbend to the outside, stay on the initial circle for the lion's share of the crossing; in fact, it may take a stern correction stroke to get the boat to change circles just as you reach the outer-bend shore. Crossing from the outside of the riverbend to the inside, you will need to do just the opposite, changing circles shortly after leaving the starting position, and making most of the crossing on the "second" circle.

FORWARD FERRIES ON A RIVERBEND

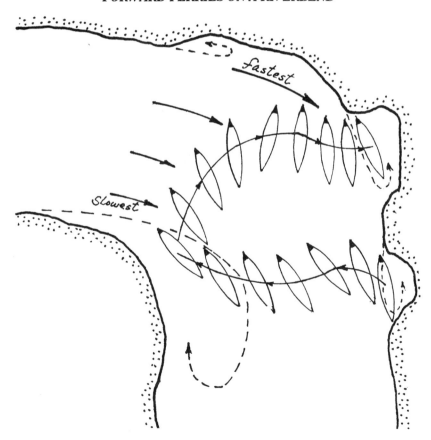

When you ferry on your circle in slow current, you may actually reach a destination across the river some distance *upstream* from your departure point, because you use power strokes throughout the maneuver, never sacrificing forward momentum to execute a sweep, rudder or pry. If, in the past, you've ferried using the "fixed angle" method, you will now find you can cross the river with far fewer strokes, and can successfully ferry much heavier current than you ever could before. That's how some paddlers make it look so easy -- their secret: *It is easy!!*

FORWARD FERRY AROUND A RIVERBEND
(sometimes called a "riverbend set")

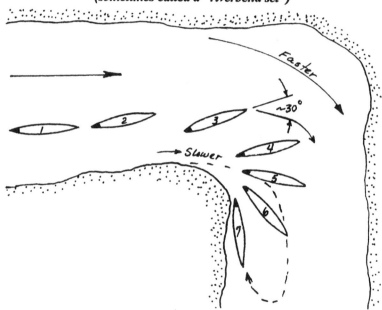

Back ferries These are ferries in which the bow is kept downstream of the stern, and the paddler strokes in reverse (back strokes) as the boat is moved laterally across the river or a part of the river. Back ferries are extremely useful for scouting a drop from your boat, or avoiding an obstacle while maintaining a downstream discipline, or positioning your boat for your next maneuver. They are useful whenever you wish to slow the downstream movement of the craft. Back ferries are

188

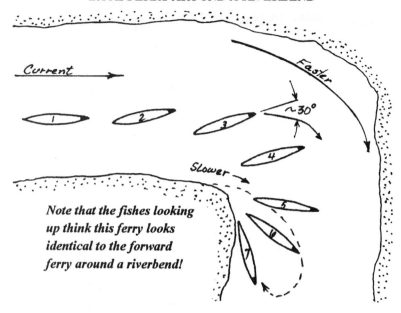

Note that the fishes looking up think this ferry looks identical to the forward ferry around a riverbend!

underutilized by many playboaters because they have never invested the time to become comfortable and skillful with their reverse paddling. The current can be used to your advantage in the same way as on forward ferries. Study the following illustrations of back ferries -- note how useful they are!

BACK FERRY TO AVOID OBSTACLES

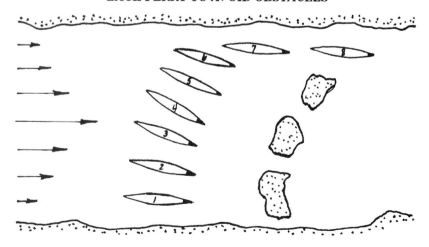

189

BACK FERRY INTO AN EDDY

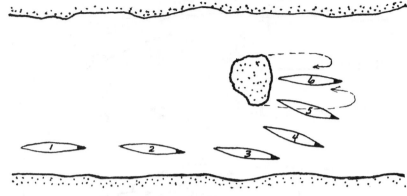

BACK FERRY INTO POSITION FOR AN EDDY TURN

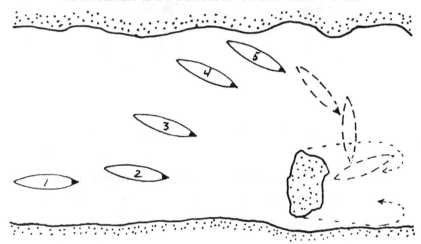

BACK FERRY TO A SHORELINE EDDY TO AVOID A HAZARD

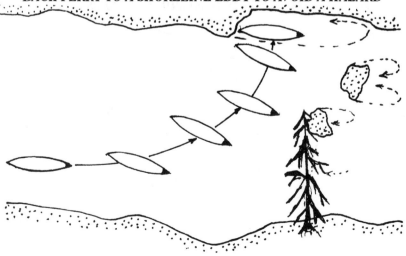

Peel-outs Peel-outs are one of the most common playboating maneuvers you'll do. They are exciting because they usually take you across a crisp eddy line so there's a dramatic change in the current hitting your bow... which is why they are also the most common cause of unpremeditated fish counts by beginners! Peel-outs are simply the U-turns you learned on the pond, transferred to the river. Paddling forward, you begin in an eddy with an upstream discipline (facing upstream) and end in the main current with a downstream discipline (facing downstream). Peel-outs are also done in reverse -- starting with a downstream discipline, and ending facing upstream. In either direction, a peel-out is a type of C-turn, and therefore employs circle paddling. As the boat crosses the eddy line, it must already be carving a circle and traveling with good forward momentum. You'll feel the entering current on the bow when you "crash" the eddy line -- acting on the boat to sharpen the turn. The greater the current differential, the more acutely the boat will want to turn as you cross it. Anticipate and increase your boat lean! You can control how tightly the craft turns by the degree of boat lean and distance of your strokes from the hull. Maximize your lean for a tight turn; minimize your lean and stroke far from the hull to keep the turn more gradual.

PEEL-OUTS

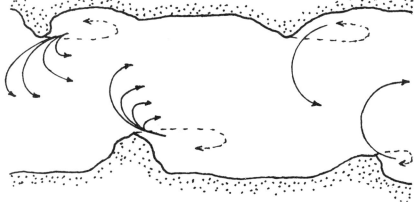

At this point, it's worth learning two more terms: *leaving current* and *entering current*. Identify these currents to plan your maneuvers appropriately. The leaving current is the current your boat is *leaving* as you cross an eddy line or differential. While in the leaving current, you should achieve good momentum, and get your boat turning in the desired direction with the appropriate boat lean. The entering current is the current your boat will be in after crossing an eddy line or differential. Always establish the appropriate momentum and boat lean for the *entering current* before crossing into it so this current will not capsize your boat. Doing so will save you the embarrassment of counting fish at every eddy line!

PEEL-OUTS

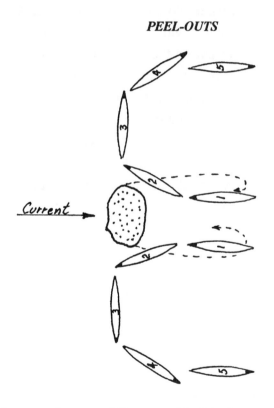

Back to peel-outs... "Go out with SAL" -- Leave the eddy with Speed, Angle, and Lean. In other words, as you position your boat in the eddy for the peel-out, remind yourself that you must:

192

(1) develop strong forward momentum (*speed*) before crossing the eddy line, (2) set your boat at a shallow *angle* to keep from spinning downstream the moment you hit the entering current, and (3) *lean* appropriately. You're likely to hit all three of these points successfully as long as you establish forward momentum on your circle *while still in the leaving current.*

The reason for peeling out *with speed* is that the greater your momentum with respect to the current, the greater your control over the course of the boat. When you cross a current differential with weak forward momentum, the river takes charge of your course. Never dilly-dally on an eddy line, as Tom's mom would say!

The reason you want a *shallow angle* is that this reduces the amount of lateral exposure of your boat to the entering current. Make it a habit to _always_ peel out at a shallow angle. This keeps all your options open, from (a) maintaining an upstream discipline and ferrying, to (b) executing a large C-turn that takes you most of the way across the river, to (c) paddling a tight little C-turn back into the eddy you just left. When you exit an eddy at a *wide* angle, say, almost perpendicular to the current, the entering current hits your bow and pushes it downstream the moment you cross the eddy line.

Finally, lean simply to prevent fish counts. Since you'll be on a circle, you will already be leaning your boat in the direction you're turning. Increase the lean when the turn becomes sharper -- whether due to your maneuver (such as a Duffek stroke) or due to the entering current acting on the bow of your boat.

Practice doing peel-outs using *all* the U-turn techniques you learned on the pond! When using a Duffek or a reverse sweeping low brace (RSLB), which are both turning braces, the blade must be anchored *in the entering current*. Peel out of the eddy, and the very first stroke after your paddle crosses the eddy line should be the turning brace, if you choose to use one. In fact, you'll get where you want to go on most peel-outs with just power strokes (forward and control strokes) -- but the Duffek and RSLB are great fun when you want a crisp turn!

Eddy turns   While most beginner fish counts occur during peel-outs, the greatest beginner frustration derives from eddy turns -- or rather, *foiled* eddy turns! An eddy turn is a U-turn that begins in the main downstream current, and ends in an eddy. The goal is to come to a stop in the eddy. Many paddlers set their sights on a particular eddy, try to turn their boat into it, and complete the maneuver so far below the obstacle that they are still in the main current. Another failure is the mid-river eddy turn that crashes *both* eddy lines, leaving the paddler in the mainstream current once again.

There are three keys to successful eddy turns: (1) Make sure you're paddling *on your circle* as you approach the eddy, (2) start with *strong forward momentum*, and (3) aim for the *top* of the eddy, where the upstream current will be strongest and the resulting spin will be the most exhilarating.

Start carving a circle while in the leaving current -- remember, that's the main current, whereas during a peel-out the leaving current was the eddy current. This will ensure that your boat is already turning in the correct direction and you already have the appropriate boat lean for crossing the current differential into the entering current. In addition, carving a circle will give you good forward momentum, which is the second "key to success."

It requires some real positive thinking for beginning paddlers to paddle forward hard when they feel they're already going downriver fast enough. But the paddler who tries to coast on his approach to an eddy turn will find he *continues* to coast, right on past the eddy. You only have control of your boat's course when you have strong momentum *with respect to the current*. Traveling at the same speed as the current is equivalent to sitting still!

EDDY TURNS

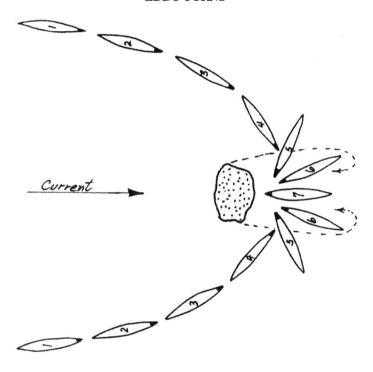

Plan a course that will land your boat in the very top of the eddy -- when paddling in Class II+ rapids, try to miss the rock by half an inch! This will help you to catch the eddy, since even if you miss your target by six or eight feet, you'll still make it into most good-sized eddies. And, as mentioned earlier, the current differential is much crisper, yielding a faster spin, at the top of the eddy. Best of all, as you develop precision on the river, this technique will enable you to catch even the smallest eddies, greatly increasing the number of playboating options available to you!

The angle of your boat as you cross the current differential will influence the sharpness of the spin. A wide angle exposes the side of your craft to the lateral force of the entering current as you cross the eddy line, and results in a quicker turn. Use this to your advantage to catch those "micro-eddies." The smaller the eddy, the wider the angle of entry you will need in order to successfully "catch" it. Plan your approach so that you execute a greater portion of the total turn in the leaving current while circling toward the eddy... but don't turn so far that you lose your downstream discipline before crossing the eddy line, or you will wind up actually entering the eddy on a forward ferry rather than an eddy turn.

S-TURNING THROUGH AN EDDY
Combining an Eddy Turn with a Peel-out

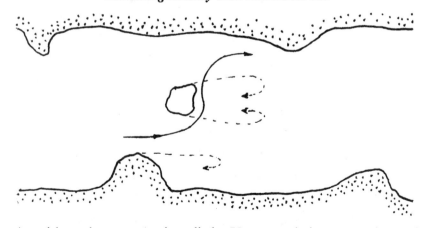

As with peel-outs, practice all the U-turn techniques you learned on the pond. The main difference is that on a peel-out, you continue to paddle after making the U-turn, whereas you might want to be able to come to a stop when you complete an eddy turn. Advanced playboaters only occasionally come to a full stop in an eddy -- they blend an eddy turn with the subsequent peel-out for a continuous, graceful turn into and immediately out of the eddy -- but the full stop should always be an option. Learn how to hit the brakes as you enter an eddy: Increase your boat lean as you "crash" the eddy line to expose the underwater portion of your hull to the opposing current. Your boat will spin on a dime, then come to a full stop if you let it. This concept should sound familiar; see the descriptions of the reverse sweeping low brace in the chapters on Solo and Tandem Canoeing.

The final thing you'll want to remember during eddy turns is to hold your boat lean until the boat comes to a complete stop and the stern stops moving laterally. The stern often continues to skid out after the bow stops moving, like the end of a whip. If you level your boat during this skid, you might wind up counting the fish in the eddy!

Using eddies to change direction Paddlers are constantly changing direction to prepare for their next maneuver. Here are two easy techniques for reversing your boat discipline quickly, one using white eddies and one using black eddies. White eddies are more fun because you simply current-broach your boat just above the eddy, and drop one end of the boat into the reversal. The other end, still being in the main flow, spins downstream. Keep the boat *level* during this turn. To turn using a black eddy, you'll have to paddle in (either forward or in reverse) to get half of the boat into the eddy; the boat will spin as the other end remains in the downstream current. When using a black eddy to change direction, lean into the turn.

Sideslips Sideslips are useful for maneuvering your craft around an obstacle without changing its original course discipline. See illustration. They are graceful maneuvers, and require minimal expenditure of energy. Many paddlers do not use them simply because they have never mastered stationary draws on the pond! But the ACA has good reasons for requiring sideslips of Instructor Candidates before they can become certified -- Sideslips greatly increase one's options in technical rapids, are an asset when jet-ferrying, and they're _fun_.

SIDESLIPPING

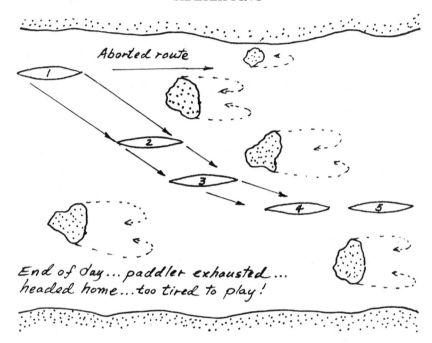

Aborted route

End of day... paddler exhausted... headed home...too tired to play!

Practice sideslips by paddling downriver toward an obstacle. About ten or twelve feet above the obstacle, initiate a sideslip to your right or left, and pass by the obstacle. In tandem canoeing, the forward sideslip is initiated by the bowperson. You should become equally comfortable sideslipping in both directions, so all options are open to you on the river. Try it in various current speeds, and see how close you can come to the obstacle before starting your sideslip, and still miss it. How soon you have to start sideslipping depends on how fast you're going, or more precisely, your "momentum with respect to the current."

Jet ferries Jet ferries are usually executed at the base of a steep rapid where the downstream current hits slower-moving water, creating a series of standing waves. The paddler uses a single standing wave to quickly move the boat lateral to the current. These are "no-stroke" ferries! If properly aligned at the outset, the boat is jetted or shot across the river while riding the upstream face of the wave. The easiest way to jet-ferry a wave is to position your boat bow-upstream, in an eddy or calm water, with your bow alongside the wave you wish to ride. Angle your boat as in a forward ferry, then once on the wave, open it up to about 45 degrees. Paddle forward, placing your bow in the trough of the wave. You will feel gravity pulling you in. Note the boat positions in the illustrations on page 200.

Don't let your bow hit the downstream face of the wave above the one you're riding; you may have to lean back to prevent this. If that downstream face you're avoiding is steeper than 45 degrees, your bow will tend to catch it and be pushed down, turning your would-be jet-ferry into a crooked pop-up... another fun move, though slightly unnerving when you're not expecting it!

At this point, solo boaters simply set a stationary draw (or cross stationary draw) on the downstream side of the boat. Tandem boaters set both paddles in their coasting positions; the stern paddler controls angulation as needed with a stern sweep or shallow-water pry. Lean your boat downstream, and enjoy the ride! Remember, even if this works perfectly, you only get a "nine" if you don't have a great big grin on your face! Practice jet-ferrying in both directions. For a real challenge, try jet-ferrying with the stern upstream of the bow. Remember, it's best to control the boat angulation with correction strokes in the eddy resistance end of the boat!

JET FERRY

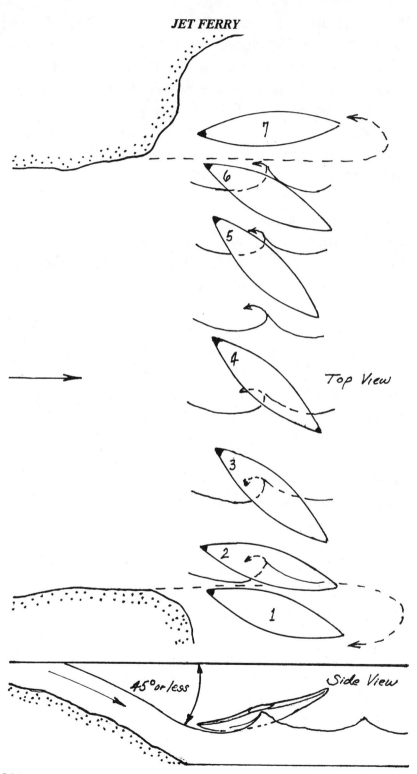

Top View

45° or less

Side View

Parallel surfing Never heard of surfing on a river? You haven't *lived!* Surfing is an extremely popular playboating maneuver in which the paddler rides the opposing forces of gravity and current on a standing wave or at the top of a hole. It is similar to ocean surfing except in the ocean, the wave moves while the water is stationary. In the river, the water moves while the wave is stationary!

The smooth water that either creates the hole or is just above the standing wave must be at an angle of 45 degrees or less. (See illustration.) Otherwise, the hole will be so steep that the bow will tend to dig into the current creating the wave, resulting in a pop-up.

Here's how to surf: Hop on the wave's trough from a position alongside it, as if you intended to jet-ferry. But as soon as your bow is set in the trough, align your boat *exactly parallel to the current*, so you won't jet across the wave. If the wave is "weak," i.e., not holding your boat strongly, lean forward to increase the weight in the bow. If the wave is pulling you in *too* far, prevent your surfing from turning into a pop-up by leaning back to reduce the weight in the bow. Balance all the forces acting on your boat, and you will stay in place while the water crashes all around you!

To stay aligned with the current, set your blade as far back toward the stern as possible, and close to the boat. Adjust the blade angulation according to the correction you need to make: Set the leading edge of the blade closer to the hull than the trailing edge to turn your bow toward the side the blade is on; angle the leading edge farther from the hull to turn the other way. In tandem canoeing, the bowperson can do little to help maintain the boat's position except to fine-tune the position with an occasional stationary draw or stationary pry; a nice way to

PARALLEL SURFING
Top View

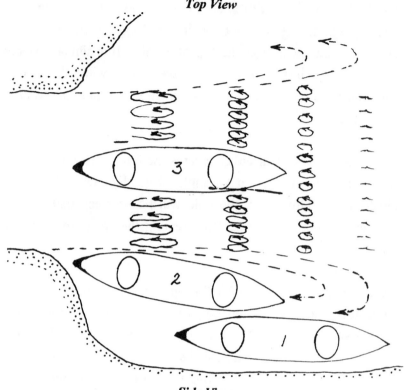

Side View

YA-HOO!

express his faith in the sternperson is for the bowperson to perform a headstand on his pedestal!

Decked-boaters, you can advance from surfing to *shredding* the wave by combining jet-ferries and *cutbacks*. Shredding the wave is a form of surfing in which the paddler jets back and forth along the length of the surfing wave, reversing direction with a forceful change in boat direction near the ends of the wave. This works best in a heavily-rockered boat with a low-volume stern and hard chines. Ideally, the trough you're surfing (measured from crest to crest) should be at least as long as your boat. On big water, you'll find huge, smooth troughs two or three boat-lengths long.

Kayakers, to execute a nice cutback, start jet-ferrying across the wave with good momentum. You'll be holding your angle (preventing the boat from current broaching) with a stern rudder on the upstream side of your boat. You'll also be leaning the boat upstream on the jet-ferry. As you approach the end of the wave, bring the blade close to the hull and execute a strong push (the beginning of a reverse sweep) to drive the stern away from the blade. At the same time, lean back and switch to a slight upstream boat lean. This will *stern pivot* your boat (i.e., it will slice the stern down into the water, causing the bow to turn in mid-air). The bow now turns freely, and heads you back in the other direction. Pull hard with your abdominal muscles to help lift and turn the bow.

Helpful hint: A moment before changing the boat lean, convert the blade position to a Duffek anchored opposite your body (somewhat aft of the usual Duffek position). This provides a solid anchor to prevent capsizing if you "counter-lean" your boat a bit too far.

Canoeists, start with a jet-ferry toward your offside. You'll be holding your angle with a stern rudder. Switch directions with the same powerful push followed by a Duffek as described above At the same moment, switch boat lean, and lean back to stern-pivot the boat, heading back to your onside. Now, ferrying toward your onside, you'll be holding your angle by forward stroking or with an onside stationary draw, anchored as far aft and as close to the boat as possible. There are two ways to initiate the cutback: (1) Execute a powerful stern sweep or, (2) place a cross Duffek opposite your torso (farther aft than the usual Duffek position). In either case, again lean back and heel the boat slightly upstream for a stern pivot. Now you're headed back on your offside jet ferry.

On narrow waves, you'll have to execute the cutbacks quickly to keep the bow from digging into the wave above the one you're riding. If the bow *purls* (begins to pop-up), try heeling the boat on edge (at least 45 degrees) and leaning back and the bow usually slices back to the surface.

On a larger wave, you can lean forward or back to shift your boat up or down the face of the wave. Try starting at the bottom of the trough at one end of the wave, and riding up the face to the crest at the other end, where a radical cutback will redirect you back down the wave face. It's a blast!

Link cutbacks to the left and right -- slowly and gracefully, or fast and hard. Either way, you're shredding! You'll push your limit as your strokes and boat leans begin to work in harmony.

Side surfing One step beyond parallel surfing, side surfing is a bit like riding a bucking bronco in the middle of the river. The boat is positioned perpendicular to the main current. The surfing trough must be a bit longer than the boat for this to work well. Always check the shape of the trough before going in. As you study a potential side surfing hole from above, it should be either a straight line or "smiling" at you. Such a hole will be easy to exit, whereas a "frowning" hole may be difficult to get out of once you're in. As in parallel surfing, the angle of descent of the smooth water creating the hole should be 45 degrees or less.

SIDE SURFING

There are two common ways to get into the side surfing position. One way is to current-broach your boat (turn perpendicular to the main current) above the hole, and as your boat begins to fall into the hole, set you boat lean *prior* to landing in the hole. (See below for specifics of the lean.) The other way is to enter the wave or hole as if you intend to parallel surf, then drive the stern into the hole with a reverse sweeping low brace. Caution: If you have too much forward momentum, your boat may exit the hole the minute you get in it. Just mosey in as if tiptoeing up behind a River Devil, and wait for gravity to pull you in.

The paddler J-leans to keep the bottom of the craft flat on the smooth water creating the hole, and sets a brace on the downstream side; kayakers can do a high-bracing or low-bracing scull, or a combination of both. Solo canoeists will initially want their boat positioned so they can low-brace on their onside. Facing the other way in the same hole, the canoeist must stabilize his boat with a cross sculling high brace.

Exit the side-surfing hole by sculling with a greater blade angle in one direction than the other. Sometimes you will work like crazy to get in a hole, only to find you have to work even harder to get out! Learn to stroke only as much as necessary to hold your boat in the hole. Many people toss their paddle and side-surf with just their hands. This is a great way to develop sensitivity to current forces on the side of the boat. We advise you to learn to "hands roll" before you try this!

Hole spins   Often called *three-sixties,* these consist of side-surfing facing one way, then spinning the craft to side-surf facing the other way, without ever completely leaving the hole. Many paddlers have so much fun riding the hole that they'll sit in a hole and spin until another paddler demands a turn at it! Start by side-surfing the hole, facing either shore.   To reverse your orientation, force your boat to one end of the hole by sculling with a wider blade angle in one direction than the other. When the leading end of the boat hits the downstream flow just beyond the end of the hole, it will spin that end downstream. You may have to paddle (forward or back) to prevent the rest of the boat from exiting the hole.   The moment your boat gets beyond parallel to the current, hip-snap to the opposite boat lean, and scull or sweep the entire craft back into the hole. Side-surf in the new orientation until you're ready for another spin.   Practice spinning in both directions!

Pop-ups   These maneuvers take your boat into the Third Dimension, one end of the boat plunging underwater to get the rest of the craft *and the paddler* airborne!   Make sure the site is

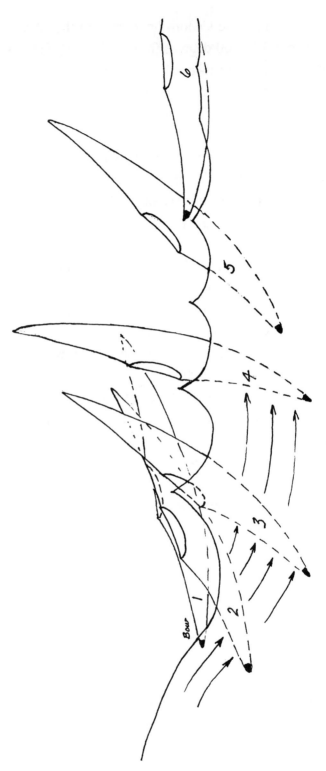

appropriate. The smooth flow creating the hole or wave should be about 30 to 60 degrees from horizontal, and the river must be at least half a boat-length deep and unobstructed for a stretch running from the pop-up wave or hole to four boat-lengths downriver.

Also make sure there are no boaters within several boat-lengths of where you intend to execute the pop-up, as the boat will head downstream with tremendous momentum, and can seriously injure anyone in its path.

Ferry at a shallow angle out to the pop-up area, align your boat with the current, and, if it's a good pop-up hole, gravity will pull your bow into the upstream face of the trough. You will have to paddle forward and lean forward to get into a weaker hole. The goal is to drive your bow into the smooth water at the top of the formation with enough force to literally sink the bow, so the current "catches" the top of the boat (deck or flotation). The boat must not be tipped to the left or right. The water will exert a powerful downward force on the deck, pushing the stern up into the air. The current will continue to drive the boat downstream and, if the current doesn't turn your pop-up into an ender, the boat will come down right-side-up! Once you initiate a pop-up, about the only way you can keep from doing an ender is to lean back in your boat; but if the current is powerful enough, you'll do an ender whether you intend to or not. As your boat comes down from the pop-up, use your momentum to perform a reverse sideslip to re-enter the bottom of the eddy from which you started the whole maneuver. See illustration.

Enders These are pop-ups-plus-a-plunge. They begin in the same way as a pop-up, but the bow is pushed so far under the boat that the boat lands on the water upside-down. The paddler

208

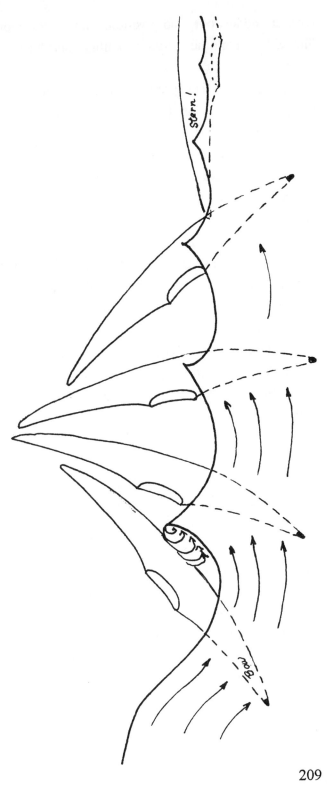

rolls up, eddies out, and positions himself for another round... in line with all the other paddlers waiting their turn!

Pirouettes This is a prevent-a-plunge ender. When the boat is straight up in the air (see Ender Illustration, position #3), the paddler reaches forward and executes a cross sweep to spin the boat 180 degrees so his body is facing downstream. Whether in a canoe or a kayak, here's how the sweep is done: Reach down/forward to the bow, place the working blade across your bow, anchor it in the water, and then sweep it across the deck. Instead of the cross sweep, some playboaters execute a back stroke or reverse sweep. Either stroke will spin your boat on end like a ballerina on one toe. If it's a one-eighty, you'll land right-side-up! Regardless, be prepared for a righting action!

Here's the challenge: When you become proficient doing pop-ups and enders, practice burying the stern underwater instead of the bow. In other words, practice the maneuvers in reverse. Have fun!

Running dams or steep ledges Waterfalls can be extremely dangerous, but they also can be a joy to run. They are formed by water flowing over a dam or steep ledge in the river. Paddlers frequently run 30 to 40 foot drops successfully, which the authors of this book consider somewhat insane. In general, drops of more than eight feet should be run only by highly skilled boaters. _Never_ go over a vertical drop with your boat current broached. Also be sure you understand all the following variables before you consider running a waterfall: (1) the pool size above the dam or ledge, (2) the height of the dam, (3) the volume of water flow, (4) the size of the reversal at the base, (5) the uniformity of the reversal, (6) the depth of the water at the base, (7) the ease of rescue, and (8) the required skill level of the paddler.

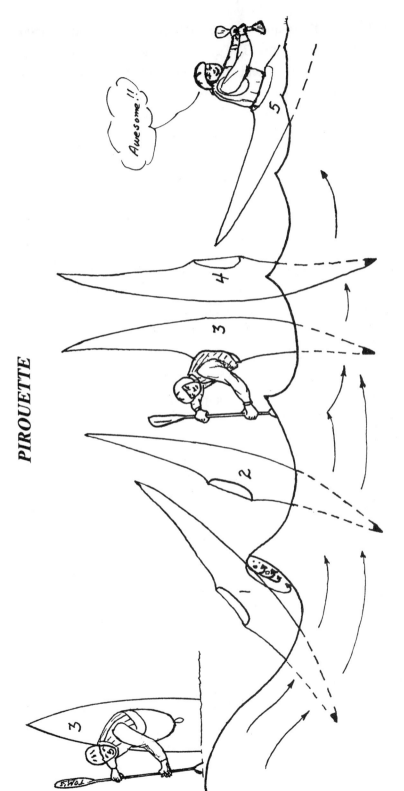

The pool above the dam must be long enough for you to gain good forward momentum. The faster you go over the dam, the better -- because the boat will stay more nearly horizontal, and as a result not go very deep into the water at the base of the drop. Also, good forward momentum will help you to "jump" beyond the hole. Ideally, you should land at or below the dividing line between the bottom of the reversal and the downstream current, so you are not caught in the reversal. This forward momentum will still be with you when you land, helping you to get out of the reversal if you land near the bottom of it.

A boat going over slowly will tip to vertical and be submerged in the reversal. A current-broached boat will also be trapped in the reversal. If you decide to run a waterfall, align your boat with the main current and paddle hard forward; just before going over the lip, lean back and pull up on your legs to lift the bow. Don't stroke in the air, as this will shift your weight to one side and you might land on the edge of your boat or upside-down. You must have a good wide route or a choice of routes for the drop to be safe, because the horizon line prevents you from identifying any landmarks seen when you scouted the drop from shore.

Riding pillows Class III and IV rivers present river features not seen in milder currents, including pillows above steep cliffs and large rocks. These are cushions of water four to 18 inches high, formed by water "piling up" on the upstream side of a ledge or rock. Sometimes these pillows are unavoidable and other times, they're actively sought out by playboaters. To ride a pillow current-broach your boat directly above it. As your boat floats into the pillow, lean *toward* it with a sculling brace, just as you would do if you were accidentally pinned against the rock. You'll stop at the cushion (without touching the rock) and stay upright as long as you hold a good downstream lean. Use your sculling brace, or your momentum as you approach the pillow, to give you your desired exit off the pillow.

Ascending rivers What is it about rivers that makes paddlers always want to go *down*stream? There are many skills to be developed by spending time ascending rivers. Most rivers that are Class II or easier can be ascended. As in all playboating maneuvers, the key is to read the river and use the currents to your advantage! In order to ascend a river, you must keep your correction strokes to a minimum. You should spend all your energy stroking in the frontal resistance end of the boat -- all forward and control strokes. Stay in the paddler's pie!

Your general strategy will be to hop from the top of one eddy to the tail of another eddy a short distance upstream, and minimize the time spent in the main current flow. Use the upstream current in the eddy to help you develop upriver momentum before crossing the eddy line. And keep in mind that the downstream flow is slower near shoreline than at mid-river obstacles, so the easiest ascent is often made by eddy-hopping along a shore.

Plan ahead; use ferries to get to the bottom of a string of eddies that you can use to "hop" upriver. If you need to jump an eddy wall, exit the eddy with strong momentum and a shallow angle. Just before the bow hits the wall, lean back and un-weight your bow so it will rise up above the eddy wall. Not only is ascending rivers fun in itself, but it will increase your playboating options -- you can run through a rock garden, ascend it, and then run an entirely different route through the same stretch of river.

Now you know why it can take a good playboater all day to go just one mile down the river -- there's so much to do! You can exercise your mind as well as your body, inventing a hundred different ways to run a nice technical rapid. That's the whole idea of intelligently challenging Mother Nature. As with your "pond homework," you will have to invest time before becoming proficient at river playboating maneuvers, but what sweet rewards await you! Be patient with yourself. Repeat your maneuvers and experiment constantly. Remember the goal: Catch Every Eddy... Surf Every Wave!

RIVER RESCUE

Unpremeditated spills are an inevitable part of whitewater playboating. In addition, boats can get pinned or swamped, paddles can break against obstacles, and other miscellaneous breakdowns occur. Developing calm, competent responses to these situations is as important as developing a good forward stroke... although hopefully they won't be needed as often!

PREVENTION

The greatest safety lies in preventing accidents before they happen. In the case of whitewater playboating, that mostly means preventing unintended capsizes whenever possible. Experienced playboaters often capsize intentionally, especially when playing in holes and surfing waves -- confident that they can quickly roll their boat back up. But until you have a strong roll, try to stay upright!

Every paddler should take an American Canoe Association River Rescue Workshop, which covers the two subjects of river safety and rescue techniques in far greater detail than provided in this book. Contact the ACA for workshop information.

Prevention is the key. So let's start with some strategies for preventing a capsize when it seems imminent. Then we'll discuss ways to rescue yourself and your boat when you *do* wind up swimming with the salmon.

Don't depend on others. Whitewater playboating is a solo, or at most, tandem sport. This also applies to rescue situations; a paddler should never expect help when he capsizes, but should develop the skills to get himself, his boat, and paddle to shore on his own. Dependence on others can be a recipe for disaster.

Boat lean. Probably the most common reason for capsizing is incorrect boat lean. *Always* lean in the direction the craft is turning. This should become a reflex. The hardest thing for beginners to remember is to lean into the turn regardless of whether or not it's the direction they *want* to be turning in. They must lean into the turn, *then* correct their course.

Crossing differentials. The faster the boat is moving and the sharper the turn, the greater the lean needs to be in order to prevent a capsize. This is especially true when crossing a crisp eddy line. When gaining momentum to peel out into a strong current, anticipate that the boat will turn more sharply as the bow encounters the entering current, and lean your boat accordingly.

Watch the "ball bearing end." Maintain boat lean until the boat completely stops turning. New paddlers should keep this in mind whenever coming into an eddy. The paddler often levels his boat because the bow has stopped turning, but the stern is still skidding laterally, and he immediately finds himself counting fish!

Close Encounters with Rocks. Another common reason for capsizing is Close Encounters With Rocks. This is most likely to occur when the craft becomes current-broached (at a right-angle to current flow), but can also occur when a paddler chooses the wrong route through a rapid. If you do broach on a rock, your boat may wind up pinned by the current against the upstream side of the rock. The first thing you should do if you find yourself in this situation is to *keep calm* and lean downstream. If the obstacle -- usually a rock -- is above water and is near your pivot point, reach out immediately and hug the rock! Be One with the rock, and you will succeed in keeping your side of opposition

BROACHING

Type
Possible result

AMIDSHIP

DOUBLE END

STRAINER

217

elevated. (That's the side of your craft farther upstream.) This might prevent you from capsizing.

Use the current to free one end. It is often possible to push off the rock by moving whichever end of your boat is being hit with more current farther into the open current. This is the ideal solution for the single-broached craft. When the boat is pinned upstream of obstacles at both the bow and the stern, it is said to be *double-broached.* This is a more difficult position from which to free a boat. Again lean downstream and, if one end is nearly free, it may be possible to shift the boat position by jerking the upper body, to dislodge that end. The boat will then pivot free of the other obstacle. Be prepared for a "righting action" when the boat pops free!

Climb out if necessary. If the craft cannot be released from a broach position, the paddler may be able to climb out onto the obstacle, and then free the boat. If the water is less than knee-deep, it may be safer and more effective to step into the river *upstream* of the boat. Never step into moving water that is more than knee-deep. And never step into water downstream of your boat -- *under no circumstances should you risk getting pinned between your boat and a rock.*

Wait for others. If all these efforts fail, wait for assistance from others. While waiting, try to get yourself out of the water to reduce body heat loss.

SELF-RESCUE

The Roll. The most common type of self-rescue is the boat roll. When should you learn to roll your boat? When you want to start paddling heavy water in which swimming to shore is particularly difficult. Or when you want to paddle the beautiful but ice-cold rivers fed by melting snow. Or when you are getting to know all your local fish by name, and they nod sympathetically every time your head reappears underwater. Be sure to read the chapter on the Three Hundred Sixty Degree Roll!

Know your rescue priorities. Until you've learned to roll, you will have to wet-exit and swim to shore, towing your boat and paddle with you. If you run into difficulty and can't get everything to shore, know your priorities. First and most important, get yourself safely to shore. Second in importance is your paddle -- hang onto it if you can do so without endangering yourself. Third, try not to let go of your boat. It's less important than your paddle, because it's so easy to spot downriver, and is likely to come to a stop anyway on an obstacle or in an eddy. Least important is to rescue any other gear that may have fallen out when you capsized. (Properly packed, nothing should fall out!)

The swimming rescue. Here's how to carry out a self-rescue:

...First, exit the boat. See the chapters on Kayaking and Canoeing for specific technique.

...Select the safest shore to swim to -- usually the near shore, but there are exceptions. For example, a beach on river right and a vertical ledge on river left dictates that you go to river right! And, it is usually safer and easier to get out on the inside shore of a riverbend than the outside shore, because the water is shallower and the current is milder on the inside shore.

...Use a "lifeguard stroke," i.e., a shallow-arm sidestroke using the arm closer to shore, and swim vigorously.

...Face downstream as you swim to shore; this ensures that you will see obstacles downstream of you, and enable you to identify a safe landing site. *The proper swimming arm is the right arm if you're rescuing to river right, and the left arm if going to river left.*

...Hold both your boat and paddle in the hand farther from shore. An open boater should hold onto his painter at least three feet from his boat so he has a clear view downstream. Keep the non-swimming arm extended as you swim to shore. This is safer than keeping your gear close to your body.

...As you swim to shore, if it looks like you're going to impact a downstream object on your present course, stop, and resume swimming in an upstream direction so the boat will swing downstream of your body. Then just float with the current until you can safely resume your swim to shore. Always keep your boat downstream of your body to keep from getting pinned between a rock and your boat.

...Stand up only when you reach calm water that is *less than knee-deep.*

Sometimes you'll capsize in heavy water above a pool. In this situation, it may be safest to float through the rapid, and self-rescue as soon as you reach the pool. To float safely in whitewater, position yourself on your back with your body straight, and keep your feet on the water's surface. This will minimize your risk of injury -- your helmet and lifevest protect you from rocks, and the feet cannot be caught on a rock. Use your feet to fend yourself away from any rock you're about to hit, and if you still have your boat, make sure you fend to the same side as the boat.

There are two situations where it is extremely important to abandon the feet-first floating position. One is when you are about to go over a ledge. As you approach the ledge, tuck your body into a ball. Then, at the bottom of the drop, you will not risk trapping a foot in an underwater crevice. The other time to change position is if you find yourself unable to avoid a strainer. In this situation, switch to a head-downstream position, and do the crawl stroke until you reach the strainer, then use your arms to actively pull yourself up to the top branches of the strainer. This prevents getting caught underwater.

BOAT-ASSISTED RESCUE

A boat-assisted rescue is one in which a fellow paddler in a boat assists a boater who has capsized, helping to get the swimmer and his equipment to shore. The rescuee should always assume that no one will be available to help him, and initiate his own self-rescue procedure, as outlined above. Doing so reduces the work of the rescuer.

There are three common types of boat-assisted rescue: (1) bumping, (2) towing, and (3) boat-over-boat. These techniques are suitable for all playboating craft, unless otherwise indicated.

Bumping. This is the most common form of assistance. Bumping assists the capsized paddler, but does not relieve him of his self-rescue responsibilities. The rescuer simply bumps or pushes the capsized boat to help the swimmer tow it ashore. The rescuer should maintain the capsized boat's ferry angle (upstream end closer to shore). It is usually best to push the boat near its pivot point or slightly upstream of the pivot point. If the boat is bumped along its downstream end, the ferry angle will be lost, making it harder for the swimmer, not easier. It is easier to bump with a tandem canoe or a kayak than with a solo canoe, because the latter craft is propelled with only one blade.

Towing. When a rescuer tows a rescuee to shore, he is assuming a far greater responsibility than when bumping; he should not offer a tow unless he is capable of hauling the rescuee and his boat to shore faster than the rescuee could carry out an independent self-rescue. Towing requires the power of two blades in the water, so a solo canoeist cannot really be expected to offer this form of assistance. The swimmer holds his boat and gear in one hand, and grasps the rescue boat's stern grab loop or painter in the other. He should face downstream as he would during a swimming self-rescue, and *kick vigorously*. The rescuer paddles to shore on a forward ferry. Other boaters can still assist by bumping.

Boat-over-boat. This form of rescue is best carried out in the pool at the base of a rapid, not in the rapid itself. It must be practiced on a pond before being attempted in the river. The rescuee goes to one end of his capsized boat -- to the stern if it's a kayak -- while the rescuer paddles to the other end, and positions his boat perpendicular to the capsized boat. The swimmer pushes down on his end, while the rescuer lifts the other end of the boat, breaking the airlock. Then the rescuer pulls the capsized boat over the his front deck or gunwales, just in front of his body. The capsized boat is pushed across the rescuer's boat until it is balanced; this empties out most of the water. More water is emptied from the boat by rocking it back and forth. The rescuer then rolls the boat upright, and slides it back into the water toward the rescuee.

Finally, the empty boat is positioned parallel to the rescuer's boat; the rescuer holds the cockpit edge or gunwale nearest his boat to stabilize the boat while the rescuee climbs back in.

Almost all shore-based rescues are carried out with throw bags. These bags contain rescue lines for assisting swimmers to shore. The rescuer holds the free end of the line as he throws the entire bag out to a swimmer. As the bag flies through the air, the rest of the line is deployed from the bag.

Throw bags are easy to use and should be carried by every responsible playboater, especially the paddler who ventures into Class III-V rapids where there is a higher probability that he may be needed to assist others. Since shore-based rescue systems are generally arranged after scouting a rapid from shore, it is perhaps wise at this point to review the conditions under which one should scout. Remember, you alone are responsible for your own safety. *Inspect each drop you plan to run rather than let someone else describe it to you.*

Scouting. Study the rapid from shore before deciding whether to attempt it, and to plan your route through it, whenever you have any of the following conditions: (1) you have a poor view of the rapid from above, (2) you hear an unusual amount of noise below where you are presently playing (you might even begin to feel a bit queasy), (3) you see a horizon line, and perhaps mist in the air just below it, (4) you are paddling a familiar river immediately after a flood and you need to check some of the drops for new strainers, or (5) you have noticed a rise in the water level and you are not familiar with the rest of the river at the new level.

Scouting procedure. Your paddling party should go ashore well above the drop. Empty out any water in your boat (etiquette, in case you opt out of running the drop and a friend decides to paddle your boat), and take your paddle and throw bag with you along the shore. Your paddle serves as both a walking stick and a means of signaling "all clear" to boaters as they wait in line to run the rapid. If possible, first scout from the bottom of the rapid because it's easiest to determine your probable running strategy from this vantage point, then move up along the shore and try to get a look at your selected route from your paddling eye-level, looking downriver.

When do you set up the shore-based system? Having decided to attempt the rapid, if there is even a slight possibility that anyone in the group may capsize and be unable to roll his boat, you should set up a shore-based rescue system. Make sure everyone knows it is being set up and on which shore. No one should enter the rapid until all the shore-based rescuers are completely readied.

The first paddler to run the rapid should be the most experienced boater, who then positions himself in the calm water below the anticipated capsize area, ready to assist in the event that other paddlers attempting the drop let go of their boat or paddle.

Where do you place the system? Select a site somewhat below the area where a paddler is most likely to capsize, so he has ample time to initiate his self-rescue. Select the safest shore, which should provide plenty of area for the swimmer to swing into shore, and sufficient shoreline or shallow water for a series of lines to be deployed from different locations.

How do you set up the system? Under ideal conditions, a minimum of three rescuers stand ready to throw their lines. Depending on current speed and the amount of available space on shore as well as river rescue space, the rescuers position themselves five to twenty feet apart. Each rescuer needs firm

SHORE–BASED RESCUE

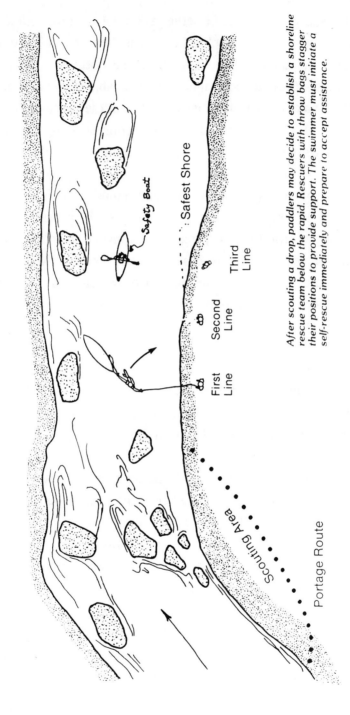

Safety Boat

Safest Shore

First Line

Second Line

Third Line

Scouting Area

Portage Route

After scouting a drop, paddlers may decide to establish a shoreline rescue team below the rapid. Rescuers with throw bags stagger their positions to provide support. The swimmer must initiate a self-rescue immediately and prepare to accept assistance.

226

footing and room along the shore to shift his position downstream as needed to adjust the tension on the line when pulling a swimmer to shore. Each rescuer should "clear" his line before the first paddler enters the drop; this is done by simply deploying the line across the river and then carefully packing it back into the throw bag. This assures that the line is properly packed and wet; a wet line deploys better because of the added weight.

The primary line is the line closest to the anticipated capsize area. The rescuer holding this line should be experienced and in charge of the other rescuers. The primary line is generally the first one deployed when a swimmer needs assistance. The secondary line is ready for the next possible assistance, and the tertiary line is thrown last, if needed.

How do you throw a rescue bag? It is assumed that if you own a throw bag, you are practiced in its use and you know your consistent and effective throwing distance... which you can learn in your backyard with a friend (or foe) running slowly back and forth at varying distances from you! Have your friend hold his arms stretched out and exposed to you as you attempt to throw the bag beyond him so that the line lands somewhere over his body or outstretched arms, just as you should do at the river. Most people discover that their best accuracy is with an underarm throw. Swing your arm as if deploying a bowling ball, releasing the bag at about 10 o'clock (6 o'clock being straight down). A few people throw their bags overhand and still fewer throw them sideways. The choice is yours, as long as you're accurate! From our experience, the consistently effective throwing distance for most paddlers is only 25 to 45 feet.

What are your responsibilities as the rescuee? If you are forced to wet-exit your boat, *immediately proceed with your* _self-rescue._ It is best to assume that any assistance that may be attempted by others will never materialize. Also, since you are responsible for your own welfare, you have the right to decline assistance from others. If you feel that the rescuer is inexperienced and may do you more harm than good, simply proceed with your self-rescue. But if you want help, you need to assist the rescuer too. Hold the rescue line with your swimming hand so you continue to face downriver and _kick aggressively with your feet._ You have the choice of releasing your boat and, if necessary, your paddle. Try hard to get everything to shore if you can. But YOU are the most important! And when you do finally reach shore, make it a habit to signal "I'm okay" by raising both arms over your head to form a big "O". Your friends will want to know if you're more than psychologically damaged! They will be relieved to see this signal and will return it with delight!

What are the responsibilities of the rescuer? Before you throw a bag, yell "Rope" or the swimmer's name to alert him that a rope is coming. You, as the rescuer, are likely to be stressed a bit too, and this excitement can result in a poor throw that misses the target completely. If this occurs, the secondary line should be deployed, since it is positioned farther downstream where the swimmer and his upset boat are drifting. Throw only one line at a time. Throwing multiple lines simultaneously only causes confusion and possible entanglement. You should keep a few extra feet of line from being deployed, so if you run out of shore space, you will have extra line which can be "fed out" to maintain appropriate pulling pressure. Bear in mind that when you are swinging the swimmer in to shore, he is holding onto your line with only one hand while you are usually using both hands to pull; more often than not, you will have to relax the tension to keep the swimmer from losing his grip. Do this first by moving along the shore, and finally by releasing some of the line you originally kept on shore. Above all, don't force the swimmer to let go of his boat by pulling the line in too hard, and don't let others help you, as they will only increase the tension that must be matched by the swimmer.

What are the characteristics of a good throw-bag? A good throw bag is constructed of lightweight rip-stop nylon and is just large enough to hold about 60 to 70 feet of line. Most outfitters carry a yellow polypropylene rescue line of 5/16 or 3/8 inch in diameter that floats on the water surface and is intended for such use. Rescue bags can be purchased completely assembled or you can easily construct your own. See your local dealer for construction details and materials.

Where can you get additional information on river rescue? The premier text on this subject is a book called *River Rescue*, by Les Bechdel and Slim Ray. It is available at most outfitting stores or directly from its publisher, the Appalachian Mountain Club, 5 Joy Street, Boston, MA 02108. You can order the book from the A.M.C. by calling (800) 262-4455.

PADDLING THE RIVER
FOR SAFETY AND PLEASURE

The thrill of playing in the midst of nature's arteries derives partly from an awareness that one is taking a certain amount of risk just by being there. Intelligence, skill, physical fitness, appropriate river selection, and proper equipment are the major factors that reduce risk to an acceptable level.

Many of the techniques you've read about up to this point have been described in terms of upper body or lower body functions. But don't underestimate the importance of a third region that we call the "*upper upper* body"! *Use* it. Intelligent decisions make the difference between fun and catastrophe on the river. Think about the risks associated with a particular run -- Are the river conditions favorable, is your personal gear adequate for the weather, are you well-rested and clear-headed that day? One of the best paddlers we know recently canceled a long-planned run down a Class IV-V river, because she knew she didn't have the best mental concentration for it that day. It was a difficult, admirable decision, and possibly spared her serious injury.

A lot of people say that common sense isn't all that common anymore. We're hoping that's because a disproportionate amount of it is being applied on the river, along with "river sense," which is an empathy with the river that one develops after enough time on and *in* the water. It enables a paddler to know almost intuitively where a channel lies, whether to paddle hard through a hole, or avoid it altogether. If you don't "feel right" about running a rapid, apply some introspection; there's probably a good reason for the way you feel.

The importance of *skill* in whitewater playboating cannot be overemphasized. This is a very skill-intensive sport. Invest plenty of time to hone your technique on flatwater or very easy rapids before paddling heavy water or highly technical rapids.

Physical strength and stamina will also help you in playboating. It's not a "muscle" sport in which one attempts to overpower the river, but strength does help on maneuvers in strong currents. And stamina enables you to play the river longer. As with downhill skiing, when you're tired, it's not only less fun -- the sport becomes far more dangerous. Most ski accidents happen on the last run of the day, and the weary playboater who falls out of his boat at the take-out, scraping shins for the first time all day, is a familiar river sight. Stamina is essential for safety as well as enjoyment.

Another physical attribute that plays an even greater role than strength or stamina is kinesthetic sensitivity. This is the ability to sense and balance your own body movements, anticipating their effects on boat and paddle -- as well as sensing the movements of the boat as if it were an extension of your body. To a large extent, this seems to be something we are born with. But it can be developed, particularly if you spend plenty of time practicing on a pond and on very gentle rapids; try to "tune in" to the cause-and-effect of every movement in these non-threatening waters.

Select rivers that are challenging but don't exceed your ability. Be honest with yourself and others about your skill level. This will make playboating more enjoyable, as well as safer for everyone involved. Remember that you put others at risk too, when you put yourself in a situation where your friends may be called upon to rescue you or your boat.

Whitewater playboating has become a high-tech sport. Materials and designs have advanced so that paddlers are now making moves and paddling rivers once thought impossible and un-runnable. Safety has also been enhanced -- as in the larger cockpits found on contemporary kayaks so paddlers can more easily wet-exit, and are less likely to feel trapped in the boat. Take advantage of these advances. Above all, be sure the equipment you use offers maximal *safety* on the river.

In closing, we wish you a long and rewarding playboating career. We hope this book helps you to understand the language and concepts of playboating, and inspires you to take on all the physical and intellectual challenges the sport has to offer. Remember playboating is very dynamic -- what's right today may be wrong tomorrow! That's why there is no true distinction between "learning to playboat" and "playboating" itself -- the best paddlers are in a permanent state of "learning by doing." We hope you'll be among them. See you on the river!

WHITEWATER GLOSSARY

This glossary is designed to cover the contemporary language of whitewater playboating. It also is in some ways an index, as definitions often refer the reader to a relevant section of the text. In addition, when a word appearing in a definition is itself defined elsewhere in the glossary, it appears in bold type if that word is closely related and we feel it will help the reader if that definition is read also.

ABAFT - Behind, toward, or on the stern or rear of a boat. Astern, aft of.

ABEAM - At right angles to the craft's centerline. A boat moving *abeam* moves perpendicularly to the centerline. Also, the measurement of the width of the boat at its widest point. This is also referred to as the boat's *beam*.

ABOVE - Upriver from.

ACA - American Canoe Association, 7432 Alban Station Blvd., Suite B-226, Springfield, VA 22150-2311. Tel. (703) 451-0141. A nonprofit, educational organization serving the public since 1880, in the areas of conservation, safety, instruction and competition. An advocate for river access and protection as it relates to the paddling community, the ACA is America's largest nonprofit organization dedicated to serving paddlesport.

AFT - At, near, or toward the stern. Behind.

AGROUND - A boat touching the bottom, as on a rock, ledge, beach, shoal, or in shallows. Not waterborne.

AIRLOCK - Suction within an open boat when it is overturned in the water. Makes the boat difficult to right or rescue.

AMIDSHIPS - One of the three general regions of the hull, the other regions being bow and stern. The general area midway between the bow and the stern. Often shortened to midships.

ANCHOR - A paddler loads or *anchors* his paddle at the beginning of the powerphase, and then brings the boat to this anchor during the completion of the powerphase. Paddles do not move significantly through the water during a stroke; rather, the boat moves to the paddle. See **Newton's 3rd Law of Motion.**

ASTERN - Behind the boat. At or toward the rear. Abaft.

ATHWARTSHIP - The width of a boat at a given point along its length. Also, the distance between the **gunwales**, measured at right angles to a canoe's centerline. Used as "what is the *athwartship* measurement at the front of the cockpit?"

AWA - American Whitewater Affiliation, P. O. Box 85, Phoenicia, New York 12464. A volunteer, non-profit organization of paddlers and clubs interested in whitewater paddlesport. Primarily involved in river protection and boaters' rights with respect to river access.

BACK BRACE - Lower-back support in a kayak. See chapter on Playboating Equipment.

BACK FERRY - See **downstream ferry.**

BACKFACE - Technically, this is the blade surface *not* bearing a force during a powerphase to move the boat. However, in 1983, the American Red Cross definitively named each blade surface as either the **powerface** or the **backface.** The **backface** now is that blade surface used to execute a back stroke, while the powerface is that blade surface used to perform a forward power stroke. This has aided the teaching of paddling because each stroke can be explained as either using the backface or the powerface.

BACK PADDLE - To paddle in reverse, using any type of reverse stroke (the blade moving away from the stern and toward the bow during the powerphase of the stroke). Can be done to slow the downstream movement of the craft when the bow is downstream of the stern, or to carry out a maneuver such as a back ferry when traveling around a river bend.

BACKROLLER - A broad water reversal, such as that found below a dam or ledge. A type of **hole.**

BACK STROKE - A commonly used power stroke which uses the backface of the paddle and generally follows the reverse course of the forward stroke. See also **back paddle.**

BAIL - To remove water from a craft by use of a bailer cup, tin can, bucket or sponge.

BANANA BOAT - A playboating craft which has considerable **rocker** and ends higher than midship. Often used to describe an open or decked boat which is so designed in order to decrease lateral resistance at its ends to pivoting.

BAR - A riverbed accumulation of sand, gravel, or rock usually located along the inside bend of a river.

BEAM - The width of a craft at its widest point, usually measured at or near the middle. See **Abeam.**

BEAR AWAY, BEAR OFF - To move away from something, such as an object or the wind.

BELAY - To wrap a line around a rock, tree, or a person's waist in order to slow or stop slippage. Used in river rescue operations.

BELOW - Downriver from.

BIG WATER - Large volume, fast current and big waves, often accompanied by huge reversals and extreme general turbulence. The term suggests immense volume and extremely violent current (and wide-eyed paddlers!).

BLADE - The broad, flat section of a canoe or kayak paddle, which is used by the paddler to apply a force or anchor to move the boat.

BOAT-DESIGNED CIRCLE - That size circle which a particular playboat will carve when paddled on a circle using only forward strokes and minimal boat lean toward the side to which the boat is turning. The size of the circle depends on the hull design; greater curvature and a shorter waterline produce a smaller boat-designed circle, and the boat with such a circle will be easier to turn but harder to paddle in a straight line. See chapter on The Circle Concept.

BOIL - Water swelling upward in convex mounds. Usually formed by underwater objects and/or water of lesser velocity below the surface current. Appears similar to boiling thick liquid. Often found on the downstream side of undercut rocks. See chapter on How to Read the River.

BOOF - To paddle over an obstacle with enough speed to land the boat flat (and hopefully upright!) on the other side.

BOTTOM - The relatively horizontal portion of a boat hull. That portion of the boat below the chine and extending halfway up the chine.

BOULDER GARDEN - A rapid strewn with boulders, creating an area of numerous obstacles, eddies, wave formations and current differentials that permit complex, creative playboating. Also referred to as a rock garden. See chapter on River Playboating Maneuvers.

BOW - The area in the forward end of a watercraft, fore of the **amidship** area.

BOW JAM - An open canoe bow **static stroke** used to move the canoe away from the side on which the paddle is placed in the jam position. The blade is jammed vertically into the water against the side of the canoe, and held at an angle so that water is deflected forcefully away from the canoe; the canoe responds by turning away from the blade. Only effective if the bow is experiencing **frontal resistance**.

BOW LINE - A line, sheet or tether attached to the bow. Bow painter. See **painter**.

BOWPERSON - Person who paddles a tandem craft from the bow pedestal or seat.

BRACE - A static and/or dynamic stroke used to stabilize a boat. A brace can be high or low. [See Kayaking and Canoeing chapters for details of paddle position.] One "throws" or "hangs" a brace to prevent the craft from tipping over (or wishes one had done so).

BRACING STROKE - Any of several paddle strokes providing stability against the capsizing force of a sudden change of the current hitting one side of the boat. Also may be used for turning. Can be a high brace, a low brace, or a turning high brace; in canoes, can also be a cross high brace, cross low brace, or cross turning high brace.

BROACH - To turn a craft broadside to oncoming waves or obstructions. To swing or be swung at right angles to the flow of water is to be current broached.

BROACHING - Turning broadside to oncoming waves or obstructions with the current forcing the craft against a rock or other immovable object, and potentially pinning it there.

BUOYANCY - The ability to float. Flotation bags, styrofoam and other means of air-trapping in a boat will increase its buoyancy when swamped.

BY THE HEAD - A craft is said to be "by the head" when loaded more heavily in the bow than in the stern or aft. Helpful when paddling into the wind.

BY THE STERN - A craft is said to be "by the stern" when loaded more heavily in the stern than in the bow or fore. Helpful when paddling downwind.

C-1 - A solo decked canoe; the paddler kneels while using a paddle with a single blade. **Volume** is similar to kayak playboats but boat is usually flatter and wider (70 cm or about 27 1/2 inches).

C-2 - A tandem decked canoe in which both paddlers kneel and use single-bladed paddles.

"C" STROKE - A solo correction stroke which resembles the letter *C* (or an inverted *C*) which starts at the bow and ends at the stern. It begins in approximately the same catch position as a forward stroke, but a foot further out from the centerline. The stroke initially draws the bow to the blade. The paddler then brings the blade through a continuous arc under the boat, then away from the boat in the stern; the powerface is used continuously. This stroke is used primarily to get the boat moving forward from a standstill and turning toward the side on which the stroke is executed.

CANOE - In reference to whitewater playboating, and in comparison to kayaking, a canoe is a craft paddled from a kneeling position, with the use of a single-bladed paddle. Most playboating canoes are **banana boats**.

CARVING A CIRCLE - Whitewater playboats are designed to "carve a circle," not to **track** in a straight line. One carves a circle by initiating the desired circle and then controlling the size of this circle by a combination of boat lean and forward control strokes. The size of the circle is determined mostly by the degree of boat lean but also by the control strokes executed on the inside of the circle being carved. It is also influenced by the design of the hull; see **boat-designed circle**. See chapter on The Circle Concept.

C.F.S. - Cubic feet per second. A unit of water flow used to indicate the volume of water flowing per second past any given point along a river. A cubic foot of water is about 7.5 gallons or 62 pounds.

CAPSIZE - To overturn.

CARRY - A **portage** where a boat is carried around an obstruction in the river or between two waterways. Also the route followed by such a carry.

CATCH POSITION - The position of the blade when in the water and ready to begin a powerphase.

CENTER OF BUOYANCY - The point of resolution of all upward forces counteracting the downward pressure of the weight of the watercraft, its cargo, and crew.

CENTER OF GRAVITY - The point of resolution of all downward forces or weights contained within a watercraft, including the weight of the craft itself.

CHANNEL - The course that a significant portion of the water follows. Usually the deepest and fastest flow. Sometimes referred to as the navigable route, but this is not necessarily true. See chapter on How to Read the River.

CHINE - Curved portion of the boat hull where the bottom meets the side. The sharpness of this curvature influences the stability of the boat; a sharp curve decreases secondary stability, and is referred to as *hard chines*. The benefits of hard chines are increased responsiveness to subtle changes in boat lean and greater turning ability. *Soft chines* are more forgiving of inappropriate boat lean, and can make a boat easier to roll. (See also **flare** and **tumblehome**.)

CHOKING UP - Moving the hand on the shaft nearest the **working blade** closer to the other hand. This extends the working blade farther out over the water. Used mostly when performing low shaft angle correction strokes.

CHUTE - An accelerated water flow, often compressed between two or more obstacles and dropping faster than the adjacent current.

238

CIRCLE CONCEPT - The method of executing peel-outs, eddy turns, ferries, and other river playboating maneuvers in such a way that the boat is constantly tracing an arc (part of a circle); the size of the circle is controlled by power strokes on the "inside" of the circle, reducing the need for correction strokes that would slow down the boat. See chapter on The Circle Concept.

CLASSIFICATION - A rating applied to a river or a rapid, describing its general navigability for canoes, kayaks, and rafts. See chapter on International Scale of Difficulty.

CLOSED BOAT - Any boat in which the deck completely covers the topside of the craft except for an opening called a cockpit; the space between the cockpit and the paddler's body is sealed by a sprayskirt, preventing the craft from taking on water when submerged or capsized. (Tandem closed boats have two cockpits.) Also called a *decked boat*.

COCKPIT - A hole in the deck of a kayak or canoe where the paddler sits (kayak) or kneels (canoe).

COMBINATION STROKE - A sequence of two or more strokes not separated by a recovery phase; a blended stroke maneuver consisting of two or more simpler strokes.

COMPOUND BACK STROKE - A canoe back stroke in which force is applied first to the blade's powerface and then to the backface. The paddler rotates his shoulders to begin the powerphase as far aft as possible. The paddler applies force parallel to the centerline and when the blade is just behind his hip, he rotates the blade (switching from powerface to backface) and continues it forward to the catch position of the forward stroke. This is a *compound stroke* because both blade surfaces are employed during the total powerphase. This stroke is actually a combination of the *far back stroke* and the *back stroke*. See "Reverse Travel" in chapter on Solo Canoeing.

COMPOUND STROKE - Any stroke in which force is applied first to one face of the blade and then to the other during the powerphase of the stroke, e.g., see **compound back**.

COMPOUND WAVE BLOCK - To elevate first one side of an open canoe, then the other, to prevent water from entering as the boat approaches cresting waves. The elevation is timed precisely at the point the water is about to enter from one side and then repeated again, if necessary, on the other side; a quick hip snap preforms the elevations. See **wave block**.

CONFLUENCE - The point where two or more rivers flow together.

CONTROL HAND - The hand on the grip of a canoe paddle; the right hand on a kayak paddle (except on the rare kayak paddle designed for left hand control). This hand controls the angulation of the paddle blade during all phases of a stroke, whether done on the **onside** or **offside.**

CONTROL STROKE - Any power stroke executed in the leading or frontal resistance end of the boat that keeps the boat on a desired course. The difference between a control stroke and a power stroke may be a subtle change in blade angulation or distance from the centerline of the boat; most control strokes have a powerphase essentially parallel to the centerline

CONTROL THUMB - The thumb of the control hand on a canoe paddle. This thumb is often referred to by canoeing instructors to assist their students in achieving proper blade angulation during both the powerphase and the recovery phase. In general, the control thumb points in the direction in which the blade travels during the recovery.

CORRECTION STROKE - Any stroke which is executed in the following or eddy resistance end of the boat, designed to alter the course of the boat quickly. Unlike a **power stroke**, a correction stroke generally has a low shaft angle during the powerphase; that is, the shaft of the paddle is held as nearly parallel to the water as possible.

COURSE - The desired movement of the craft from one point to another point. Also, a sequence of gates set along a river for a slalom race.

CREST - The top of a standing wave.

CROSS CURRENT - A current moving at an angle to the main current or channel. It's possible for a crosscurrent to be faster than the main one.

CROSS - An adjective used to describe any canoe stroke executed on the **offside**.

CROSS DRAW - A canoe stroke in which the paddle is crossed to the paddler's offside and anchored about two feet from the boat opposite the paddler's hip; the boat is pulled to the anchor.

CURLER - A high, steep wave that curls or falls back onto its own upstream face. Considered by most to be a form of **reversal**.

CURRENT - General movement of water in a river.

CURRENT BROACH - A craft is said to be *current broached* when it is at right angles to the direction of current flow.

CURRENT DIFFERENTIAL - Any boundary line between two currents flowing in opposite directions or at different speeds. An example of the former would be an **eddy line**. An example of the latter would be the differential between the slow current close to shore and the faster current farther from shore. See chapter on How to Read the River.

DECK - The top of a closed canoe or kayak. On a traditional open canoe, the triangular piece found at bow and stern to which the gunwales attach at their ends; often called deck plates.

DECK PLATE - See **deck**.

DECKED CANOE - Any canoe in which the deck completely covers the topside of the craft except for an opening called a **cockpit**; the space between the cockpit and the paddler's body is sealed by a sprayskirt, preventing the craft from taking on water when submerged or capsized. (Tandem decked canoes have two cockpits.)

DEPTH - The depth of a craft, measured vertically amidships from the bottom to the top of the gunwale or cockpit.

DIFFERENTIAL - See **current differential**.

DIFFICULTY RATING - Same as **classification**. See chapter on International Scale of Difficulty.

DISCHARGE - The volume of water that passes through a specific cross-sectional area in a time interval, usually measured in cubic feet per second (**c.f.s.**).

DISCIPLINE - With respect to the position of a craft on moving water, the *discipline* of the boat identifies whether the bow is upstream or downstream of the stern. See **upstream discipline** and **downstream discipline**. With respect to paddlesport, the various categories of paddling such as whitewater, sea kayaking, freestyle, etc. With respect to paddlers, what it takes to do enough "pond homework" to get the most out of this book!

DISPLACEMENT - The volume of water displaced by a watercraft, its cargo and crew.

DOUBLE BLADE - Paddle with a blade at each end; usually used in a kayak and sometimes in an open canoe.

DOWNRIVER RACE - A whitewater competition. When decked boats are used, it is generally called a **wildwater race**. Usually takes place over several miles and in water of varying difficulty, the difficulty depending on the skill of the paddlers. *Downriver sprints* are shorter races, often about one mile long.

DOWNSTREAM DISCIPLINE - An orientation of the boat in which the bow is downstream of the stern. For example, "One should maintain a downstream discipline throughout a back ferry." Opposite: **upstream discipline**.

DOWNSTREAM FERRY - Synonymous with back ferry. A maneuver in which a boat is moved laterally to a desired point by back paddling while maintaining a downstream discipline, with the stern angled toward the intended destination. The amount of angle used depends on the velocity of the current. Called a downstream ferry because the paddler is facing downstream. Called a back ferry because one is back paddling. For details, see section on River Playboating Maneuvers.

DOWNSTREAM "V" - A "V" formed on the water's surface with the apex downstream, formed by two obstacles positioned side-by-side in the river. The water deflected off the obstacles forms eddy lines in the shape of a "V". The faster current between the lines of the "V" forms a **chute** which can generally be paddled safely.

DRAFT - Depth of water required to float a craft, or the vertical distance between the waterline and the lowest point of the boat. Also called *draw*, as "My canoe only draws three inches of water."

DRAG - Frictional resistance to motion. Also called *surface* or *skin resistance*. Also, not enough water in the river to go playboating!

DRAW - See **draft**.

DRAW STROKE - A stroke designed to move the craft laterally toward the powerface of the working blade.

DRIFT - The unassisted movement of a boat caused by currents in the water and/or wind.

DROP - A section of rapids which is usually steeper and/or more obstructed than the surrounding sections. A sudden pitch or unusually sharp dip in a section of rapids. An abrupt descent in a river. See **falls**.

DRY PACK - A waterproof storage pack or bag often carried in a whitewater playboat.

DRY SUIT - A waterproof outerwear garment worn by cold-weather paddlers. Designed to prevent water from entering inside the suit, it keeps the torso, legs and arms dry. Dry suits come as full suits, dry-tops and dry-bottoms. Perspiration and/or gasket leakage necessitates that the paddler wear synthetic wicking underwear to collect moisture.

DUFFEK STROKE - A high bracing stroke first used in the kayak by Milovan Duffek of Czechoslavakia. Now used in all playboating craft mainly to enter or leave an eddy. It is sometimes called a **hanging draw** or a **turning high brace**.

DUFFEK SYSTEM - A combination stroke sequence used when entering or leaving eddies. The entire system consists of the Duffek which initially is static, then a dynamic draw of the bow to the blade, followed immediately by a forward stroke.

DYNAMIC STROKE - Any stroke in which the blade position is changed with respect to the boat position during the powerphase, as in a forward stroke, a draw, or a sweep. Can be effective whether or not the craft is initially in motion or in moving water. Opposite: **static stroke**.

EDDY - Area below an obstruction either in the river or along a shoreline, or on the inside of a riverbend where the current either stops or moves upstream (relative to the main river flow). Most eddies are fairly calm but some can be dangerous, particularly if the eddy flow is severe.

EDDY CUSHION - The billowing water that pads the upstream face of exposed rocks and other obstructions in the river.

EDDY FLOWER - A term used to tease paddlers who take a passive approach to learning the sport, rather than actively playing the river. There is no substitute for *practice* in this skill-intensive sport!

EDDY HOPPING - One of the most exciting facets of whitewater playboating, going from eddy to eddy while paddling downstream or upstream. Also a means of scouting rapids from the boat, and safer than paddling straight downriver in unfamiliar waters. See chapter on River Playboating Maneuvers.

EDDY LINE - The boundary line between the swift downstream main current and the circulating or upstream current within an eddy; this line is created by the shear between opposing currents. See chapter on How to Read the River.

EDDY RESISTANCE - The resistance created by swirling water that attempts to fill in the hole created by the water displacement of a moving craft. Often called *tail suction* since the boat drags along some water. The following end of the boat (i.e., the stern when traveling forward, the bow when traveling in reverse) is referred to as the *eddy resistance end*.

EDDY TURN - A maneuver used to enter an eddy. Also referred to as *eddying out* or *catching an eddy*. The craft most commonly enters the eddy with a **downstream discipline** and abruptly turns upstream (in reference to the mainstream flow). See chapter on River Playboating Maneuvers.

EDDY WALL - An eddy line created by extreme current differentials. A wall of water is formed along the boundary near the obstacle creating the eddy. Also called an *eddy fence*. See chapter on How to Read the River.

ENDER - A playboating maneuver in which one end of the boat is forced into the smooth water at the top of a hole, causing that end to be driven down by the current while the other end pops up into the air, and the entire boat flips 180 degrees, causing the paddler to land upside-down on the water. See chapter on River Playboating Maneuvers.

ENTERING CURRENT - When about to cross a current differential, the *entering current* is that current the boat will be in after crossing the differential. Usually used in reference to entering or leaving an eddy -- when entering an eddy, the upstream current in the eddy is the entering current. When leaving an eddy, the mainstream flow is the entering current. (Also see **leaving current**.)

EVEN KEEL - A properly balanced craft, neither down by the head nor by the stern. Also called *even trim* or *well trimmed* when observed from the side.

FACE - A flat side of a paddle blade. The side used for the propulsion phase in the forward stroke is called the **powerface**. The side used for the propulsion phase of the back stroke is called the **backface**. Also refers to the slope of a wave.

FALLS - A drop over which water descends freely at least part of the way. In some parts of the country, heavy noisy rapids are often termed *falls*.

FAR BACK - A powerful back stroke often used to stop forward movement of a canoe; consists of the first half of the **compound back stroke**. The paddler rotates his shoulders and places the blade in the water "far back" behind him and, applying the force on the powerface, brings the paddle toward his body but parallel to the centerline, stopping at his body. Recovery is underwater.

FAST WATER - Generally a term describing noisy rapids with or without obstacles.

FEATHER - To return the paddle to the **catch position** with one edge of the blade leading, so the blade slices through the air or water with a minimum of resistance. The edge farther forward is called the *leading edge*; the following edge is called the *trailing edge*.

FEND - To push off from an object; to fend off.

FERRY - A maneuver for moving a boat laterally across a current. The upstream end of the boat is angled toward the destination shore or eddy, while the paddler stops or minimizes downstream movement of the boat by paddling in the opposite direction from the current (i.e., forward strokes if the bow is aimed upstream or back strokes if the bow is aimed downstream). The current's deflection off one side of the boat assists in shifting the boat's position toward its goal. The stronger the current, the more nearly the boat must be aligned with the current, to prevent the boat from **current broaching**. See chapter on River Playboating Maneuvers.

FISH COUNT - What paddlers do when they err on the river and tip over!

FLARE - The outward-curving contour of the sides of an open boat to provide secondary stability; hulls with greater flare generally have more secondary stability than those with less flare.

FLOOD - Any rising which causes the river to flow out of its normal banks. It is not advisable to paddle a flooded river due to the increased number of **strainers** along the river banks.

FLOTATION - Air-trapping material placed in an open or decked boat to keep it floating high when upset or swamped. Air bags are most common and weigh the least, but a variety of foam-type materials are used also. The flotation displaces some of the water a capsized craft would normally hold. The flotation, therefore, prevents the capsized boat from being severely damaged and it also makes the boat more maneuverable, whether paddled or towed to shore.

FOOT BLOCK - A foam, metal or plastic brace on which the paddler supports his onside foot during the powerphase of a stroke. There is a foot block for each foot in a well outfitted boat, whether a canoe or kayak. Such a brace helps the paddler bring the boat up to the paddle (anchor) by applying pressure on the brace during the powerphase of a stroke. See chapter on Playboating Equipment.

FOOT BRACE - See Foot Block.

FOOT PEG - Similar to Foot Block but this term is more common in referring to a kayak with plastic or medal adjustable braces.

FORWARD STROKE - The power stroke used in paddling a craft directly ahead. See specific chapters on kayaking and canoeing for details.

FREEBOARD - The distance from the waterline to the top of the gunwale of an open boat or to the seamline of a decked boat. The measurement is taken where the gunwale or seamline is closest to the water.

FRONTAL RESISTANCE - The resistance or pressure experienced on the **displacement** or **leading end** of the boat created by the water and air the boat is entering. When traveling forward, the bow is referred to as the *frontal resistance end* of the boat; when traveling in reverse, this would be the stern.

GATE - Narrow, short passage between two obstacles. Racing gates are poles supported by wires above the river, separated by at least 1.2 meters (about 4 feet). Gates are color-coded. The boat must be moving downstream as it goes through green gates. Red gates must be taken paddling from downstream to upstream, and are usually in or near an eddy.

GAUGE - A device used to measure the water level of a river. Often located at dams or under bridges. Paddlers often mark rocks or other obstacles to create their own gauges, or they may use a **gauging station**.

GAUGING STATION - Streamside device installed by the Army Corps of Engineers for measuring the flow of water.

GRAB LOOP - Loop of strap material at each end of a kayak or decked canoe, used for pulling or carrying the craft, in water and on land. Also, loop at front of sprayskirt where it attaches to cockpit, used to pull the skirt free of the boat during a **wet exit**.

GRADIENT - The average drop of a river generally expressed in vertical feet per mile.

GRIP - Top of a canoe paddle shaft which is held by the **control hand**.

GUNNEL - See **gunwale**.

GUNWALE - Strip along the top of a canoe's side, extending from bow to stern, where the deck and topsides meet. Also refers to the top of the sides of a canoe. The canoe gunwale is actually a longitudinal frame providing strength and support.

HAIR PADDLER - A boater who enjoys running Class V and VI rivers, and is not yet inhibited by the realization that he is a mere mortal.

244

HANGING DRAW - The original name of the **Duffek stroke**; also known as a **Turning High Brace**. See **Duffek**.

HARD CHINES - See **chines**.

HAYSTACKS - Large standing waves often with exploding crests which accompany deceleration of a current. See **standing waves**. See chapter on How to Read the River.

HEAVY WATER - See **big water**.

HELMET - A required playboating accessory for protecting the noggin.

HIGH BRACE - Any of a number of strokes which assist the paddler in keeping his boat upright; all high braces apply force to the powerface during the powerphase. Generally, during the powerphase of a high brace, the paddler's knuckles are up and his elbows are below the shaft of the paddle. See "Righting Action Strokes" in the Kayaking and Canoeing chapters.

HIP PAD - A supporting piece of foam encircling the back half of the paddler at his hips as he sits on the seat or pedestal, and attached to the walls of the boat. Enhances lower body connection to the boat. See chapter on Playboating Equipment.

HOLDING POSITION - Attempting to stop or arrest the downstream movement of the craft. Craft moves slower than the current, thus creating **frontal resistance** on the upstream end of the boat.

HOLE - A type of current reversal, generally caused by heavy water flowing over an obstacle, which creates a depression or hole on the downstream side of the obstacle. Holes vary in size; most can be used in whitewater playboating, though some should be avoided due to their capacity to trap a craft. See chapter on How to Read the River.

HORIZON LINE - The apparent line between the river's surface and the sky or scenery downriver that is seen where a river drops suddenly. Usually accompanied by increased noise and/or mist. The river immediately below a horizon line is hidden from the paddler's view. Scouting is advised.

HULL - The frame or body of a craft, exclusive of **outfitting**.

HUNG UP - Said of any craft that is caught on an obstacle but not **wrapped**.

HYDRAULIC - A general term for different types of reversals, eddy fences, and other places where there is a powerful current differential. Sometimes used in the plural to refer to the whole phenomenon of big water where massive waves, violent currents, and large holes are the primary obstacles. Also, a **keeper** created by a sudden drop of water over a dam, rock or ledge, causing a recirculating current to be formed on the surface below the obstacle.

HYPOTHERMIA - A serious, life-threatening physical condition caused by a lowering of the body core temperature. Paddlers should be concerned at the earliest symptoms, which include shivering and cold extremities (which may be evident by inability to attach one's sprayskirt around the cockpit, or to touch the thumb tip to each fingertip in sequence). Such early symptoms dictate immediate attention to prevent further lowering of body core temperature. Later symptoms include slurred speech, impaired mentation, bluish skin, dilation of pupils, decrease in heart and respiratory rate, extreme weakness, and uncontrolled shivering.

INSIDE BANK - In a river bend, the edge of the river with the slower and shallower water. If a river is turning left, then the inside bank is on **river left.**

INVERTED J - A reverse canoe stroke which uses the backface of the paddle, executed in the following or eddy resistance end of the boat by the tandem bow or solo paddler. Sometimes called a *reverse J.*

JET FERRY - A type of ferry in which the paddler takes advantage of the slope on the upstream side of a wave and the force of gravity to shoot or "jet" along the wave trough lateral to the main current flow. See also **ferry.** See chapter on River Playboating Maneuvers.

J-LEAN - The body position used to lean or heel a kayak or canoe. The paddler curls his torso laterally, while exerting upward pressure on either the knees against the deck (kayak) or the thighs against the thigh straps (canoe), while keeping the upper body approximately over the centerline to prevent a capsize. See diagram in Concepts of Paddling.

J STROKE - Stroke used by the tandem stern or solo canoeist to correct for **yaw** when paddling forward. When properly executed, the stroke is a continuous smooth action which not only provides forward motion but also "pushes" the boat away from the blade in the eddy resistance end, thus correcting for the yaw created at the beginning of the stroke.

K-1 - A kayak designed for the solo paddler; most kayaks are K-1's.

K-2 - A kayak designed for two paddlers; becoming more common.

KAYAK - In reference to playboating, and in comparison with a canoe, a craft paddled in a sitting position, with the use of a double-bladed paddle. Most playboating kayaks are **banana boats**.

KEEPER - A severe current reversal capable of trapping a boat. Similar to but more powerful than a **stopper**. See also **hole**. See chapter on How to Read the River.

KNEE BRACES - Any support type structure, attached to the floor of a canoe or under the deck of a kayak, that prevents lateral movement of the paddler's knees.

KNEE CUPS - Support pads to protect a canoeist's knees and prevent them from moving laterally. Usually constructed of cross-linked polyethylene, closed-cell foam; U-shaped to fit snugly.

LEAD BOAT - The boat leading a group down the river. The lead paddler often selects the general course to be followed by the others. See chapter on Group Organization on the River.

LEAN - To heel or tip the boat to one side to stabilize or maneuver it. Generally done to elevate the **side of opposition**, and/or to facilitate turning of the boat by altering the shape of that portion of the hull below the waterline. See chapter on Concepts of Paddling.

LEAVING CURRENT - When crossing a current differential, the *leaving current* is that current the boat is in before crossing the differential. Usually used in reference to entering or leaving an eddy -- when entering an eddy, the leaving current is the mainstream current. When leaving an eddy, the leaving current is the upstream current in the eddy.

LEDGE - A rock stratum that acts as a low dam or series of dams. Also, the river may flow around or under shoreline ledges that extend into the river.

LEE, LEEWARD, LEEWAY - A *lee* is a protected area downwind or downstream of an obstruction which breaks the normal direction and force of the wind or water. *Leeward* means downwind. *Leeway* refers to the drift of a boat downwind.

LEFT BANK - See **river left**.

LIFEVEST - Personal flotation device or PFD. Worn like a vest, it provides flotation when swimming, as well as upper body protection, warmth, and increased visibility to other paddlers. Should be *worn* at all times when paddling. The U.S. Coast Guard requires one PFD per boater in all craft in all bodies of water or waterways.

LINE - To work a craft downstream by means of ropes from shore; used to move the boat through rapids or shallows the boater does not wish to paddle.

LIST - Leaning or tilting of a craft due to improper positioning of crew and/or gear rather than due to external forces.

LOAD - The initial placement of the canoe paddle into the water on the forward and cross-forward strokes. The load angle on both strokes should be about 70 degrees from horizontal. See **anchor**.

LOW BRACE - A righting action stroke in which the blade is nearly flat on the surface. The paddler's knuckles on both hands are down, his elbows are above the shaft, and he applies force to the backface of the paddle. In all low braces, the blade exits the water with the powerface facing aft. In a canoe, the control thumb points forward during the execution of the brace. See **righting action stroke**.

MANEUVER - Term given to the movement of the boat as a result of a stroke, series of strokes, or current formations. For example, a draw stroke executed opposite the hip of a solo paddler results in a maneuver called an **abeam**. There are calm water maneuvers such as spins, abeams, circles, forward straight, reverse straight, forward and reverse sideslips, and U-turns; and there are river play maneuvers which include forward and reverse eddy turns, parallel and side surfing, upstream and downstream ferries, jet ferries, C-turns, S-turns, pop-ups, and enders.

MEANDER - A river is said to *meander* when it forms looping bends as it dissipates its energy.

MOUTH - Area where a river joins another body of water.

NEWTON'S THIRD LAW OF MOTION - *For every action, there is an equal and opposite reaction*. In paddling, the *action* is the force applied in a specific direction on one of the blade surfaces by the paddler; the *reaction* is the movement of the boat in the opposite direction of that force.

NOSE CLIPS - A device placed on the nostrils to keep them closed. Necessary for some people when capsized to protect against sinus infections, or undue distress.

OC-1 - Solo open canoe.

OC-2 - Tandem open canoe.

OFFSET - With respect to a kayak paddle, the angle between the two blades seen when one peers down the length of the paddle from one blade tip to the other. Contemporary playboating paddles generally have an *offset* of 45 to 60 degrees. See chapter on Playboating Equipment.

OFFSIDE - In kayaking, the side opposite the working blade. In canoeing, the side opposite the paddler's designated paddling side; **cross strokes** are executed on the offside.

ONE HUNDRED DEGREE RULE - A rule of thumb that states that when the sum of the air temperature and the water temperature is less than 100 degrees Fahrenheit, there exists risk of hypothermia in the event of a capsize, and precautions should be taken accordingly. Consider the river as one Class higher in difficulty when the air-and-water sum is less than 100 degrees.

ONSIDE - In kayaking, the side of the working blade. In canoeing, the paddler's designated paddling side.

OPEN - Undecked or uncovered.

OPEN CANOE - A canoe not closed or decked at the top.

OTTER ENTRANCE - The launching of a playboat by getting in on land, then sliding down the bank into the river like an otter.

OUTFITTING - A general term for the items used in, or the process of, fitting a paddler properly in his craft for optimum boat control, safety and comfort. Kayak outfitting includes a seat pad, hip pads, thigh cups, a back brace, and flotation. Playboat canoe outfitting includes a pedestal or saddle, thigh straps, knee cups, toe or foot blocks, and flotation.

OUTSIDE BANK - In a river bend, the side toward which centrifugal force pushes the current. The side of the river bend with the deeper and faster water. When the river bends to the left, the outside bank is **river right.**

PADDLE - The tool used to propel a boat in the desired direction. Paddles come in many shapes, sizes, and materials. Kayak paddles have a blade at each end; canoe paddles have a blade at one end and a grip at the other end. See chapter on Playboating Equipment.

PADDLE SENSITIVITY - The ability of a paddler to employ the paddle to make his craft respond positively, precisely, and quickly to the many variables encountered along the river. This response becomes a conditioned reflex as the paddler gains experience. The paddler is then said to have a high degree of paddle sensitivity.

PAINTER - A length of highly visible rope attached to an end of a canoe. A canoe may be moored, towed, lined, or rescued using a painter. The rope should float and be at least 5/16 inch diameter. The minimum length should be two-thirds the length of the canoe; it is advisable to have a painter on each end of the boat. Painters should be secured in or on the boat at their respective ends in such a way that they are readily available in the event of an unpremeditated spill.

PEAR GRIP - A canoe paddle handle shaped in the form of a flattened pear, more common in touring than in whitewater.

PEDESTAL - Foam or plastic seat which supports a canoeist's derriere. See chapter on Playboating Equipment.

PEEL-OUT - A maneuver in which one exits an eddy by tracing an arc (carving a circle) so that the paddler reverses the **discipline** of the boat; in a forward peel-out, the bow is upstream while in the eddy, then is downstream of the stern after the peel-out. In a reverse peel-out, the stern is initially upstream, and ends up downstream as the boat is paddled in the reverse arc. See chapter on River Playboating Maneuvers.

PFD - Personal Flotation Device; see **lifevest**.

PILLOW - A smooth bulge on the river's surface created by water flowing over an underwater obstruction.

PITCH - A section of a rapid steeper than the surrounding sections; a **drop**. Sometimes used to describe a pronounced drop or steep rapids. Also, paddlers frequently *pitch* their blades during a power stroke by angling the powerface slightly away from the boat during the powerphase. That is, the edge of the blade nearer the boat is further aft than the edge of the blade farther from the boat. A pitched stroke is a type of control stroke. See **slice**.

PIVOT - To turn or **spin** the craft with little forward or astern movement. To turn on a point. Paddlers *pivot* their boats using **sweep strokes** and/or **stern sweeps**.

PIVOT POINT - The balance point of the total mass or weight of the craft. A specific point on the bottom of the craft below the center of gravity and the center of buoyancy. See chapter on Concepts of Paddling.

PLAYBOATING - Recreational boating technique used in whitewater. Paddlers maneuver about the obstacles, using ferries, eddy turns, and peel outs executed in both forward and reverse directions. Playboating also includes the use of wave formations, holes, and various types of reversals to perform such activities as surfing, jet-ferries, pop-ups, enders and 360 degree hole spins. Playboating is used in formal workshops to obtain the highest skill level achievable in whitewater boat control.

PLAYSITE - A rapid offering paddlers the chance to practice or simply enjoy a particular maneuver or set of maneuvers. When the playsite is fun enough, and easily accessible from shore, some "river runs" have the put-in and take-out at the same spot!

POGIES - Gloves worn by cold weather paddlers which permit the bare hands to directly grasp the paddle. Often called Bonnie Hots; originally designed by kayak racer Bonnie Losick in 1979.

POOL - A deep, quiet stretch of river, slower and deeper than the surrounding sections.

POP-UP - A playboating maneuver in which one end of the boat is forced into the smooth water at the top of a hole, causing that end to be driven down by the current while the other end pops up into the air, often lifting the boat as high as 60 to 80 degrees from horizontal. If the submerged end is pushed all the way under the paddler and the end in the air goes a full 180 degrees, the maneuver is an **ender**. See chapter on River Playboating Maneuvers.

PORT - The left side of a craft as one faces forward in the boat.

PORTAGE - The act of carrying a boat and its associated gear around an obstacle or from one body of water to another. Also, the place where the boat has to be taken from the water and carried on land around an obstruction or dangerous spot in the river.

POWERFACE - Technically, this is whichever blade surface bears against the water during the powerphase of a stroke. In 1983, however, the American Red Cross definitively named the blade surfaces, and the American Canoe Association adopted this nomenclature. For the purpose of teaching paddling, this has been a good strategy. Now the powerface refers to that blade surface used to bear against the water on the forward stroke. See **backface** for a description of the other blade surface.

POWERPHASE - That part of a stroke that bears water pressure against a blade surface. (See also **recovery phase**.)

POWER STROKE - A stroke used to propel a craft forward or backward. Such strokes have a high shaft angle during the powerphase and are executed in the frontal resistance end of the boat. The most common strokes are the forward stroke and the back stroke. See also **control stroke**.

PRIMARY STABILITY - The stability of the boat when not being leaned to either side. A flat bottom boat has excellent *primary stability*. A boat with *no* primary stability would be one that was perfectly round on the bottom. See also **secondary stability**.

PROPULSION PHASE - The phase of any stroke during which the blade is in the water and force is exerted on the blade. The major components of most strokes are the propulsion phase and the **recovery phase**.

PRY - Any stroke that uses the paddle shaft as a lever against the gunwale or seam of the boat. Force is exerted on the backface by pulling hard toward the centerline with the upper hand. The craft moves away from the blade.

PUT-IN - The starting point of a river run.

RAPID - A fast, turbulent stretch of river, often with obstructions but without an actual waterfall. A section of a river characterized by a steep gradient and increased water speed.

READING - See **river reading**.

RECOVERY - The act of preparing for the **powerphase** of a stroke. In canoeing, the blade is usually **feathered** during the recovery phase, and the blade can be in or out of the water. In kayaking, one blade is in the recovery phase while the other, the **working blade**, is in the powerphase.

RESISTANCE - In playboating, the friction or forces between a craft and water or air. There are three types of water resistance acting on a moving craft: (1) frontal or head-on resistance, (2) surface or skin resistance, and (3) eddy or tail suction resistance.

REVERSAL - A place where the current swings upward and rotates back on itself. Some reversals take the form of flat, foamy, surface backflows immediately below large obstructions, while others consist of steep waves that curl heavily back onto their own upstream faces. Reversals are also called **hydraulics, stoppers, keepers, white eddies, roller waves, backrollers, curlers, sidecurlers,** and **holes**. Although some of these terms are used loosely to refer to any sort of reversal, others carry more precise meaning and refer to specific types. See chapter on How to Read the River.

REVERSE J - A modified canoe back stroke used for traveling in a straight line, in reverse. The J action occurs in front of the paddler and always in the **eddy resistance** end of the canoe. Used by the solo or tandem bow canoeist.

REVERSE SWEEPING LOW BRACE - A stroke in which the paddle blade is "swept" from the stern toward the bow, with the shaft held at a low angle, to spin the bow of the boat toward the side on which the stroke is being done. The backface is placed on the water at a "climbing angle," i.e., the blade edge nearest the bow is elevated. See details in chapters on Canoeing and Kayaking.

RIFFLES - Shallow water running over a gravel or sand bottom and creating small waves. Could be termed gentle rapids, ripples, or sandpaper.

RIGHTING ACTION STROKE - Any stroke executed in order to prevent a "fish count." Righting action strokes include the **high brace**, the **low brace**, and the **righting pry**.

RIGHTING PRY - A **pry** executed near the paddler's **onside** hip in order to prevent the craft from capsizing to the **offside**.

RIVER DEVILS - Critters that live in, on, and about water. They spend most of their energy causing havoc with unwary paddlers, their favored result being to witness the facial expressions of underwater paddlers!

RIVER ETIQUETTE - Practices established informally by paddlers to maximize enjoyment and minimize friction between boaters. See chapter on Paddlers' Personal Responsibilities.

RIVER GODS - Violent enemies of the **River Devils** but good friends of playboaters. They assist paddlers toward the development of positive river karma and try to help them to have enjoyable river experiences. They get very upset when a playboater doesn't "Catch every eddy and surf every wave!"

RIVER LEFT - The side of the river on one's left when facing downstream. Referred to as river left whether one is *actually* facing downstream *or* upstream. Also sometimes referred to as the "left bank."

RIVER RATING - See **classification**.

RIVER READING - The art of identifying water formations and currents by recognizing patterns on the water surface, and understanding the obstructions or gradients that cause them. A paddler "reads the river" in order to plan playboating maneuvers or possible routes through a rapid. See chapter on How to Read the River.

RIVER RIGHT - The side of the river on one's right when facing downstream. Referred to as "river right" whether one is *actually* facing downstream *or* upstream. Also sometimes referred to as the "right bank."

RIVER SIGNALS SYSTEM - A set of signals using either a paddle or just one's arms to send messages from one boater to another. Developed by the **American Whitewater Affiliation**, these signals should be known by all playboaters, as they can prevent serious accidents. See chapter on Paddlers' Personal Responsibilities for illustrations of these signals.

RIVER STRATEGY - Term given to the plan for running a river or rapid; such a plan generally utilizes several **maneuvers** depending on the playability of the river/rapid.

ROCK GARDEN - A rapid strewn with rocks, creating an area of numerous obstacles, eddies, wave formations and current differentials that permit complex, creative playboating. Also referred to as a boulder garden. See chapter on River Playboating Maneuvers.

ROCKER - The upward sweep of the keel line toward both ends of a boat. In general, the more underwater rocker a boat has, the more easily it will pivot, because the lateral resistance to pivoting is reduced or eliminated at the waterline ends. See chapter on Playboating Equipment.

RODEO - A competitive event which takes playboating to the extreme. First held in 1976 on the Salmon River, there are over ten such events held annually today. Freestyle, or hot-dogging at a playspot is the feature attraction. There are women's and men's events for all skill levels.

ROLLER WAVE - A **reversal**. This term is used to mean both **curler** and **backroller**.

ROOSTER TAIL - A type of wave formation caused when two side currents flow together forcing water up and into the shape of a rooster's tail. Such a wave formation also may be formed by a pointed underwater obstacle just below the surface. Rooster tails are usually avoided.

RUDDERING - Holding the paddle blade stationary in the water at a fixed angle for the purpose of steering or turning. Since this is a **static stroke**, the craft must be moving faster than the current for it to be effective.

RUN - A stretch of fast, usually rough, water. Also used to refer to the passage through such water. Also used to describe a particular river trip. Also, the act of making a trip.

SAL - Speed, Angle, Lean. An acronym used in teaching whitewater playboating, to remind beginning paddlers to leave or enter each eddy with momentum (speed), proper boat angle (with respect to the current), and correct boat lean. Another way of reminding students is to *"set your circle in the leaving current as you paddle into the entering current."*

SCOUT - To look over a rapid before running it. This can be done from the boat or from shore. See chapters on How to Read the River and River Rescue.

SCULL - To propel a craft a short distance laterally by moving the paddle in a continuous back-and-forth motion. Applying force to the **powerface** moves the a boat toward the side on which the blade is working; this is a forward scull. Applying force to the **backface** moves the boat away from the working blade; this is a reverse scull. See "Abeams" in Kayaking and Canoeing chapters.

SEAMLINE - Where the deck and hull meet to form the edges of a closed boat.

SECONDARY STABILITY - The stability (i.e., the tendency not to capsize) of a boat when heeled to one side. See also **primary stability**. V-shaped hulls have good *secondary stability;* a round-bottomed boat would have neither primary stability nor secondary stability.

SELF RESCUE - The act of rescuing oneself after capsizing; getting oneself safely to shore without assistance. An experienced paddler usually rescues not only himself, but also his boat and paddle. See chapter on River Rescue.

SHAFT - The part of a paddle between the blades, or between the blade and the grip.

SHAFT HAND - In canoeing, the hand holding the paddle shaft. The lower hand as opposed to the **control hand**, which is on the grip.

SHALLOW WATER DRAW - A tandem stern or solo canoe **correction stroke** used to move the stern of the canoe toward the working blade. The shaft is held relatively low with a horizontal insertion of the blade into the water behind the paddler; a force is exerted on the powerface, toward

252

the side of the canoe. Sometimes called a *stern draw*.

SHALLOW WATER PRY - A tandem stern or solo open canoe **correction stroke** used to move the stern of the canoe away from the working blade. The blade is inserted behind the paddler close to the boat, with the shaft as horizontal as possible. Holding the shaft against the gunwale with his shaft hand, the paddler aggressively pulls the grip toward his offside, thus applying force on the backface to push the craft away from the blade.

SHEER - The upward curve of the sides of a hull from amidships to the ends. Usually observed along the gunwales when viewed from the side.

SHOAL - A build-up of riverbed forming shallow water. Usually found near the **inside bank** of bends in the river.

SHOCK CORD - Elastic cord used in securing paddles and other equipment; "bungie cord."

SHOOT - To maneuver over falls or down a rapid, as in "shooting the rapids."

SHUTTLE - The process of placing cars at the start and destination points of a river run.

SIDECURLER - A **reversal** parallel to the main current, formed by a side current passing over a rock as it enters the main channel.

SIDE OF OPPOSITION - That side of the craft experiencing greater lateral resistance (pressure) exerted by water; a craft traveling forward or in reverse always turns *away* from its side of opposition. To prevent a **fish count**, it is usually wise to "elevate the side of opposition," that is, to **J-lean** the boat away from that side.

SIDESLIP - To shift one's boat laterally while maintaining forward or reverse momentum and the boat's initial **discipline**. Also, the lateral movement of a craft due to momentum or river current, as in the sideslipping that occurs during an eddy turn - actually due to the momentum of the **center of gravity** of the craft, which causes the center of gravity to continue in its initial direction, often continuing even after the craft has completed the turn. See "Sideslips" in Kayaking and Canoeing chapters.

SKID PLATE - A composite material, usually of heavy duty kevlar, put on the very ends of a canoe to prevent damage to the craft during its rigorous whitewater life!

SKIRT - See **sprayskirt**.

SLACK WATER - Stream flow without rapids or riffles; **a pool**.

SLALOM - A race against time in which a paddler must negotiate a specified course designated by 25 pairs of vertically suspended poles (**gates**). The gates are colored either green or red. The color of the gate determines the direction in which it must be taken. Touching a gate is penalized by adding five seconds to the final score. Missing a gate costs the racer 50 seconds. Slalom classes are determined by boat type, sex of paddlers, age category, and ability levels. Fastest adjusted time wins.

SLAM - Smile, Lean, Angle, Momentum. As in, "SLAM or you'll dunk!" Acronym used by instructors to remind students that they should set a proper boat *lean*, *angle* of exit, and boat *momentum* before crossing an eddy line during a peel-out or eddy turn. And reminds students that all maneuvers look *and* feel more successful when done with a *SMILE!* Also see **SAL**.

SLEEPER - Submerged rock or boulder just below the surface, usually marked by little or no surface disturbance.

SLICE - A stroke in which the the blade is set at about a 45 degree angle or less with respect to the centerline (as opposed to the 90 degrees during the powerphase of a normal power stroke), with the blade angled *away* from the boat. This angulation drives the paddle to the side of the boat as soon as force is applied; the powerphase continues with the shaft and/or part of the blade rubbing the boat. Water is forced away from the craft, turning the bow away from the blade. A technique for adjusting course or angular momentum of the craft. Also, using both forward and reverse slices sequentially, they can be used to execute tandem canoe offside spins or solo canoe offside abeams.

SLUICE - Similar to **chute**.

SNEAK - To take an easier route around a difficult spot. Often takes the form of maneuvering down one side of a big rapid in order to avoid the turbulence in the center.

SOLOING - Paddling a craft alone, as opposed to tandem paddling.

SPIN - To rotate a craft about its **pivot point**.

SPRAYSKIRT - A garment worn about the waist of a decked boat paddler, which attaches around the rim of the cockpit to make it watertight.

STAIRCASE - A stretch of river where the water pours over a series of drops that resemble a staircase.

STANDING WAVE - A stationary wave formation at right angles to the current flow. Standing waves are caused by the deceleration of current that occurs when fast-moving water flows into slower-moving water. They usually occur in sets, and although they remain in a fixed position, the water rushes through them. The height of these waves is measured vertically from the trough to the crest. See **haystack**.

STARBOARD - The right side of the craft as one faces forward in the craft.

STATIC DRAW - A **static stroke** used either to **sideslip** or to turn, in which the blade is placed with the powerface angled to face the bow, similar to the angle of a **Duffek stroke**.

STATIC STROKE - Any stroke that exerts a force without movement of the blade. There must be movement of the boat and/or current passing by the boat for this to be effective. Opposite: **dynamic stroke**.

STEM - The sharply curved section at the end of a boat which often slices through the water when paddling forward or backward. Most contemporary playboats have so much **rocker** that the stems rarely even touch the water!

STERN - The rear section of a watercraft.

STERN DRAW - A **correction stroke** designed to bring the stern to the blade; a sweep starting at a 45 degree angle to the centerline behind the paddler and ending when the stern comes to the blade. It is used by solo paddlers and the tandem stern paddler. Sometimes called a *shallow water draw*.

STERN SWEEP - A **correction stroke** designed to bring the stern to the blade; a sweep starting at a 90 degree angle to the centerline opposite the paddler and ending when the stern comes to the blade. It is used by solo paddlers and the tandem stern paddler.

STOPPER - A **reversal** powerful enough to stop a craft momentarily. Also called a *stopper wave*. The usual strategy is either to avoid stoppers or to paddle through them forcefully, keeping the boat at right angles to the reversal.

STRAINER - Any obstacle such as brush, fallen trees, bridge pilings, or other material that retains solid objects while allowing water to flow through. Can trap a boat or a paddler, either on the surface or underwater, and therefore is potentially lethal. Because the underwater component of a strainer often cannot be seen from the surface, any branches extending into or out of the water should always be avoided.

STROKES - The various manipulations of the paddle which propel a craft in the desired direction. In most strokes, the blade actually braces the water, moving only a few inches through the water during the **powerphase**; the blade thus serves as a leverage point against which the boat is propelled along its course.

SURFACE RESISTANCE - The resistance created by water and air friction against the surface of the boat. Also, the resistance created by the friction between the air and the water on the surface of a river. See **drag**.

SURFING - The act of riding the upstream face of a wave. The current tries to force the boat up to the crest of the wave, while gravity pulls the boat toward the wave trough. A dynamic equilibrium may be achieved whereby, by bracing and ruddering, a boater can ride or surf for an extended period. Also used to **jet ferry**. See chapter on River Playboating Maneuvers.

SWAMP - To fill (a boat) with water without capsizing it.

SWEEP BOAT - The last boat in a group, assigned responsibility for assisting other boaters if help is needed; the sweep boat carries first aid and other rescue supplies, and should be paddled by someone competent to assist in rescues. See chapter on Group Organization on the River.

SWEEP STROKE - A low-shaft-angle stroke used for turning and/or pivoting. May be a forward sweep, a reverse sweep, or a stern sweep. See "Spins" in Kayaking and Solo Canoeing chapters.

TAKE-OUT - The ending point of a river run. Also, all that any playboater has enough energy for after a great day on the river!

TAKING RESISTANCE ON THE RECOVERY - An underwater power stroke **recovery** in which the blade is not parallel to the centerline; rather, it is angled with the leading edge farther from the hull than the trailing edge. The resistance created while bringing the blade to the catch position for the next power stroke causes the boat to turn toward the blade. Often done by canoeists on the cross forward stroke when they wish to turn more sharply to their offside.

TANDEM - Two paddlers per craft, as opposed to solo paddling.

T-GRIP - A handle shaped in the form of a "T". Generally provides better control of blade angulation in whitewater than the pear-shaped grip of touring canoe paddles.

TECHNICAL - Word used to describe a rapid in which there are many intricate passageways requiring considerable maneuvering. A technical rapid may be a good **rock garden**. This term also refers to a paddler's ability, as in, "That individual is a good technical paddler."

THIGH STRAP - Seat-belt-like material that runs diagonally over a canoeist's thighs as he kneels in the boat. Essential for connecting the whitewater canoeist to the boat. To lean the boat, the paddler **J-leans** while forcing his thigh upward against the thigh strap on the side opposite the desired boat lean. See chapter on Playboating Equipment.

THREE W'S - Wind, Weather and Waves are three elements of nature that can be hazardous for paddlers. See chapter on Paddlers' Personal Responsibilities.

THROAT - The flare of the paddle shaft where it starts to form the blade. The area between the shaft and the blade. Also, where Kel's heart is when beginning a big drop!

THROW BAG - Specially designed bag containing a throw line. Sometimes called a *stuff bag*. (See **throw line**.) See chapter on River Rescue.

THROW LINE - A length of rope used in a rescue. The rope is coiled in a nylon bag in such a way that it will uncoil and come out cleanly when the bag is thrown, and is made of a material that floats. Several of these lines, scattered in different craft, can be of use when a shore-based rescue system is called for. See chapter on River Rescue.

THWART - The part of an open canoe used to provide reinforcement for the **gunwales**; thwarts are the spreaders or crossbars that extend from one gunwale to the other. Their placement and length determine not only the shape of the top of the canoe but also, to an extent, the hull's **rocker, flare** and **tumblehome**.

TIGHT - Watertight.

TIP - Bottom edge of a paddle blade.

TOE BLOCK - See **foot block.**

TONGUE - The smooth "V" of fast water found at the head or top of a rapid or between obstacles. The smooth "V" usually indicates the deepest water of a channel. Also called a *downstream "V"*. (Paddlers often seek a downstream "V" when selecting a route, but avoid upstream "V's" as these are usually formed by obstacles.) See chapter on How to Read the River.

TRACK - To paddle a boat in a straight line. Also refers to the tendency of a boat to travel in a straight line, as in, "The boat *tracks* well." Boats with their **stems** in the water (touring boats) track better than whitewater playboats. See **tracking ability**.

TRACKING ABILITY - Ability to paddle a straight course. Also a boat may be said to have good *tracking ability* if the design of the hull is such that the paddler can maintain a straight course with ease. The tendency of a boat to **track** easily is inversely related to the ease with which it is turned. Playboats are designed to turn readily, and therefore do not track the way touring boats do. See chapter on Playboating Equipment.

TRIM - The angle at which a craft rides on the water. For instance, down at the stern, down at the bow, or listing to port or starboard (athwartship trim). Also, a *trim* boat is one that is sitting equally deep in the water at the bow and stern, and not listing to either side.

TRIP - See **Run**.

TROUGH - The low point or hollow found between the crests of two adjacent waves.

TUMBLEHOME - The inward-curving upper portion of an open boat which produces a narrowing of the **beam** at the **gunwales**. Increased tumblehome decreases **flare**, and therefore can increase water intake and in some cases can improve the **tracking ability**. It can decrease the boat's **secondary stability**.

TURNING HIGH BRACE - A turning stroke in which the paddle shaft is held at a high angle, while the blade is placed with the powerface facing the bow. This **static stroke** causes the bow to turn toward the blade. See also **Duffek stroke**.

UNDERCUT ROCK - A rock which is shaped in such a way that water flows under a section of it. Boiling water in an eddy is an indication that one or both sides of the rock creating the eddy is *undercut;* such an eddy offers limited support for a **brace**. (See **boil**.)

UPSTREAM DISCIPLINE - An orientation of the boat in which the bow is upstream of the stern. For example, "One should maintain an upstream discipline throughout an upstream ferry." See also **downstream discipline**.

UPSTREAM FERRY - A maneuver in which the bow is kept upstream of the stern and angled toward the intended destination while the boat is moved laterally to the destination by forward paddling. Called an upstream ferry because the paddler is facing upstream; called a **forward ferry** because the paddler is forward paddling. For details, see chapter on River Playboating Maneuvers.

UPSTREAM SIDE - The side of the boat farthest upstream, when the boat is at an angle to the main current. This side of the boat may or may not be the **side of opposition** depending on which way the boat is turning!

UPSTREAM "V" - A "V" formed on the water's surface with the apex upstream. Usually formed by an obstacle just below the surface, upstream V's are generally avoided to prevent damage to the boat. See chapter on How to Read the River.

VOLUME - In reference to water, heavy or high volume means heavy water or big water. See **c.f.s.** In reference to closed boats, the amount of water in gallons that it would take to fill the boat. For example, "My kayak volume is 70 gallons."

WATERLINE - Level of the water on the craft's sides when floating.

WATERLINE LENGTH - Length of a craft measured at the waterline. This will vary with the amount of rocker and load.

WATERMANSHIP - One's ability to be at ease in, on, or about water.

WATERSHED - Land area that is drained by a particular river. Usually measured in acres or square miles.

WAVE BLOCK - To elevate a side of an open canoe to prevent water from entering when approaching an oncoming cresting wave which is about to break over one side of the boat. The timing must be precise and the hip snap quick, then the boat is returned to normal. Experienced paddlers learn to perform wave blocks and **compound wave blocks** by habit.

WEIR - Low dam built to back up or divert water.

WET EXIT - To exit one's boat after a capsize, as opposed to rolling it up. So called because in decked boats, the paddler's lower body may be dry prior to (but not after!) a wet exit.

WETSUIT - A close fitting garment of neoprene foam that provides thermal insulation in cold water.

WHITE EDDY - A **reversal**, just downstream of an underwater obstruction, characterized by a foamy highly aerated backflow at the surface. See **hole**.

WHITEWATER - The general term for a stretch of fast, rough water on a river. Whitewater is always obstructed by rocks above and below the surface.

WILDWATER RACE - A closed-boat race between two points, usually 4 to 8 miles in length on a Class III or better river.

WORKING BLADE - In kayaking, the blade which is being used to propel the craft.

WORKING HAND - The hand nearest the **working blade.** Often used by instructors to explain to a student which hand to move or use in some manner.

WRAPPED - Said of a craft that is wrapped or pinned by the force of the current around a rock or other obstruction.

YAW - When a craft is being set in motion from a complete stop, the turning of the craft away from the side on which a stroke is executed, even with a stroke executed parallel to the centerline. Also, to fail to hold a course by turning from one side to the other. Way, spelled backwards!

YOKE - A cushioned shoulder harness that clamps to the gunwales of a canoe, permitting the canoe to be carried or portaged upside-down on the paddler's shoulders. Some center **thwarts** are shaped to serve as yokes.

INDEX

NOTES

NOTES

NOTES

NOTES